CSS3
Pushing the Limits

Stephen Greig

WILEY

Publisher's Acknowledgements

Some of the people who helped bring this book to market include the following:

Editorial and Production

VP Consumer and Technology Publishing Director: Michelle Leete
Associate Director–Book Content Management: Martin Tribe
Associate Publisher: Chris Webb
Associate Commissioning Editor: Ellie Scott
Project Editor: Sara Shlaer
Copy Editor: Chuck Hutchinson
Technical Editor: Kevin Bradwick
Editorial Manager: Jodi Jensen
Senior Project Editor: Sara Shlaer
Editorial Assistant: Annie Sullivan

Marketing

Associate Marketing Director: Louise Breinholt
Marketing Manager: Lorna Mein
Marketing Assistant: Polly Thomas

Composition Services

Compositor: Indianapolis Composition Services
Proofreader: Joni Heredia Language Services
Indexer: BIM Indexing & Proofreading Services

About the Author

Stephen Greig is a hard working designer and front-end developer who is very passionate and considerate about the work he produces—a passion that is emphasized when it comes to CSS, particularly the more advanced and experimental CSS3 modules. It was his experimenting with these modules on his blog (`http://tangledindesign.com/blog/`) that paved the way for this book. Outside of his profession, Stephen enjoys sports, travelling, new experiences, and socializing with friends—who are often found in pubs! Follow him on Twitter via @Stephen_Greig.

Acknowledgments

First and foremost, Stephen would like to thank his partner Hannah, who put up with months of neglect and oversight, yet still offered a voice of constant encouragement throughout the writing of this book. Furthermore, Stephen is extremely grateful to his family for their continued support; in particular, he'd like to thank his dad, Syd Greig, for supplying many of the fantastic photographs used in the demonstrations throughout this book. The writing process was smooth and untroubled, thanks in no small part to project editor Sara Shlaer, who provided constant guidance and essential critique, playing a major part in crafting the final output. Huge thanks must also go to copy editor Chuck Hutchinson, who meticulously perfected everything he was presented with, and technical editor Kevin Bradwick, whose expertise and eagle eye ensured that all code functioned correctly and was error free.

Contents

Introduction

CSS (Cascading Style Sheets) is a core requirement in any web designer's toolkit, providing lifeless HTML with heart and soul since its inception in 1996. CSS has come a long way since then, though, and with the latest incarnation, CSS3, now boasts a vast range of impressive features that really push the boundaries of its status as a simple styling language. It doesn't just paint the walls of your web pages anymore; now, the walls move, they adjust their shapes, the paint changes color, and all these effects are achieved without reliance on the bigger and smarter cousin that is JavaScript.

What Is CSS3?

CSS3 has received an incredible amount of coverage across the web, quickly transforming it into one of the industry's most frequently used buzzwords, but it's soon to be eclipsed and outdated by CSS4, right? Wrong!

In contrast to the preceding versions of CSS (1 and 2.1), CSS3 is not one giant specification that will eventually progress to CSS4 and beyond. Instead, the decision was made to modularize the entire specification, resulting in a comprehensive collection of various modules that all fall within the bracket of CSS3. Each of these modules is now free to progress independently at its own pace, without the possibility of being held back by other features.

The modules that simply further develop features from CSS 1 and CSS 2.1 are known as *Level 3 modules*, whereas brand new features and concepts form *Level 1 modules*. They will eventually progress to Level 4 and Level 2 modules at varying paces, but the entire collection can all be referred to as CSS3. In other words, there will never be a CSS4 or a CSS5 (despite what you may have seen across the web suggesting otherwise). Rather, CSS3 can be used to refer to everything after CSS 1 and 2.1.

With that said, I hope it's plainly evident that there's a bit more to CSS3 than a few rounded corners and drop shadows. This book takes you on a deep dive into the surprising new feats you can accomplish with CSS3, such as custom patterns with CSS gradients, manipulation of elements in a 3D environment, frame-based animations, and finally, complex layouts with comprehensive new layout tools!

Who This Book Is For

This book is about taking CSS3 to the next level, using advanced techniques and concepts to truly push the various features to their limits. It does therefore assume an intermediate to experienced level in terms of your skill and knowledge of CSS. As well as being considerably comfortable with everyday CSS, you ideally have experience with some of the more mainstream aspects of CSS3 and are ready to push things forward and advance to the next level. If you already have this foundational knowledge, you're in a great position to make the most of this book.

What This Book Covers

As I mentioned previously, CSS3 has already received an astounding amount of attention, but much of it covers the same old ground. Conversely, this book takes you to the furthest corners of CSS3 to unearth the hidden gems that allow you to achieve things you didn't know were possible with only a modest styling language.

The book also offers a few short refreshers on some of the more mainstream aspects of CSS3, before I demonstrate just how far you can push these features with the help of an open mind, allowing you to craft impressively rich and creative results.

How This Book Is Structured

As I discuss each new feature throughout this book, I introduce it with care and clarity before I raise the stakes and demonstrate how to harness its real power. You get to delve into many advanced examples, rich in both visual effects and interactivity, with some that are rounded and practical and others that are highly imaginative and experimental. However, everything you learn in this book is accompanied by the appropriate guidance to ensure the skills and knowledge you acquire are not misused; after all, a very wise man once said, "with great power comes great responsibility." And who are we to question Uncle Ben?

The book is divided into four parts, each of which covers different aspects of CSS3 and the extensive range of modules that fall within this bracket. The next couple of pages break down the main sections of the book and outline precisely what's in store for you throughout the next 300+ pages.

Part I: New Toys

Part I introduces a range of new CSS3 modules, from the maturing Level 3 Selectors module to the youthful and exciting Level 1 Filters module.

- **Chapter 1: "Advanced Selectors"**—There's more to life than ID and Class selectors—much more in fact, and this chapter takes you through the lot, showing you how to target elements in ways you never thought possible!

- **Chapter 2: "New Tools for Text"**—CSS covered the basics of type from the very start, offering control over essential aspects of text such as line height and letter spacing, but now you can really satisfy the perfectionist within you thanks to a vast range of new type tools that provide a fine-grained level of control.

- **Chapter 3: "New Tools for Backgrounds and Borders"**—Ever wanted adaptable background images or crazy, decorative borders? How about elaborate patterns using nothing but CSS? Of course, you have! Well, you're in luck because this chapter walks you through many of the new features boasted by the Level 3 Backgrounds and Borders module.

- **Chapter 4: "Into the Browser with CSS3 Filters and Blending Modes"**—No longer do you have to rely on your graphical editing software to apply the simplest of image adjustments because the attention-grabbing Filters module preserves your valuable time. This chapter also provides a glimpse further into the future with the Blending Modes module, which takes image adjustments in the browser to another level entirely.

Part II: Transforms, Transitions, and Animation

CSS3 harnesses a great deal of its power within the Transforms, Transitions, and Animations modules. They combine to create the jaw-dropping effects that make you hastily inspect the code in disbelief, only to find a few simple CSS rules with no JavaScript in sight.

- **Chapter 5: "A First Look at 2D Transforms"**—Two-dimensional transforms form the basis of many impressive CSS3 experiments; this chapter walks you through the basic functionalities in detail.

- **Chapter 6: "Bringing 2D Transforms to Life with Transitions"**—The core concept and functionality of the various 2D transforms are impressive, but when combined with simple animation (transitions), they become a different beast entirely.

- **Chapter 7: "A New Dimension with 3D Transforms"**—If you thought 2D transforms were cool, then brace yourself for this chapter. The 3D aspect of the Transforms module allows you to produce truly mind-blowing visual effects with just a few lines of CSS, with no Flash or JavaScript in sight. In this chapter, you flip objects in a 3D environment, create a 3D shape, and then animate it!

- **Chapter 8: "Getting Animated"**—Transitions are great for animating from one state to another, but for anything beyond this, they're just not sufficient. The CSS Animations module steps in here to provide a truly comprehensive animation tool, allowing you to create complex, keyframe-based animation.

Part III: Getting to Grips with New Layout Tools

For all the amazing advancements in CSS over the years, there is one fundamental aspect of web design that is so elementary in concept and yet CSS has struggled to master it. But no longer! With CSS3 comes a whole host of additional layout tools, each of which aims to tackle different layout dilemmas that have long been in need of a simple solution.

- **Chapter 9: "Creating a Multicolumn Layout"**—Multiple-column layouts are extremely popular in print publications and have been for a long time, and yet a simple solution for multicolumn web pages is only just filtering into the mainstream. This chapter walks you through the module and demonstrates how to create a functional multiple-column layout.

- **Chapter 10: "Creating a Flexible Box Layout"**—CSS has traditionally struggled with basic layout requirements such as vertical centering and directional flow, but with the brand new Flexible Box Layout module comes a comprehensive new layout mechanism, finally providing you with complete control over your layout. This chapter breaks down the complexities of an intimidating module and will have you eager to try it out at the first opportunity!

- **Chapter 11: "Grid Layout, Regions, and Exclusions"**—This chapter introduces the fresh-faced Grid Layout and Regions and Exclusions modules, which are still very much in development. By the end of this chapter, you will understand the immense benefits of these solutions and will no doubt be genuinely excited by the creative freedom of the impressive Regions and Exclusions modules.

- **Chapter 12: "Going Responsive with CSS3 Media Queries"**—Responsive web design has taken the web industry by storm over the past few years. This chapter discusses the fundamental aspects such as media queries before going on to demonstrate how the new layout modules make the responsive process that much easier for you.

Part IV: Pushing the Limits

By this point, you will be bursting with knowledge and eager to apply it. This part of the book does just that, showing you how to make the most of the various features of CSS3 and really push them to their limits.

- **Chapter 13: "Getting Creative with Pseudo-elements"**—Pseudo-elements open many doors in terms of creative CSS, allowing you to form advanced shapes using minimal, semantic HTML. I show you how you can use them to preserve your HTML while creating abstract and scalable shapes and icons.

- **Chapter 14: "Using Preprocessors to Push CSS3 to the Limit"**—No matter how much CSS advances, it will always be somewhat held back by its status as a styling language, rather than a programming language. Preprocessors bridge this gap and allow you to use advanced programming functionalities such as variables, functions, and math operators in a stylesheet setting to really make the most of the various CSS3 features.

- **Chapter 15: "Creating Practical Solutions Using Only CSS3"**—Finally, this chapter brings everything together and combines much of what is covered before it to create aesthetically rich, interactive, and practical solutions that really show the potential of CSS3 in a real-world setting.

- **Chapter 16: "The Future of CSS"**—CSS is constantly developing, and this chapter provides a sneak peek into what the future has in store, such as Level 4 Selectors, native CSS variables, and more!

A Word of Caution

With a powerful tool like CSS3 that is very much open to interpretation and incredibly easy to misuse, I feel it is important to establish some ground rules early on. I add more specific cautions at appropriate points throughout the book, but let's start with a couple of general warnings.

Aim for Progressive Enhancement

Another phrase that will be etched into your brain come the end of this book is *progressive enhancement*. Nearly everything that falls within CSS3 is a work in progress, and in the majority of cases, the features can boast patchy browser support at best. This is where you must apply some common sense and ensure that you're not using these features in ways that will affect the core functionality of your website. Instead, you should use these features to enhance your website in the browsers that can handle it, while ensuring that functionality is never compromised in those that can't. In experiments, by all means go wild, but in production projects, you must use these new features wisely and with reason.

Be Smart, Be Subtle

With all these new toys, you can easily get carried away and go overboard with shiny new features such as gradients, shadows, and animation. But remember, just because you can doesn't mean you should! Some of the new features may seem exciting and open up so many new doors, but you have to be careful which of these doors you go through; you must see past the novelty factor and ensure things are not overdone. Everything danced, blinked, flashed, and changed colors in the '90s. And it was annoying. Subtlety is the way forward.

Demos and Browser Support

Most of the examples throughout this book come with live demonstrations on the companion website at `http://www.wiley.com/go/ptl/css3`, where you can inspect the end result and trawl through the full code for a better understanding. To make my life easier, I coded all the demos to work in Google's Chrome browser only, unless otherwise stated, so bear that in mind if you're about to send me an angry email about my broken code!

As I previously alluded to, the various features within the range of CSS3 modules have patchy browser support, which I note in my discussions of each feature. However, most of the major browsers are now on very quick release cycles, meaning that they're constantly gaining support for new features, so much of the compatibility data in this publication should be taken with a small pinch of salt.

A fantastic resource for the latest information on browser support is `http://caniuse.com`, which provides support data for the majority of CSS3 features discussed in this book and also shows which browser versions require vendor prefixes.

> Towards the end of the book, I coded a couple of the demos to be viewed in Opera to take advantage of its browser support for the features being discussed. However, Opera has since decided to ditch its Presto rendering engine in favor of WebKit, so from version 15, its browser compatibility situation has changed completely. So don't be thrown when you see screen shots of my examples in Opera.

If you'd like to contact me regarding anything in this book, whether you need to ask for help or just want to say hi, feel free to send an email to `steve.greig1@gmail.com`. You can also get in touch and follow my regular updates on Twitter via my handle, `@Stephen_Greig`.

Part I

New Toys

Chapter 1
Advanced Selectors

Web designers commonly get into the habit of using only a very small collection of basic CSS selectors, most notably the id, class, and descendant selectors, because that's all they need…or so they think.

It's true that you can accomplish almost everything with the class selector, but why compromise your nice, clean markup by adding unnecessary classes when you can choose from a range of more practical and efficient alternatives?

CSS3 has brought with it a whole host of such alternatives, some of which are simply wonderfully convenient and others that can make you excitedly ponder all the possibilities! What? CSS3 selectors *are* exciting!

In this chapter, you will learn about the different types of selectors, from sibling combinators to nth child expressions. With the help of practical examples, you'll be able to understand precisely what they do and how you can put them to use. I'll finish the chapter by combining many of the various selector types that will be described between now and then to create some truly advanced CSS selectors.

Child and Sibling Selectors

The child and sibling combinators are actually among the more mature features in the Selectors module; however, despite this they've had trouble in finding the same kind of mainstream attention as id and class selectors enjoy. It's about time they got a little nudge into the spotlight.

Child Combinator

Generally speaking, the cascade aspect of CSS is awesome, but sometimes you just don't need or want it. Have you ever found yourself undoing your own styles in a nested unordered list, for example? This is where the child combinator can help out. Consider this example:

```
nav ul {
    background: blue;
    border: 2px solid red;
}

nav ul ul {
    border: none;
    background: none;
}
```

If you find that you have to re-declare your styles to fight against the cascade, there is almost definitely a better way of going about the task. As shown in the following snippet, the child combinator allows you to select only the `ul` that is a direct child of the `nav` element so that the styles aren't applied to any nested `ul` elements:

```
nav > ul {
    background: blue;
    border: 2px solid red;
}
```

Simple stuff, right? Even better, this capability is supported in all major browsers, including Internet Explorer 7!

A few of the selectors discussed in this chapter, including the child combinator, have been around for a while and were actually first defined in the CSS 2.1 selector specification. However, I still see a staggering number of experienced web designers who remain oblivious to their existence, opting to stick with their trusty class and descendant selectors.

Adjacent Sibling Combinator

The adjacent sibling combinator targets the sibling that immediately follows an element. This selector has a number of uses. One common use is when you need to target, for example, the first `p` element to follow an `h1` or an `h2` in your body text, as follows:

```
p {
    margin-top: 1.5em;
}

h2 + p {
    margin-top: 0;
}
```

Nice and easy, and a practical solution to targeting elements that could otherwise be really awkward to style, particularly if some of your markup is generated by a content management system.

Major browser support for the adjacent sibling combinator is universal, again including IE7+!

General Sibling Combinator

The general sibling combinator selector is similar to the adjacent sibling combinator, but more [wait for it]… general! Whereas the previous selector targets only the sibling that *immediately* follows an element, this selector targets *any* sibling that follows an element.

Consider the following example:

```
HTML
<h2 class="important">Everything below is very important</h2>
<p>This text is very important.</p>
<p>This text is also very important.</p>
```

```
CSS
h2.important ~ p {
    color: red;
}
```

This selector targets all p elements that follow an h2 with a class of important, allowing you to apply a text color of red to all paragraphs under that particular heading.

If your first thought regarding this selector is anything like mine was, you probably are thinking "Hmm, pretty cool, but to be honest I can see this sitting at the bottom of the virtual toolbox gathering layers of virtual dust."

The reality, though, is *quite* the contrary! In fact, the general sibling combinator will prove to be one of the most vital ingredients in some of the most complex solutions you will read about in this book. Keep an eye out for its return towards the end of this chapter.

The general sibling combinator is much newer than those discussed earlier. Although it is compatible with all major browsers, Internet Explorer supports it only from version 9.

Attribute Selectors

Another method of selecting elements is through HTML attributes, in terms of whether an element has a certain attribute applied to it and/or the value of the attribute.

All the following attribute selectors have full major browser support, including IE7+.

Selecting Based on the Existence of an HTML Attribute

You can use a selector to target only those elements that have a specific attribute applied to them. The following example shows the use of a selector to target only those a elements that have a title attribute applied:

```
HTML
<a title="Contact Us" href="contact.php">Contact Us</a>
<a href="mailto:info@domain.com">Email Us</a>
```

```
CSS
a[title] {
    text-decoration: underline;
}
```

The selector would apply an underline only to the Contact Us link in this example because the Email Us link doesn't have a title attribute.

Selecting Based on the Exact Value of an HTML Attribute

More often than not, you would want to select an element based on the attribute's *value* rather than simply the fact that it exists. The most basic way of achieving this is to select based on the exact value of the attribute, as shown in the following example:

HTML
```
<input type="text">
<input type="submit">
```

CSS
```
input[type="submit"] {
    background: blue;
    color: white;
}
```

This selector targets any `input` element with a `type` attribute value that matches an exact string. In this case, the string is `submit`, allowing you to apply styles to your Submit button freely, without affecting your text input. Very useful.

Selecting Based on the Partial Contents of an HTML Attribute Value

Sometimes you might not know the exact attribute value you need to match, so you want a bit more leniency in terms of matching your HTML attributes. Fortunately, you can use a straightforward solution that allows you to select based on the HTML attribute *containing* a particular string, as shown in the following example:

HTML
```
<a href="http://twitter.com">Twitter</a>
```

CSS
```
a[href*="twitter"] {
    padding-left: 30px;
    background: url(twitter-icon.jpg) left no-repeat;
}
```

The simple addition of an asterisk means that the `href` attribute value in this example has to contain only the string `twitter` to match and apply the styling to the element. In this case, a `background-image` of the Twitter icon is added to any links that go to a Twitter URL.

Selecting Based on the Beginning of an HTML Attribute Value

You can also select based on what an HTML attribute value begins with. For example, if you want to add an icon to all external links, you select all elements with an `href` value that starts with `http`, as shown in the following code:

HTML
```
<a href="http://google.com">Google</a>
```

CSS
```
a[href^="http"] {
    padding-left: 30px;
    background: url(external-icon.jpg) left no-repeat;
}
```

As previously described, the selector targets all the `a` elements with an `href` value starting with `http`, simply by changing the asterisk to a caret (^) symbol.

Selecting Based on the End of an HTML Attribute Value

Now, perhaps you want to show an icon, such as a country's flag, depending on the domain suffix in an external link. You could select all links that direct to a New Zealand domain name, for example, by selecting all the a elements that have an href value that ends in .nz, as shown in this example:

HTML
```
<a href="http://google.co.nz">Google New Zealand</a>
```

CSS
```
a[href$=".nz"] {
    padding-left: 30px;
    background: url(nz-flag.jpg) left no-repeat;
}
```

By changing the caret symbol to a dollar sign, you can now match the string with the *end* of the href attribute, allowing you to apply a New Zealand flag to all links that go to a New Zealand domain name.

Selecting Based on Space-Separated HTML Attribute Values

Some HTML attributes allow you to specify multiple, space-separated values; one such example you likely used frequently in the past is, of course, the class attribute, which allows multiple class values.

With the help of the tilde character (~), you can select an element with an attribute containing multiple values, based on one of those values, as shown in the following example:

HTML
```
<img data-group="Gallery Dog" src="terrier.jpg" alt="Scottish Terrier">
<img data-group="Gallery Dog" src="spaniel.jpg" alt="Springer Spaniel">
<img data-group="Gallery Cat" src="white-cat.jpg" alt="White Cat">
<img data-group="Gallery Cat" src="black-cat.jpg" alt="Black Cat">
```

CSS
```
img[data-group~="Dog"] {
    border: 3px solid brown;
}
```

In this example, the HTML5 data- attribute enables you to store some information on each of the images in terms of the image's purpose (in this case, a gallery image) and to which gallery the image belongs (cat or dog).

The selector used here simply looks to see whether one of the values of the data-group attribute is Dog and then applies the appropriate styling.

Pseudo-Classes

Pseudo-classes have been around for a while in the form of :hover and :visited, among others, but now CSS3 offers a sizeable selection of brand new pseudo-classes to make the lives of web designers just that much easier.

Firsts and Lasts

First of all (excuse the pun) I touch on the ways of selecting the first or last element in a parent container—without using any classes, of course.

Picture this scenario: you've just coded a nice vertical navigation and given it a `border`. You've also applied a `border-bottom` to each of the links to act as a divider. Of course, you now have the classic issue of a double border at the end of the navigation, as illustrated in Figure 1-1 (we've all been there). You can also see the issue on the companion website, `www.wiley.com/go/ptl/css3`, in the demo file `0101-double-border.html`.

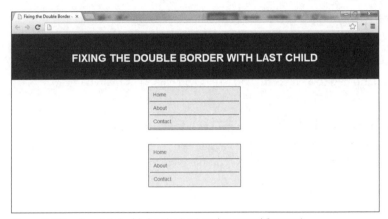

Figure 1-1 The dreaded double border (top), and corrected (bottom)

You could add a class to the last navigation item and use that to remove the `border-bottom` styling, but that approach feels dirty and wrong. Why? Because it's inefficient, adds unnecessary bytes to the markup, and would prove to be a pain when the code requires maintenance.

Enter the `:last-child` pseudo-class:

```
HTML
<ul>
    <li><a href="index.php">Home</a></li>
    <li><a href="about.php">About</a></li>
    <li><a href="contact.php">Contact</a></li>
</ul>

CSS
ul {
    border: 1px solid #000;
}

ul li {
    border-bottom: 1px solid #000;
}

ul li:last-child {
    border-bottom: none;
}
```

In this example, the pseudo-class looks for the last child in the `ul`, which is, of course, the last navigation list item, and it removes the `border-bottom` styling.

There is little need to go into any more depth with the various cousins of the `:last-child` pseudo-class because they all function in much the same way, so I just touch on them briefly. Note that all these selectors have universal support in major browsers, including IE9+, but not in earlier versions of IE unless otherwise stated.

- `:first-child` selects the first child of an element, regardless of the element type. This particular pseudo-class was first defined in CSS 2.1 and has universal major browser support, including IE7!

- `:first-of-type` looks for the first of a particular type of element in a container. For example, `p:first-of-type` would select the first `p` element, regardless of whether or not it is the first child in the parent.

- `:last-of-type`, as you might expect, does exactly the same as the preceding selector, except it looks for the *last* of a particular type of element in a container.

- `:only-child` selects an element if it is the sole child in its container. For example, in the markup for a standard navigation, each `a` element would generally be the only child of the `li` element that it inhabits.

- `:only-of-type` does the same as the preceding selector, except it selects elements if they are the only one of their type in the container. For example, if a `div` contains only an h1 and a p, each of these children would be the only one of its type.

Nth Child Selectors

The nth child selectors are great because sometimes you need a bit more flexibility than just first or last; sometimes you want to select the fifth child or the eighth child…or the 279th child. When you use `:nth-child()`, it's a cinch.

The most basic way to use `:nth-child()` is to explicitly state which child you want to select, as demonstrated in the following example:

HTML
```
<ul>
    <li>List Item One</li>
    <li>List Item Two</li>
    <li>List Item Three</li>
    <li>List Item Four</li>
</ul>
```

CSS
```
ul li:nth-child(3) {
    color: red;
}
```

In this example, the third list item text would be red. All very simple.

But what if you have a really long list with an unpredictable number of list items and you want to select the fifth-from-last item? Fortunately, another pseudo-class does just that job.

The `:nth-last-child()` selector works in exactly the same way as `:nth-child()`, except that it counts from the last child rather than the first. So `li:nth-last-child(5)` would select the fifth-from-last list item.

Furthermore, you can swap out the `-child` aspect of these selectors for `-of-type`, much like the examples discussed earlier, when you require a more specific match.

For example, consider the following code:

HTML
```
<article>
    <h1>This is a Top Level Heading</h1>
    <p>This is the first paragraph.</p>
    <p>This is the second paragraph.</p>
    <p>This is the third paragraph.</p>
    <p>This is the fourth paragraph.</p>
</article>
```

CSS
```
article p:nth-of-type(3) {
    color: red;
}
```

This selector would target the third paragraph, whereas if you use the `p:nth-child(3)` selector, it would target the third child of the container regardless of type, which would be the second paragraph.

Again, you can use `:nth-last-of-type()` to start the count from the end of the parent container, so if you use the preceding example, `:nth-last-of-type(2)` would select the third paragraph.

Taking Nth Child to the Next Level with Expressions

As well as a simple number, the nth child pseudo-class also accepts expressions for times when you require much more complex selecting patterns. These expressions take the form of $an+b$; for example, $2n+1$, which selects every odd child.

So how does this expression work? Well, think back to those exciting algebra lessons you remember with such fondness and consider the expression as a simple algebraic equation, where *n* increments by 1, starting from 0.

$(2 \times n) + 1$

$(2 \times 0) + 1 = 1$ (selects the first child)

$(2 \times 1) + 1 = 3$ (selects the third child)

$(2 \times 2) + 1 = 5$ (selects the fifth child)

$(2 \times 3) + 1 = 7$ (selects the seventh child)

[Etc.]

With the expression broken down, you can clearly see how it selects every odd child. However, I find using a different method of breaking things down makes it a little easier to immediately understand an expression at a glance.

Consider the example 5n+3 . Here, the first number (5) states that every fifth child should be targeted. The second number (3) states the location where the sequence should start. So in this case, every fifth child would be selected, starting from the third child. This example would select the 3rd, 8th, 13th, and 18th child (and so on).

Using Keywords with Nth Child

In addition to integers and expressions, the nth child pseudo-class also accepts a choice of two shorthand keywords, which are, quite predictably, odd and even.

The odd keyword is shorthand for 2n+1, as shown in the earlier example, and the even keyword can also be written as 2n+2 or 2n+0 —or simply, 2n. You might have noticed that 2n doesn't exactly need a shorthand option, but the even keyword does have the benefit of being immediately obvious to those who aren't familiar with expressions.

Using Negative Numbers with Nth Child

The nth child pseudo-class doesn't just accept positive integers; you can use negative numbers too. Your mind may be searching for a situation in which you might need to do so, but you can actually use negative numbers in some very clever ways.

Figure 1-2 shows a basic league table with 10 teams. The top spots—1 and 2—are promotion places, 3–6 are play-off places, and 9–10 are relegation spots. You need to target each of these zones to style them appropriately, so how do you do it?

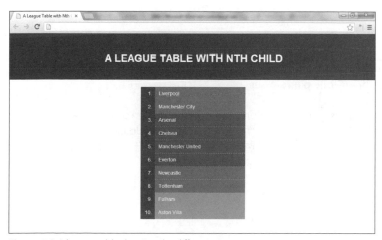

Figure 1-2 A league table showing the different zones

You could just use :nth-child() with basic integers to target each position, as demonstrated in the following code. Note that generally you would code a league table using a table, but for the sake of simplicity, an ordered list suffices for this example.

HTML
```
<ol>
    <li>Liverpool</li>
    <li>Manchester City</li>
    <li>Arsenal</li>
    <li>Chelsea</li>
    <li>Manchester United</li>
    <li>Everton</li>
    <li>Newcastle</li>
    <li>Tottenham</li>
    <li>Fulham</li>
    <li>Aston Villa</li>
</ol>
```

CSS
```
ol li:first-child,
ol li:nth-child(2) {
    background: green;
}

ol li:nth-child(3),
ol li:nth-child(4),
ol li:nth-child(5),
ol li:nth-child(6) {
    background: blue;
}

ol li:last-child,
ol li:nth-last-child(2) {
    background: red;
}
```

This code would do the job just fine, but that's a lot of selectors—eight in total. With the help of negative numbers, you can reduce that total to just three—one per rule-set.

To select the top two spots, you can use the expression $-1n+2$. Remember, the selection process starts at the second number; in this case, the second child. The first number (-1) states that every child (starting from the second child) should be selected, but in the reverse direction, therefore selecting the second item and then the first item. You can see how this equation works in the following example:

(-1×n) + 2 (you can shorten this to just $-n+2$)

(-1×0) + 2 = 2 (second child is selected)

(-1×1) + 2 = 1 (first child is selected)

(-1×2) + 2 = 0 (No selection)

To select the play-off positions (items 3–6), you need to use a bit of imagination as the desired range is isolated in the middle of the list. You can select the first six places using the method described previously, but in order to be more specific you can actually attach a *second* :nth-child() expression onto the selector! The required expression in this second pseudo-class is n+3, which ensures the selection begins at the third item, and the original –n+6 expression ensures the selection *ends* at the sixth item. Take a closer look in the following code example.

```
ol li:nth-child(-n+2) {
    background: green;
}

ol li:nth-child(-n+6):nth-child(n+3) {
    background: blue;
}

ol li:nth-last-child(-n+2) {
    background: red;
}
```

Much nicer. You can see the finished example, 0102-league-table.html, on the companion website.

The Best of the Rest

With the subject of nth child selectors all but exhausted, there are a few more pseudo-classes to discuss that can prove extremely useful, most of which haven't found their way into the mainstream just yet.

All the following selectors have universal support in major browsers, including IE9+:

- :empty selects any elements that have absolutely zero content or children.

  HTML
  ```
  <div></div> <!-- This div is empty -->
  <div> </div> <!-- This div is not empty -->
  ```

  CSS
  ```
  div:empty {
      display: none;
  }
  ```

- :not(x) is referred to as the negation pseudo-class. You can use it to select all elements except for x, where x is another selector.

  ```
  p:not(.important) {
      color: black;
  }
  ```

- :target selects an element that is the target of a fragment identifier in the document's URI. For example, if #bio sits at the end of the URI in your address bar, you can use :target to select the element in your HTML with an id of #bio.

HTML
```
<div id="bio">This is a bio</div>
```

CSS
```
div {
    background: white;
}

div:target {
    background: yellow;
}
```

Very useful and very convenient. In the case of :target, though, you gain a bit more than just convenience. I often use id attributes as anchors, allowing me to direct a link to another area on the same page, which adds the id anchor to the end of the URI, meaning it can then be styled using :target.

Have you clocked what that means? That's right—with :target, you can alter CSS styling for a particular element on-click! Using the preceding example, if you have a link with an href value of #bio, when a user clicks this link, the background of the #bio div changes from white to yellow! Huge potential there, I'm sure you will agree.

The last few pseudo-classes to address all relate to form elements, allowing you to style these elements based on their current state.

Again, all the following are supported in all major browsers, including IE9+:

- :disabled selects elements that can't be focused or selected in any way—for example, text inputs that use the disabled HTML5 attribute.

- :enabled selects elements that are in their default state and are ready to be selected. Basically, this includes anything that cannot be selected using :disabled.

- :checked targets radio buttons or check boxes that have been selected by the user.

Again, the last of these selectors stands out as a potential star performer in the brave new world of CSS3 experimentation. With a bit of help from the other advanced selectors that have been discussed, the :checked pseudo-class can be a really powerful tool that you can use to trigger CSS alterations on-click.

Also, :checked doesn't suffer from the drawbacks that can make :target awkward to work with in terms of triggering CSS changes on-click, such as ugly id's and page jumps.

Bringing It All Together

The time has come to combine some of these advanced selectors and put them to use to create a simple, interactive multiplication table (see Figure 1-3).

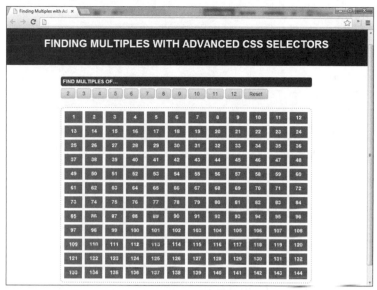

Figure 1-3 Interactive multiplication tables using only CSS

I explain how to develop this solution using only the code necessary to make it function correctly, so to see the full working demo with all the bells and whistles, open `0103-multiples-grid.html` on the companion website at `www.wiley.com/go/ptl/css3`.

The grid is simply a long list of numbers and so has been marked up using an ordered list. The button options are actually `label` elements, styled to look like clickable buttons. So how do they function as clickable buttons? Well, the `label` elements have been grouped with `input` elements (`radio` buttons to be precise) using the `for` attribute, allowing the `label` to be clickable on behalf of the hidden `radio` button.

```
<input value="2" id="two" name="multiples" type="radio">
<label for="two">2</label>

<input value="3" id="three" name="multiples" type="radio">
<label for="three">3</label>

<input value="4" id="four" name="multiples" type="radio">
<label for="four">4</label>
<!-- etc. -->

<ol>
    <li>1</li>
    <li>2</li>
    <li>3</li>
    <!-- etc. -->
</ol>
```

Now that the markup structure is in place, the buttons need to trigger the appropriate action when clicked. For example, when a user clicks the 5 button, the styling should change to highlight all numbers that are a multiple of 5.

The first step is to select the appropriate radio button:

```
input[value="5"]
```

You use an attribute selector here, so only an `input` element that has an exact `value` attribute of 5 is selected. Next, you need to modify this selector so that it targets the element only after it has been clicked:

```
input[value="5"]:checked
```

As you read earlier, radio buttons and check boxes allow use of the `:checked` pseudo-class when a user selects them, subsequently making the buttons behave like event triggers. However, now you need to somehow select the *list items* when the button is checked, which, with a glance at the markup, looks as though it could be troublesome based on the general laws of CSS.

Fear not! Remember the general sibling combinator (~)? This simple tilde character is all that you need here because, if you need reminding, it selects any siblings that follow a particular element in the parent container.

```
input[value="5"]:checked ~ ol li
```

The `ol` comes after all the `input` elements in the markup and they share the same parent, so the general sibling combinator works great in this example. As it stands, the preceding selector targets all the `li` elements when a user clicks the 5 button.

Now, you need to make it target only the numbers that are multiples of 5. You may have guessed that this is where the handy nth child pseudo-class makes a return!

```
input[value="5"]:checked ~ ol li:nth-child(5n)
```

The 5n equates to "select every fifth child"—and that's it! With that selector, every multiple of 5 in the list of numbers is selected when a user clicks the 5 button, allowing you to highlight these numbers in whatever way you want. This is what I've done in the demo.

```css
input:checked ~ ol li {
    opacity: 0.3;
    transform: scale(0.7);
}

input[value="2"]:checked ~ ol li:nth-child(2n),
input[value="3"]:checked ~ ol li:nth-child(3n) /* etc. */ {
    background: #333;
    opacity: 1;
    transform: scale(1);
}
```

> Bear in mind that in the printed code examples throughout the book, I'll be using only the un-prefixed version of properties for brevity. The live demos, however, are optimized for Chrome unless otherwise stated, as I mentioned in the introduction.

The preceding code employs some CSS3 properties to shrink and obscure all the numbers when one of the buttons has been clicked *except* for the numbers you want to highlight, as shown in Figure 1-4. The `opacity` and `transform` properties are explained in more detail in Chapters 4 and 5, respectively.

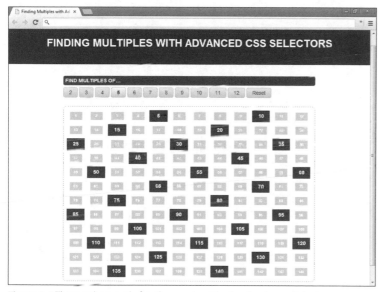

Figure 1-4 The numbers grid after the number 5 button has been clicked

Summary

The best thing about all the selectors discussed in this chapter is that they are supported in all current versions of major browsers! However, you probably know that the phrase "current version" fades into insignificance when it comes to the old enemy—Internet Explorer.

Internet Explorer 9 supports all the Level 3 selectors, which is great, but none of the preceding versions of IE support many of the new selectors…which isn't so great. This is where I bring in the first of many reminders about the term *progressive enhancement*.

The usage stats for IE8 (and possibly IE7 depending on the project and your opinion) are still too significant to ignore, so unfortunately you need to keep that in mind when the opportunity to use one of these selectors arises. Just be conscious of how your site or application will react if it is forced to ignore entire rule-sets in IE8 due to lack of support for the CSS. If it compromises the usability or functionality of the site, use an alternative. If the compromise is simply aesthetic, it is probably safe to stick with the advanced selectors and just deliver a *progressively enhanced* version of the website to the modern browsers that can handle it.

Further Reading

A complete list of CSS selectors and browser compatibility
`http://kimblim.dk/css-tests/selectors/`

Selectors Level 3 Specification
`http://www.w3.org/TR/selectors/`

Chapter 2

New Tools for Text

Typography is a highly detailed subject, and CSS barely scratches its surface. From kerning, tracking, and leading to ligatures, x-heights, and aspect ratios, you should take into account a number of factors when developing your type, whether it is a headline or body text.

Evidently, CSS has had to get to grips with a lot of typographic controls. In addition, CSS helps to develop solutions for a global platform (the Internet), meaning it also has to accommodate alternative writing cultures, such as those who write from right to left.

To its credit, CSS has done a great job so far, with many of the required type controls, such as `line-height` and `letter-spacing`, having been implemented in the early specifications. It's still playing catch-up, though, and with CSS3, you can look forward to having a whole lot more control over your type, making CSS a truly comprehensive solution for styling type on the web.

In this chapter, you will learn how to perfect your type through use of fine controls provided by the new CSS3 modules. The discussion begins with kerning and ligature tools before addressing new methods of improving your text's legibility. To finish, I walk you through the more creative aspects of the type-related CSS3 modules, such as `text-shadow` and image masking.

> **This chapter covers the cutting edge from the type-related Level 3 CSS specifications. Some of the properties and techniques covered here have limited browser support and, in a few cases, no support at all as of yet. But remember, this is about staying one step ahead of the game and being ready to take advantage of the new stuff as soon as it becomes available.**

Perfecting Your Type

Many of the new properties in CSS3 simply allow for greater control over the fonts you use, therefore ensuring that you can provide the finishing touches to your type, satisfying the perfectionist in you. These finishing touches include new controls for ligatures, kerning and some additional tools for fine-tuning your fonts.

Ligatures

A typographic *ligature* is a combination of two or more characters that would otherwise sit awkwardly together to form one glyph. This combination makes the characters more legible or simply makes them a little nicer on the eye.

Type designers often implement ligatures when a character overflows into the space of an adjacent character, causing the two letters to overlap or display in an awkward fashion. If you've read about ligatures before, you probably know that the main culprit is the *f* character, which often overhangs into the space of the following character, causing visual problems in several cases.

Figure 2-1 shows how Adobe Caslon Pro handles the *fi* characters by default (left) and with ligatures enabled (right). You can see that the default handling renders the tittle (dot) of the *i* character uncomfortably close to the hood of the *f* character. The ligature combines the tittle into the hood of the *f,* allowing for a much nicer flow between the two characters.

Figure 2-1 Adobe Caslon Pro handles the **fi** ligature nicely.

You've probably guessed by now that CSS3 has introduced a method of controlling the use of ligatures on the web! The `font-variant-ligatures` property does the job. The possible values for this property are given in the following list:

- `common-ligatures` enables the use of all common ligatures that are featured in a typeface, such as *fi* and *ff* . Note that this is enabled by default on OpenType fonts.
- `no-common-ligatures` disables the use of any common ligatures that are featured in a typeface.
- `discretionary-ligatures` enables the use of any nonstandard ligatures that the type designer has employed, which could be any combination of characters.
- `no-discretionary-ligatures` disables the use of any discretionary ligatures featured in a typeface.
- `historical-ligatures` enables the use of ligatures defined as historical in the typeface.
- `no-historical-ligatures` disables the use of historical ligatures.
- `contextual` enables the use of contextual alternates, such as joined-up handwriting in appropriate typefaces where the opportunity arises. These characters are not technically ligatures because they do not combine to create one glyph; they simply link glyphs together for aesthetic benefit.
- `no-contextual` disables the use of contextual alternates.

The following example shows how you can use the `common-ligatures` property to enable common ligatures in Webkit browsers:

```
h1 {
    -webkit-font-variant-ligatures: common-ligatures;
}
```

Unfortunately, the Webkit browsers (Chrome, Safari and Opera 15+) are, at the time of writing, the only browsers to support this property. As you can see from the preceding example, it also requires the `-webkit-` prefix to make the ligature function. However, an alternative is available; it doesn't have the same amount of ligature control but does come with other benefits—and it works in Firefox too!

I assume that news has you itching with excitement, and I get to that alternative shortly. But first, let's tackle the subject of kerning.

Kerning

Before diving in, it's back to typographic theory. Sometimes, the proportional spacing in fonts can actually appear to be off, and the characters look as if they are uncomfortably positioned due to their shapes. *Kerning* is the act of adjusting the spacing between these characters to create a more aesthetically pleasing result, as shown in Figure 2-2.

Figure 2-2 Text without and with kerning applied (top and bottom, respectively). The **W** and **A** characters without kerning applied appear awkwardly spaced.

Many fonts actually contain kerning data that corrects apparent spacing issues between certain characters, which is brilliant because it means the type designers (who know what they're doing) have already done the work for you. It would be a shame not to utilize this data, wouldn't it?

Earlier versions of CSS provided a method of controlling the *tracking* in text in the form of the `letter-spacing` property, which alters the character spacing proportionately, but the CSS toolbox has never offered a true *kerning* tool—until now!

> *Tracking* refers to the proportionate spacing between letters and words in a body of text, whereas *kerning* refers specifically to the adjustment of space between certain character pairs, such as the uppercase *W* and *A* characters.

CSS3 introduced the `font-kerning` property, which provides a method of utilizing a font's kerning data if it contains any. The best thing about this property is its simplicity, as you will gather from the following list of possible values:

- `normal` applies the kerning data to the text.
- `none` ensures that no kerning data is applied to the text.
- `auto` lets the User Agent decide whether or not to apply the kerning data.

See what I mean? All you need to do to fix those annoying character spacing issues is use the `font-kerning` property with a value of `normal`.

Don't get too excited though; reality's about to strike again. The common issue of browser support is again the problem because only Chrome, Safari, and Opera 15+ support `font-kerning`, again using the `-webkit-` prefix.

Providing your short-term memory is up to scratch, you will recall the more widely supported alternative I mentioned when discussing the `font-variant-ligatures` property. Well, that alternative also covers `font-kerning` too, so let's get to it!

Borrowing from SVG

As you've seen, CSS *does* have the tools for the job, but most browsers don't know how to handle those tools yet. For now, you need to resort to something they *can* handle if you want to enable ligatures and kerning on your web page.

This is the point at which CSS has to borrow from the SVG specification. Just as you may have called on your neighbor to borrow his lawnmower, CSS calls on its fellow web language, SVG, to help get the job done.

SVG, or Scalable Vector Graphics, is a language that allows you to describe vector graphics using XML. The language contains properties that allow you style these XML elements, much like CSS.

> **For more information on SVG, I recommend you look at the specification** (`http://www.w3.org/TR/SVG11/`)**, because in this chapter I discuss only the solitary SVG property required to do the business at hand.**

The hero of the hour is the `text-rendering` property. "It looks just like a CSS property!" I hear you cry. That it does, but the values are slightly different because they use the camel casing method for word separation rather than hyphenation.

> **Camel casing refers to the use of uppercase letters to separate words, such as** `propValue` **instead of the hyphenated method,** `prop-value`**.**

The value you need in this instance is, quite appropriately, the `optimizeLegibility` value, which does exactly what it suggests. It attempts to improve the legibility of your text by enabling the font's ligatures and kerning data, thereby achieving the same results as the two CSS3 properties discussed previously. The following snippet shows how you might apply the property:

HTML
```
<h1>WAR on waffles</h1>
```

CSS
```css
h1 {
    text-rendering: optimizeLegibility;
}
```

The results are particularly satisfying (see Figure 2-3), solving what can be really frustrating spacing issues with minimal effort.

Figure 2-3 Text without and with optimized legibility applied (top and bottom, respectively). You can see that alterations have been made in terms of the **WA** kerning pair and the **ffl** ligature.

> If you're scratching your head at the phrase used in this example, here's some explanation. The uppercase character pair *WA* is one of the worst offenders in terms of inappropriate spacing, and the word *waffles* utilizes a lovely three-character ligature. I do not advocate war and certainly have nothing against waffles! Quite the contrary actually.

Remember that when something sounds too good to be true, it usually is! Don't get too downhearted; It's not that bad, but this method does come with certain sacrifices.

The `text-rendering` property basically makes a decision on what the browser should prioritize when rendering text. You can optimize in terms of speed (`optimizeSpeed`), geometric precision (`geometricPrecision`), and of course, legibility (`optimizeLegibility`). So when you use the `optimizeLegibility` value, you are effectively choosing the aesthetic quality of your text over speed and performance.

Don't let that choice put you off too much, though; just be mindful when you want to make this trade-off. If, for example, your web page is huge and performance is crucial, it's probably not the best idea to apply the property straight to the `body` element. Instead, be selective of your usage and apply it only where you think it is really required. For small-scale sites such as personal websites and portfolios, I wouldn't expect the sacrifice in speed to be noticeable enough to cause you any worry.

One last issue to address regarding the `text-rendering` property: remember I mentioned the slightly improved browser support compared to its CSS3 alternatives? Well, Firefox implements its support slightly differently than its Webkit competitors.

Firefox applies the property by default, using `optimizeLegibility` for text with a `font-size` of `20px` or larger and `optimizeSpeed` for anything smaller. Personally, I like this approach because I feel font data that improves legibility *should* be tapped into by default if possible, and the `20px` threshold provides a nice balance, ensuring larger text renders without unnecessary imperfections, while performance doesn't take too much of a hit. I'd like to see the other browser vendors following Firefox's lead on this one.

Maintaining Legibility with Aspect Values

Legibility continues to be the main goal here, as the discussion moves on to *aspect values*. So what is an aspect value? Put simply, it is a font's x-height in relation to the full font size; that is, if a font's x-height is exactly half that of the full font size, the aspect value for that font would be 0.5.

The calculation required is therefore a simple one: the x-height value divided by the full font size equals the aspect value. Figure 2-4 provides further visual explanation.

The x-height of a font is the height of its lowercase x character. Simple!

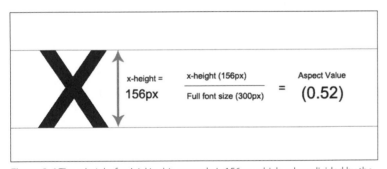

Figure 2-4 The x-height for Arial in this example is 156px, which, when divided by the total 300px font size, gives an aspect value of 0.52.

You may already be pondering the issue at hand: how do you actually get the x-height of the font to carry out this simple calculation, without attempting to manually measure it?

Fortunately, the CSS3 Fonts specification (`http://www.w3.org/TR/css3-fonts`) outlines a clever and simple method of finding a font's aspect value, without your having to calculate the x-height value. With that in mind, it's time to introduce the property that actually uses a font's aspect value: the `font-size-adjust` property. I get to how and why it makes use of the value soon, but first, consider the following code example, as outlined by the specification:

HTML
```
<p>
    <span>x</span>
    <span class="adjust">x</span>
</p>
```

```css
CSS
p {
    font: 300px Arial;
}

span {
    border: 1px solid red;
}

.adjust {
    font-size-adjust: 0.5;
}
```

The preceding code renders two span elements side by side with a red border, allowing you to see whether the adjusted span is bigger or smaller than the other span element. Figure 2-5 shows that with a font-size-adjust value of 0.5, the second span element is slightly smaller than the other, indicating that the aspect value you're looking for must be slightly higher than 0.5.

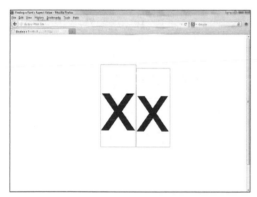

Figure 2-5 The two span elements do not align with a font-size-adjust value of 0.5.

With the font-size-adjust value amended slightly to 0.52, the two span elements align perfectly, and after you've found a value that aligns the two span elements, you've found your font's aspect value!

As you can see, this technique involves a bit of trial and error, but it should prove to be a relatively quick and easy way of identifying your font's aspect value. Alternatively, if the font you're using is well known, the aspect-ratio information is likely to be available already; Google is your friend here.

Okay, so now you know how to get the aspect value. You even know which CSS property makes use of the aspect value, but what does it actually *do* with that value?

As mentioned at the start of this section, the goal is to improve legibility. Consider a font stack consisting of Verdana and then Times as a fallback, with a font-size of 200px. Times has a smaller aspect ratio compared to Verdana, causing it to appear as though it is smaller and therefore less legible even though the font-size value hasn't changed.

You wouldn't generally use this combination in a font stack because Times is a serif font and Verdana is a sans serif font, but this example benefits from a bit of contrast in this regard.

Clearly, legibility is an issue if Times is required as a fallback font because the `font-size` that suffices for Verdana isn't suitable for Times.

At this point, you can call upon the `font-size-adjust` property and the aspect value. Verdana's aspect value is 0.55, so you just need to apply this value to the font, allowing all fallback fonts to adjust to this aspect value, as demonstrated in the following example:

```
p {
    font: 200px Verdana, Times;
    font-size-adjust: 0.55;
}
```

As described, this technique ensures that your text will maintain its legibility when the browser is forced to utilize fallback fonts, as shown in Figure 2-6.

Figure 2-6 Verdana (left) and Times (right) at exactly the same font size without and with the font-size-adjust property applied (top and bottom, respectively)

The only browser that currently supports the `font-size-adjust` property is Firefox, but it's a really useful tool and a vital one if CSS is serious about being a truly comprehensive solution for styling type on the web, so I expect to see other browsers picking up this property sooner rather than later.

More Control with More New Toys

The Level 3 Fonts specification is reasonably extensive and varied, so if I cover the whole thing in the same level of detail as the preceding sections, this chapter would occupy most of the book and would, without doubt, bore you to sleep before you make it anywhere near the end.

Thankfully, I think a few stand-outs from the spec warrant a bit more coverage, and I feel they would slot into your everyday toolkit quite nicely, as opposed to the rest, which satisfy slightly more obscure needs. I cover three of these most useful properties in this section.

Font Stretch

The `font-stretch` property has nine possible values, none of which carry out any kind of unfavorable squashing or stretching of your text as the name might suggest. The possible values are

- `ultra-condensed`
- `extra-condensed`
- `condensed`
- `semi-condensed`
- `normal`
- `semi-expanded`
- `expanded`
- `extra-expanded`
- `ultra-expanded`

If a font includes faces of varying widths, such as those in the preceding list, you can choose to utilize one of the alternative width faces using the `font-stretch` property. To reiterate, this property does not artificially squash or stretch the font if the specified face width does not exist. For example, if a font contains only three face widths (the `condensed`, `normal`, and `expanded` faces) and you attempt to select `extra-condensed`, the browser simply applies the closest existing face width—in this case, `condensed`.

Browser support for the `font-stretch` property is currently limited to Firefox and surprisingly…Internet Explorer from version 9!

Synthetic Font Styling

When a font doesn't include a bold or an italic face, you can force the effect synthetically by simply applying a `font-style` with a value of `italic`; however, this effect only slants the standard face, forcing the type to take a shape it was never intended to take. The result can often look less than appealing, so CSS3 has offered a new property to take care of this issue where required.

The `font-synthesis` property allows you to specify whether or not a font can be styled synthetically in terms of weight and style (italics). The possible values are

- `none` disables all synthetic styling.
- `weight` allows synthesized bold faces.
- `style` allows synthesized italics.

And with this description, you've reached the first property covered in this book that currently has no support among the major browsers. I included coverage on the `font-synthesis` property despite this fact because I believe it has a genuine role to play in the world of type in web design.

By the Numbers

Have you ever used the font named Georgia? If you have, which I imagine is pretty likely, you have probably noticed that the numeric characters fluctuate in terms of their position in relation to the baseline (see Figure 2-7).

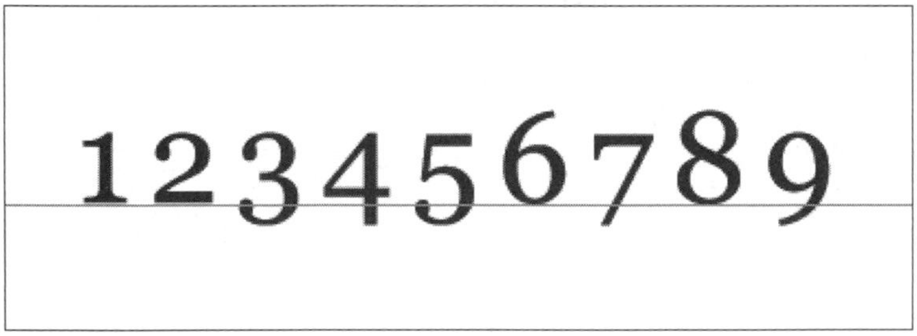

Figure 2-7 Some of Georgia's numeric characters sit on the baseline, whereas others extend below it.

Numbers that take this format are referred to as *old-style numerals*, whereas those that sit consistently on the baseline are known as *lining numerals*. Several fonts these days have both formats built in to the font data, allowing you to choose which format you'd like to use…if you have a way to access this data.

CSS3 has, of course, opened this door for you with the help of the `font-variant-numeric` property. You use this property with a simple value of either `old-style-nums` or `lining-nums` to achieve your desired outcome.

Changing the position is not the only thing the `font-variant-numeric` property does, however; it also taps into data that can affect how your numerals render in a tabular format if the font contains that data. The values you can put to use here are `proportional-nums` and `tabular-nums`, with Figure 2-8 showing the effect of these styles.

But wait—there's more! The `font-variant-numeric` property can also determine the appearance of any numeric fractions in your text. The values that do the job here are `stacked-fractions` and `diagonal-fractions`, the effects of which are illustrated in Figure 2-9.

	Lining	Old-Style
Proportional	409,280	409,280
	367,112	367,112
	155,068	155,068
	171,792	171,792
Tabular	409,280	409,280
	367,112	367,112
	155,068	155,068
	171,792	171,792

Image courtesy of the W3C
Figure 2-8 Tabular data using proportional-nums (top) and tabular-nums (bottom) as well as lining-nums (left) and old-style-nums (right).

Image courtesy of the W3C
Figure 2-9 Data using stacked-fractions (left) and diagonal-fractions (right)

These properties truly add versatility to your toolbox, but again, major browser support is currently nonexistent. If you had grand ideas of putting this to good use in your next project, you will have to hold your fire and keep an eye on the browser support situation.

Hyphenation
The lack of hyphenation on the web has never really been a huge issue, especially when compared to print media, where real estate is really at a premium, but hyphenation can be a useful tool that CSS needs to accommodate to ensure a full range of typographic control.

As I've already alluded to, hyphenation can be particularly useful when real estate is limited, such as in narrow text areas or on small-screen devices. It can also help to eliminate ugly *rags* in blocks of text, as shown in Figure 2-10.

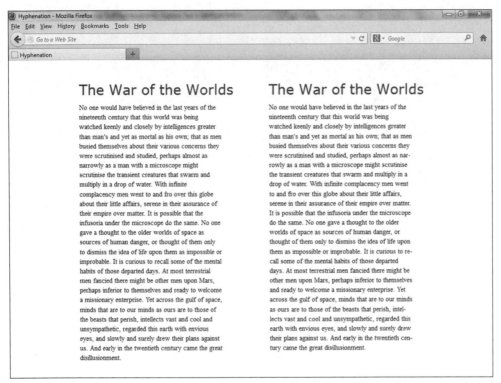

Figure 2-10 A block of text without hyphenation forming a rag (left) and a block of text with hyphenation eliminating the rag (right)

You can achieve hyphenation by hard-coding soft hyphens (`&shy;`) into your HTML to explicitly identify possible hyphenation opportunities, but that's clearly an extremely tedious process that no sensible coder would use.

An alternative method is evidently required, so CSS3 introduced the appropriately named `hyphens` property, which accepts the following values:

- `manual` states that hyphenation should be applied only where soft hyphens are manually added in the HTML.
- `auto` utilizes a language-dependent hyphenation resource to determine where hyphens can be appropriately inserted into words.
- `none` disables all hyphenation.

In addition to these rules, don't forget to set a `lang` attribute on your `html` element so your document knows what language it's dealing with and so it can apply the appropriate hyphenation rules. A basic example would be `lang="en"`.

Happily, the `hyphens` property is supported in Firefox, Safari, and Internet Explorer 10! Bear in mind that you need to use the appropriate browser vendor prefixes (`-moz-`, `-webkit-`, and `-ms-`, respectively) to ensure support in these browsers at present.

If you don't have much interest in typography, you may have found this chapter hard going so far, but you cannot afford to underestimate its importance. Websites are completely based around their content, and good typography is a big part of ensuring this content is well delivered. It's extremely fortunate for you as a web designer that CSS has implemented so many new methods of controlling the various aspects of type in your websites.

But everyone knows that most of the excitement that has surrounded CSS3 since its emergence is due to the new presentational features it introduced, and when it comes to text, this is no different.

With everything discussed so far, you can satisfy the perfectionist within you, but now it's time to get creative.

Writing Modes

One of the more interesting modules that has caught my eye is the Writing Modes specification. There's little point in building you up to let you down, so the first point to establish is the browser support situation—or lack thereof! The new features in this specification (the `writing-mode` and `text-orientation` properties) are currently not compatible with any of the major browsers, but they have enough potential to warrant their inclusion here.

This specification's true purpose is to cater to all types of international writing modes, such as right-to-left and vertical, in addition to the standard left-to-right/top-to-bottom system used by Western languages. If you're thinking you won't be creating any Arabic websites any time soon and therefore planning on skipping this section—not so fast! Take a look at the effects that can be achieved in Figure 2-11, and the cogs may just start turning in your creative engine. Latin script modes may not have any language-based requirements for these options, but I'm sure you can think of other use cases in which vertical writing modes could be of considerable value!

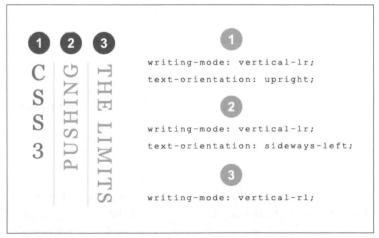

Figure 2-11 Examples of what can be achieved with the writing-mode and text-orientation properties

The Direction Property

There are three core parts that contribute to a writing mode, the first of which is the direction property. This property simply states whether the text flows from left to right or from right to left, accepting a value of either ltr or rtl to achieve the desired direction.

The Writing Mode Property

Things start to get interesting with the writing-mode property, which determines the block flow progression in a block container; that is, it specifies whether lines of text should flow horizontally from top to bottom (the default behavior) or vertically from left to right, for example. This property accepts the following values:

- horizontal-tb dictates that lines of text should flow horizontally from top to bottom.
- vertical-rl states that lines of text flow vertically, like columns, starting from the right side. The default behavior of this rule is also to rotate the characters 90 degrees.
- vertical-lr states that lines of text again flow vertically, but starting from the left side. The characters are also rotated 90 degrees by default.

The Text Orientation Property

The final piece in the writing modes puzzle is the text-orientation property. As I just mentioned, the vertical writing-mode values rotate all glyphs by 90 degrees; the text-orientation property, however, provides control over this aspect of your text, accepting the following values:

- upright is, of course, the initial value and the standard glyph orientation.
- sideways-right rotates the characters by 90 degrees in a clockwise direction, as is the default behavior for the vertical writing modes.
- sideways-left allows you to rotate the characters 90 degrees in a counterclockwise direction.

You can see that this module is certainly not limited to usage involving non-Latin writing modes and could be called upon to produce interesting effects.

SVG to the Rescue!

Again, SVG can be called on to save the day—well, kind of. SVG has its own `writing-mode` property with a different range of possible values, allowing for the same results that you can achieve using the CSS `writing-mode` and `direction` properties. It does, however, lack any kind of `text-orientation` functionality. You can read more about the values and how they work on the Mozilla Developer Network website (`https://developer.mozilla.org/en-US/docs/CSS/writing-mode`), which discusses both the SVG and CSS version of the `writing-mode` property.

The glimmer of hope that is offered by the SVG version is that of browser support. However, it's supported in only one major browser, which, believe it or not, is Internet Explorer! Not only that, IE has had support for this property in some capacity since version 5.5! Take a moment to pick your jaw up off the floor.

To conclude this discussion on writing modes, I recommend taking a look at the SVG property and playing around with that in IE to ensure you understand the concept and some of what you can achieve with writing modes. Keep an eye on browser support for the CSS module, too, and you will be in good stead to jump onto this straight away when browsers start to pick it up.

Looking Good Is Half the Battle

As already mentioned, the areas of CSS3 that have received the most attention are those that have the capability to create rich visual effects that reduce the need for graphics editors because you can achieve the same results directly in the browser with just a line or two of basic CSS.

Text Decoration

First, the `text-decoration` property, which has been around since the inception of CSS, has had a few more strings added to its bow in the Level 3 Text Decoration specification.

Chances are that at some point you have used the `border-bottom` property as a means of decorating your text because it was the easiest way to apply a dotted or dashed underline, for example. This method hasn't caused any harm over the years, but it is a *bit* of a hack when you really consider it. And when you have a property that exists explicitly as a means for decorating your text, that should really be the tool that does the job, not the `border` property.

You guessed it—the `text-decoration` property now comes with some new sister properties allowing you to specify the position of the underline (or overline as the case may be) as well as its color and style. The new properties are

- `text-decoration-line`—Possible values are `none`, `underline`, `overline`, and `line-through`.
- `text-decoration-color`—This property's initial value will match the color of your text but can ultimately be any color value.
- `text-decoration-style`—Possible values are `solid`, `double`, `dotted`, `dashed`, and `wavy`.

These three properties can be combined into the shorthand `text-decoration` property. Unlike the `border` property, this property does not enable you to specify the width of your line because the width is calculated in relation to the size of the text it is decorating. You may have noticed an unfamiliar value among the style options in the form of the `wavy` value. It may be new to CSS, but if you've ever spelled a word wrong in Microsoft Word (and who hasn't?), you have seen this type of underline before.

The `text-decoration-line` property can accept both the `underline` and `overline` values, much like applying `border-bottom` and `border-top` to text. However, you should be very cautious when using these properties together because if there's a chance of your text wrapping onto multiple lines, you may experience problems with overlapping (see Figure 2-12).

Support for these properties is minimal once more, with Firefox the only browser to offer any compatibility, albeit only through supporting the three separate properties with the `-moz-` prefix, but not allowing the shorthand `text-decoration` property.

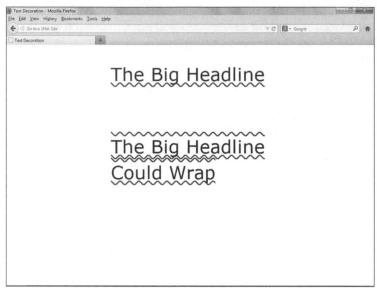

Figure 2-12 Underlined text using the new wavy text-decoration value (top). When both underline and overline are applied, this can cause issues with wrapping text (bottom).

Masking Background Images Over Text

Now this one is *really* cool. The `background-clip` property is part of the Backgrounds and Borders CSS3 module and is discussed in more depth in the next chapter, but you can also use it to enhance your text in a big way.

The specific value of `background-clip` I address here isn't actually part of the W3C specification at the moment but was introduced by the Webkit team. They implemented support into their Chrome and Safari browsers, which is how many of the new, experimental features start out. The feature I am describing in this instance is the `text` value of `background-clip`, which effectively allows you to mask an image over some text, as illustrated in Figure 2-13 (or file `0201-background-clip-text.html` on the companion website at `www.wiley.com/go/ptl/css3`).

Figure 2-13 The image (bottom) has been masked over some text (top).

So how is this effect achieved? First, you need to apply your background image:

HTML
```
<h1>The Big Headline</h1>
```

CSS
```
h1 {
    font: 300px Bebas;
    background: url(bg.jpg);
}
```

Next, you need to make this background image take the shape of the text rather than the container. This is the point at which the background-clip property comes into play:

```
h1 {
    font: 300px Bebas;
    background: url(bg.jpg);
    -webkit-background-clip: text;
}
```

Now the background image has taken the shape of the text, but it's in the *background;* that is, it's behind the currently opaque, black text. So as it stands, there is no change, but the fix is a simple one:

```
h1 {
    font: 300px Bebas;
    background: url(bg.jpg);
    -webkit-background-clip: text;
    color: transparent;
}
```

Now the text color is transparent, so the background image behind it (which has masked over the text) is visible. Success! But that causes a problem in the non-Webkit browsers because the text will be transparent, but the background image won't have masked over the text (it will have simply filled the container as normal). In that case, the text will be invisible on top of the standard background image.

Fortunately, Webkit provides a solution in the form of the -webkit-text-fill-color property, which allows you to specify a text color that will take effect only in Webkit browsers that support this technique, ensuring that the other browsers fall back to the standard color property value. It looks like this:

```
h1 {
    font: 300px Bebas;
    background: url(bg.jpg);
    -webkit-background-clip: text;
    color: #000;
    -webkit-text-fill-color: transparent;
}
```

Text Shadow

Finally, one of the more mainstream parts of the Level 3 Text Decoration module is the `text-shadow` property, which seems to have filtered its way through into the everyday toolkit of most web designers. Its capabilities are much broader than some might believe, though, because any number of multiple, comma-separated shadow values can be combined extremely creatively to produce some impressive effects.

The first of these effects that I describe is the 3D text illusion, which was pioneered by Bootstrap creator Mark Otto (`http://markdotto.com/playground/3d-text/`). But before I begin, here's a quick recap on the basic `text-shadow` syntax:

```
text-shadow: 1px 1px 3px #000;
```

The first two values determine the horizontal and vertical distances of the shadow (in that order), the third value specifies the blur radius of the shadow, and the final value dictates the shadow's color.

You often need your shadows to be subtle and have an element of transparency to them, which calls for the introduction of `rgba()`, an alternative method of specifying color values to the traditional hexadecimal approach. This method requires the red, green, and blue values for a color as well as an alpha transparency value, with 1 being opaque and 0 completely transparent.

```
text-shadow: 1px 1px 3px rgba(0, 0, 0, 0.3);
```

The preceding example would apply a black 1px `text-shadow` at 30 percent opacity.

Anyway, onto 3D text…

Creating 3D Text

Creating 3D text is actually really simple, even if at first glance things seem a bit complicated. Multiple shadows are obviously required, with the vertical shadow value increasing by a pixel each time. Having the shadow colors get slightly darker each time also helps because this creates a more realistic, gradient-like effect. For the final result, take a look at the demo (`0202-3d-text.html`).

```
h1 {
    text-shadow:  0  1px  0  #ccc,
                  0  2px  0  #c5c5c5,
                  0  3px  0  #bbb,
                  0  4px  0  #b5b5b5,
                  0  5px  0  #aaa,
                  0  6px  0  #a5a5a5;
}
```

The preceding snippet provides the basis for your 3D text, simply setting six sharp shadows extending vertically, which get ever so slightly darker with each one to increase the illusion of depth in the actual text. The result so far is demonstrated in Figure 2-14.

Figure 2-14 Very basic 3D text, using multiple vertical shadows

Text shadows have been used to form the 3D text, but they're not actually being utilized as *shadows* in the final output, which, ironically, causes the object to lack realism and depth. So you need to add a few more shadows to the text to act as *real* shadows being cast by the 3D object:

```
h1 {
    text-shadow: 0 1px 0 #ccc,
                 0 2px 0 #c5c5c5,ifconf
                 0 3px 0 #bbb,
                 0 4px 0 #b5b5b5,
                 0 5px 0 #aaa,
                 0 6px 0 #a5a5a5,
                 0 7px 3px rgba(0, 0, 0, 0.3),
                 0 10px 10px rgba(0, 0, 0, 0.2),
                 0 10px 20px rgba(0, 0, 0, 0.15),
                 0 20px 20px rgba(0, 0, 0, 0.1);
}
```

The additional shadow values make use of the blur radius and the rgba() color functionality to subtly spread the shadows around the 3D object as if this text were the cause of these shadows. Figure 2-15 shows the final result.

Figure 2-15 The final 3D text output, made up from 10 text shadows

Creating Outer Glow

On the opposite end of the spectrum from creating a sense of 3D environment with sharp shadows, you can also make great use of the blur aspect of `text-shadow` to create some pretty cool effects, such as an outer glow, as you can see from the demo file `0203-outer-glow.html`.

To create this effect, you need to start by building a few shadow layers that will form the glow around the text in your chosen color, as shown in the following code:

```
h1 {
    text-shadow: 0 0 30px rgba(33, 207, 255, 1),
                 0 0 40px rgba(33, 207, 255, 0.8),
                 0 0 60px rgba(33, 207, 255, 0.5),
                 0 0 100px rgba(33, 207, 255, 0.3);
}
```

This code snippet creates the basis for your outer glow, but the text is sitting very abruptly on top of the blur and doesn't really blend into it, causing a distinct lack of actual *glow* (see Figure 2-16).

Figure 2-16 The outer glow is currently lacking in actual **_glow._**

To remedy this situation, you simply need to add some stronger white layers with a much smaller radius to give the actual text that extra shine, producing the final result as displayed in Figure 2-17.

```
h1 {
    text-shadow: 0 0 10px #fff,
                 0 0 20px rgba(255, 255, 255, 0.3),
                 0 0 30px rgba(33, 207, 255, 1),
                 0 0 40px rgba(33, 207, 255, 0.8),
                 0 0 60px rgba(33, 207, 255, 0.5),
                 0 0 100px rgba(33, 207, 255, 0.3);
    color: rgba(255, 255, 255, 0.8);
}
```

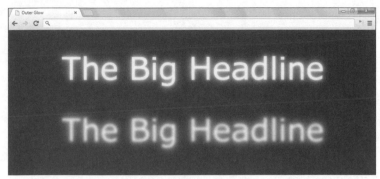

Figure 2-17 The final outer glow effect (top). You could also make the text color transparent to create a blurred text effect (bottom).

Two more `text-shadow` values have been added before the others, but they are a more intense white color than the rest, increasing the glow factor. I've also taken down the opacity of the text color by 20 percent just to take the edge off the text and allow it to blend a little better. If you were to make the text color completely transparent, you could create a pretty interesting "blurry text" effect:

```
color. transparent;
```

When you understand the syntax, which is far from complex, you can evidently be extremely creative with `text-shadow`, much more so than the examples I've detailed here. Go wild, but remember to make sure it degrades gracefully in browsers that don't support the property.

With `text-shadow`, you can at last rejoice in universal support from the current major browser versions. However (there's always a catch), Internet Explorer supports the property only from version 10, which at the time of writing is way behind its preceding versions in terms of usage stats.

Summary

To summarize, there are a lot of new type related features in the CSS3 modules, some of which provide an intricate level of control such as the kerning and ligature tools, whereas others open up possibilities in terms of decorative styling such as shadows and image masking.

I discussed a lot in this chapter that currently has very limited or, in some cases, nonexistent browser support. But don't worry! This just means that you're on the cutting edge of what CSS has to offer, and when browser support does pick up, you will be first on the scene.

Experimentation is one of the best ways to learn, so seek out any shreds of browser support you can and tinker away to your heart's content! In most cases, you can even employ the techniques in production sites, just as long as functionality isn't compromised in unsupportive browsers.

Further Reading

Fonts Level 3 Specification
`http://www.w3.org/TR/css3-fonts/`

Cross Browser Kerning Pairs & Ligatures
`http://aestheticallyloyal.com/public/optimize-legibility/`

Aspect Ratio Table of Common Fonts
`http://webdesign.about.com/od/fonts/a/font-aspect-ratio-table.htm`

Text Level 3 Specification
`http://www.w3.org/TR/css3-text/`

Writing Modes Level 3 Specification
`http://www.w3.org/TR/css3-writing-modes/`

Text Decoration Level 3 Specification
`http://www.w3.org/TR/2012/WD-css-text-decor-3-20121113/`

Chapter 3

New Tools for Backgrounds and Borders

Thanks to CSS3, you can now take advantage of a much more advanced spectrum when it comes to control over your backgrounds. Moreover, in a considerable percentage of situations now, the background image has even been rendered redundant thanks to new CSS features such as rounded corners, drop shadows, and gradients, to name but a few.

If you've only recently broken into the industry, you may be understandably naïve to the pain once suffered by many a web developer who was tasked with implementing shadows, rounded corners, and fancy borders from a design into code. However, I feel most of you will be all too familiar with an age when image slices were the only real option, and I expect you let out a cold shudder as the memories of inefficiency and inconvenience resurfaced!

CSS3 has transformed what was often a tediously drawn out process into the typing of one or two lines of code. This solution obviously means a more efficient process, a more maintainable layout, fewer HTTP requests, and better performance. Great stuff.

In this chapter I go from the more basic capabilities of CSS3 background and border properties to the cutting-edge features for the future, and finish by getting creative and experimental, truly pushing the limits of backgrounds in CSS.

More Control with CSS3 Backgrounds

To begin, I start the discussion with a few related properties that allow you to control the way your backgrounds are displayed in terms of scale and in relation to the CSS box model. The first of these properties is the `background-clip` feature.

Background Clip and Background Origin

To understand the `background-clip` property (which isn't too difficult, I promise), you must consider the laws of the box model.

I assume that if you're reading a book on advanced CSS, you already have a decent grasp of this topic. But if you need a quick refresher, take a look at the spec (`http://www.w3.org/TR/CSS2/box.html`); a quick glance at the images should suffice.

The `background-clip` property basically allows you to specify which parts of the box model your background should cover. The acceptable values are detailed in the following list, and the effects are illustrated in Figure 3-1:

- `border-box` is the default value, which causes the background to cover all the border, padding, and content areas of an element. Keep in mind, though, that the background is always rendered beneath the border layer, so with a standard, opaque border, your background won't visibly flow into the border portion of the element.

- `padding-box` forces the background to cover only the padding and content areas of an element, so it will not flow into the border areas of an element.

- `content-box` ensures the background will cover only the content area, meaning the padding area will be transparent.

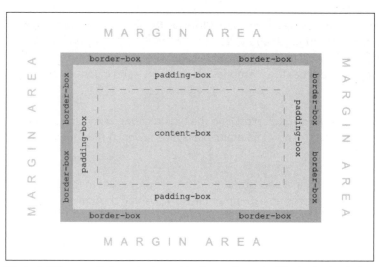

Figure 3-1 The areas that your background will cover for each of the background-clip properties

One frequent use case for this type of background control is to achieve semi-transparent borders for elements that may appear on top of other content on the page, such as a modal box or *lightbox* type feature (see demo `0301-background-clip-padding-box.html` on the companion website at `www.wiley.com/go/ptl/css3`). Figure 3-2 shows the effect in action, and the following code snippet demonstrates how to achieve it:

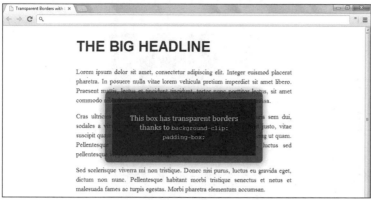

Figure 3-2 The borders are semi-transparent, allowing partial visibility of the content behind the modal box and providing an edge of realism to the design.

HTML
```
<div>
    <p>This is a modal box with semi-transparent borders</p>
</div>
```

CSS
```
div {
    background: rgba(0, 0, 0, 0.95);
    color: #ccc;
    border: 20px solid rgba(0, 0, 0, 0.7);
    background-clip: padding-box;
}
```

The `padding-box` rule is crucial here because it crops the background area of the element down to just the padding area. Without it, the black background of the `div` would expand behind the border, meaning the border's transparency would allow for only the background color to shine through rather than the content behind the element.

One more issue to address here is the use of background images. If you are using a background image and you want to apply a semi-transparent border *inside* the image, using the logic described previously, you just need to use the `background-clip` property with a value of `border-box`. But wait! If you've been paying attention, you remember that `border-box` is the default value for `background-clip` anyway, so it's not even required for this use case. So what's the problem here? Take a look at Figure 3-3 for the answer (you can also view the demo file at `0302-background-origin.html`).

This behavior may seem strange and unexpected, but there is some logic behind it. Consider the following question: when you are using the `background-position` property, where does your background image sit with a value of `top left` (or `0 0`)? It sits at the top left of the *padding* area, not the border area, so this is why the background image in Figure 3-3 starts at that point.

Figure 3-3 The example on the left shows that the background image flows into the right and bottom borders but not the top or left borders. The example on the right shows the desired effect.

This is the point where the `background-origin` property comes into play. Unsurprisingly, this property allows you to specify what position the background image should start from—that is, where exactly `top left` is in terms of `background-position`.

The `background-origin` property takes exactly the same values as `background-clip`, and as you already discovered, its initial value is `padding-box`. But to remedy the situation in Figure 3-3, you need to use the `border-box` value so the background image's starting point is at the top left of the border area, not the padding area. The code therefore looks like this:

```
.box {
    background: url(trees.jpg) no-repeat;
    border: 20px solid rgba(0, 0, 0, 0.7);
    background-origin: border-box;
}
```

Both the `background-clip` and `background-origin` properties have universal major browser support (Internet Explorer from version 9) and do not require any vendor prefixes!

Background Size

The appropriately named `background-size` property affords you the capability to scale your background images in whichever way you want to, which is extremely useful and very much required. Too often have web designers had to save multiple versions of one image to be able to serve different sizes where needed. Yet another issue solved by CSS3!

The property works simply, accepting two length values. The first value declares the width; and the second, the height. If only one length is specified, it is applied to the width of the background image, and the height value computes to `auto`, which maintains the image's aspect ratio. The lengths you specify aren't limited to pixel values, so feel free to use percentages or ems, which benefit from being much more adaptable.

The aspects of `background-size` that have crept into the mainstream in recent times, however, are the keywords and their respective capabilities.

The `contain` keyword basically makes the background image as big as possible while ensuring that both the width and height of the image fit inside the container, as well as maintaining the image's aspect ratio. This means that the entire background image is *always* visible.

The `cover` keyword has gained momentum thanks to current design trends involving huge full-width background images. It does exactly as you might expect, covering the *entire* element no matter what. It equates to either `auto 100%` or `100% auto`, depending on the container's dimensions, ensuring that the aspect ratio of the image is maintained. Figure 3-4 shows the `cover` keyword in action (`0303-background-size-cover.html`).

Figure 3-4 The background will always fill the entire viewport thanks to the cover value of background-size.

The code is wonderfully simple too, as shown in the following snippet:

```css
body {
    background: url(trees.jpg);
    background-size: cover;
}
```

You'll be pleased to learn that `background-size` is, again, supported in all the major browsers, including Internet Explorer 9+.

Understanding the Background Shorthand

Before you move on, it's probably wise to touch on the shorthand syntax for the `background` property, which is getting rather overwhelming and complex now considering the sheer number of properties it combines, new and old. You can see what I mean when you look at the following code:

```
background-image: url(image.jpg);
background-position: 0 -100px;
background-size: cover;
background-repeat: no-repeat;
background-attachment: fixed;
background-origin: border-box;
background-clip: padding-box;
background-color: #333;
```

Now that's a lot of properties just to style a background—too many. Fortunately, you can combine them all into the shorthand property using the following syntax.

```
/*

bg-image bg-position / bg-size bg-repeat bg-attachment bg-origin bg-clip

*/

background: url(image.jpg) 0 -100px / contain no-repeat fixed
            border-box padding-box #333;
```

This syntax is relatively basic with mostly space-separated values, but that forward slash could do with some explanation, as well as a couple of more important points that should be noted:

- The forward slash separates the values for `background-position` and `background-size`. You can include the latter in the shorthand only if *both* `background-position` and `background-size` are present, whereas you can include `background-position` on its own. So it's either both or just `background-position`.

- Regarding the two box values for `background-origin` and `background-clip`, if only one value is specified, it is applied to both properties. If both are declared, as in the preceding code snippet, the first value is for `background-origin` and the second for `background-clip`.

- The rest of the values are pretty flexible in terms of their ordering and can also be omitted if they're not required.

Handling Box Breaks

In this instance, a *box break* refers to an element breaking onto a new line or a new column, for example. The easiest way to understand this concept is to picture an inline element with its own background and padding styles—a span element, for example. At a line break, this `span` element is broken onto two lines, which causes the box and its styling to be literally split into two parts, but the two fragments still behave as if they were one continuous box in terms of styling.

At this point, the `box-decoration-break` property can provide a bit more control. Its initial value is `slice`, producing the effect described previously with the element's styling being sliced in two.

It accepts just one other value: `clone`. This value treats each fragment of the broken element as if they are separate entities, applying the full styling to each part individually, as shown in Figure 3-5 and in the demo at `0304-box-decoration-break.html`.

Figure 3-5 The default slice value (top) and the clone value (bottom) applied to an inline element

Sometimes you might find this property of use for inline elements, as in the preceding example, but a more likely use case involves the new CSS3 multi-column layout feature (see Chapter 11), which would come with large-scale column breaks rather than simple line breaks, presenting a much more considerable problem.

Browser support is currently pretty limited for `box-decoration-break`, with Chrome and Opera the only browsers to offer support, using the `-webkit-` prefix.

Into the Future with the Image Function

The `image()` function is very much one for the future with no current browser support, but it does showcase the kinds of capabilities you can look forward to when more and more of the CSS3 modules are implemented by the browser vendors.

You can use the `image()` notation as an alternative to the `url()` function when calling background images; it boasts much more functionality than its widely used counterpart. The first example of this additional functionality is the ability to specify portions of an image to use, resulting in a similar output to what is often achieved with the `background-position` property when working with sprite images.

However, whereas using `background-position` with sprites allows you to move the background image around so that only a portion of it is visible within the parameters of an element, the `image()` function employs a method that does not suffer from these drawbacks. It simply specifies the portion of an image it wants to use and that's it, no matter what the dimensions are of the element it is applied to. So how does it do that?

```
background-image: image('sprite.png#xywh=0,80,40,40');
```

The call to the image location uses a media fragment identifier to clip the image down to a specific portion and use that portion as an image in its own right. As the preceding line of code suggests, the portion to crop is specified using four pixel-based values, which operate as follows:

- The `x` value dictates how far across from the left edge the clipped image should start.

- The `y` value specifies how far down from the top edge the clipped image should start.

- The `w` value then declares the width of the clipped image.

- Finally, the `h` value states the height of the clipped image.

So, in the previous line of code, the clipped image would be 40x40 pixels and would start at the left edge and 80px down from the top. The result is illustrated in Figure 3-6.

Figure 3-6 The area of the image that is clipped out from the rest of the image to use as a standalone image

Another capability of the `image()` function with great potential is specifying fallback images if, for whatever reason, the preferred image cannot be loaded. The syntax is extremely simple; the images are simply comma-separated in the order they should be called upon, as displayed in the following line of code:

```
background-image: image(primary.svg, secondary.png, tertiary.jpg);
```

A further advantage of the `image()` function over `url()` is the ability to also provide a fallback background color. For example, consider the following code:

```
div {
    background: url(semi-transparent-black.png) #000;
    color: #fff;
}
```

Imagine the background image used is a black background but at 75 percent opacity. The `background-color`, which is only supposed to be used as a fallback in case the image fails, is a solid black color that would then be visible underneath the semi-transparent background image. This is obviously an issue; an ideal solution would be to employ the black background color as a fallback only when the image has failed to load. You guessed it—this is exactly how the `image()` function operates.

```
div {
    background: image(semi-transparent-black.png, black);
    color: white;
}
```

Here, the fallback background color is simply moved inside the `image()` notation, which ensures the color will be put to use only if the image fails.

Multiple Backgrounds

The necessary tools to apply multiple background images to a single element were introduced in CSS3, addressing an obvious and long-existing requirement.

I'm sure you've been in situations that have had you yearning for multiple background support, ultimately having to resort to adding extra markup (*presentational* markup—yuck!) or employing other creative measures.

The Syntax for Multiple Backgrounds

You can find countless uses for multiple backgrounds, from layered backgrounds, to one background image to sit at the top left of an element and another to sit in the bottom right. For the latter use case, consider a `blockquote` element, which you want to decorate with an opening quote image in the top left corner and a closing quote in the bottom right. A previously frustrating scenario is eased with help from the new multiple backgrounds feature:

```
blockquote {
    background: url(quote-open.png) top left no-repeat,
                url(quote-close.png) bottom right no-repeat;
}
```

As you can see, the syntax is extremely easy to grasp because any additional background images are simply appended onto the existing rule and separated with commas.

Layered Backgrounds

For this example, take a look back at the maximized background image in Figure 3-4 that was created in the section describing the `background-size` property. The rays of sunshine highlight certain areas of the scene rather nicely, creating a lighter, more spacious environment, but what if you want to make the scene a little more eerie and atmospheric? I added a black-to-transparent gradient PNG image to overlay the bottom half of the image to help achieve this effect (see Figure 3-7 and the demo at `0305-multiple-backgrounds.html`).

Figure 3-7 I added a black-to-transparent gradient to overlay the bottom half of the maximized background image.

The following code block demonstrates how the additional image layer is applied using the logic from the initial example:

```
body {
    background: url(gradient-overlay.png) bottom repeat-x fixed,
                url(trees.jpg) 0 0 / cover;
}
```

An important point to note when layering background images is the way in which the ordering works. If you have a similar mindset to me, you may have expected the first background image to be applied as the bottom layer, with any additional image calls being added on top of this original image. However, as is evident in the preceding code example, the opposite is, in fact, true. The first specified background image is actually the *top* layer, and the last is the bottom layer.

Animating Multiple Backgrounds

The technique to animate multiple backgrounds allows you to produce effects that truly push the limits of what is now capable using only CSS. Here, I discuss the animation aspect of this technique in terms of the end result; however, I address the technicalities of the animation in great detail when I pick up this example again in Chapter 6, which focuses solely on the CSS3 transition properties.

Figure 3-8 attempts to demonstrate the effects of the animation, but the printed page obviously isn't the most suitable medium for presenting moving elements, so head over to the companion website and view the demo file `0306-animating-multiple-backgrounds.html` to see the technique in its true glory.

Figure 3-8 The process of the animation, from its start position (left) to the end state (right)

Pretty cool, wouldn't you agree? Three background images are required to achieve this effect: the main image, the left cover piece, and the right cover piece, which are marked up as shown in the following snippet:

```
HTML
<div>
    <p>Trees</p>
</div>

CSS
div {
    width: 295px;
    height: 295px;
    border-radius: 50%;
    background: url(cover-left.jpg) no-repeat,
                url(cover-right.jpg) right no-repeat,
                url(trees.jpg) 0 0 / cover;
    transition: 1s;
}
```

> If you're wondering how the popping text works, you'll have to be patient as I get to that in Chapter 6!

Remember, because the main `trees.jpg` image needs to be the bottom layer, it is declared last in the background image stack. This then ensures that the cover images appear on top, hiding the main image from view by default.

Regarding the `border-radius` property (which, of course, sets rounded corners), if the element's `width` and `height` are equal, a `border-radius` value of `50%` ensures that the element is rendered as a perfect circle.

Finally, the transition property (which requires all the various vendor prefixes) ensures any changes to these initial values are animated. So, if one of the initial property values is altered when the `div` is hovered, for example, the change between the two states is gradual. As mentioned previously, I discuss the transition property in depth in Chapter 6.

```
div:hover {
    background-position: -295px -100px, 295px 100px, 0 0;
}
```

Okay, so what's happening here? Basically, three `background-position` value pairs alter the positioning of the three background images when the `div` is hovered. The ordering of these values must be maintained from the initial `background` declarations, which should make it apparent to you that the `cover-left.png` image has been moved up and across to the left, and the `cover-right.png` image has been moved down and across to the right.

Remember, this alteration is animated thanks to the `transition` property, causing the two covering images to slide away in opposite directions, revealing the main `trees.jpg` image behind them!

How easy is that?! Just a few lines of pretty basic CSS! That is the power of CSS3.

Finally, you will be pleased to learn that multiple backgrounds are now supported across the board in the current major browser versions! Internet Explorer once again supports the property from version 9.

New Tools for Borders

CSS3 includes two new sets of properties to spice up borders. The `border-image` properties enable some great tricks for—surprise—using images in your borders. The `border-corner-shape` property makes it simple to curve, notch, bevel, or scoop your borders.

Border Image

The `border-image` property is one of those features that you've probably heard a lot about, but you're not actually sure how it works. Obviously, I'm generalizing, but the reason is that it's not something you can just scan over for 30 seconds and then know exactly how to use it; the concept requires time and consideration to be fully understood so you can use it to its full potential.

When I first came across `border-image`, I expected a simple image slice that would be tiled to fill the border area and that would be it. Fortunately, the property is a lot more sophisticated than that and allows for so much more!

Each of the five `border-image` properties has an important role to play in ensuring your border is rendered exactly how you want it:

- `border-image-source` works just like `background-image`, using the `url()` notation to locate the image that will be used for the border.

- `border-image-slice` accepts up to four number or percentage values, with the former representing pixels (or vector coordinates for vector images), although the `px` unit is not accepted. This property divides your image into nine slices—one to use for the top border, one for the bottom border, one for each side, four for the corners, and then the remaining middle section, which is not used. This property does, however, accept another value in the form of the `fill` keyword, which utilizes the otherwise discarded middle section as the background of the element. Are you still with me? Either way, you will almost certainly benefit from some kind of visual explanation of this aspect of `border-image`, which is provided with Figure 3-9.

- `border-image-width` again accepts up to four number or percentage values, specifying the width of each border. You can also use the `auto` keyword, which simply uses the widths of the image slices specified with `border-image-slice`.

- `border-image-outset` specifies how far a border image is allowed to extend outside an element's border area into the margin area of the element.

- `border-image-repeat` states how the image slices should tile, the acceptable values for which are as follows:

  - `stretch` doesn't tile the image slice, simply stretching it as much as necessary to fill the border area.

  - `repeat` tiles the slice until the border area is full.

  - `round` tiles the slice while ensuring that a whole number of tiles is used to fill the area. If the area cannot be filled using a whole number of tiles, the slice is scaled up or down to ensure that it can.

  - `space` also tiles the slice while ensuring that a whole number of tiles is used to the fill the area. However, in contrast to the preceding rule, if the area cannot be filled using a whole number of tiles, the remaining space is distributed in equal measures around the tiles, so the slice is not rescaled.

Figure 3-9 The border image is divided into nine sections using the border-image-slice property.

Obviously, you don't want to include all these properties every time you want to use an image for your borders. As ever, there is a shorthand property; a few examples of which you can see in the following code:

```
/* The Syntax ---

source slice / width / outset repeat

*/

border-image: url(border.png) 20 10 40 30 / 15 15 20 20 / 10 5 space;

border-image: url(border.png) 10 20 / auto / 5 15;

border-image: url(border.png) 45 fill / auto round;
```

As you can see from the preceding examples, if you don't need to explicitly state a value for some of the properties, you can simply omit them, ensuring they default to their initial values.

How does all this work in action? The most challenging part of understanding border-image is probably the way in which the actual image is sliced up before being put to use, but when you get your head around that part, it all becomes much easier to master.

You can see from Figure 3-9 how the border-image-slice values slice up the image into nine portions that can you then treat as standalone images in their own right. Figure 3-10 shows the final result (0307-border-image.html) using the code from the following snippet:

```
div {
    border-image: url(border.jpg) 45 fill / auto repeat;
}

/* This is the same as… */

div {
    border-image-source: url(border.jpg);
    border-image-slice: 45 fill;
    border-image-width: auto;
    border-image-outset: 0;
    border-image-repeat: repeat;
}
```

Before I wrap up this discussion of border-image, look at Figure 3-11, which uses a different example to illustrate the difference between the round and repeat values of border-image-repeat. Whereas the previous example would have shown zero change between the two values, it's quite evident that this type of image relies heavily on your acknowledging the functionalities of the repeat values. It's also worth bearing in mind that the default value for border-image-repeat is stretch, a very different effect in contrast to background-repeat, which has an initial value of repeat. So remember not to fall into that trap!

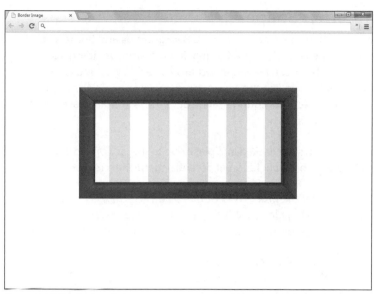

Figure 3-10 The final result

Figure 3-11 A border image using the round value of border-image-repeat (left) and the repeat value (right)

Major browser support exists, but it's patchy. Firefox comes closest, supporting the entire feature apart from the `space` value of `border-image-repeat`, whereas Chrome, Safari and Opera fail to support both the `space` and `round` values. Internet Explorer offers no support whatsoever (yep—even IE10!).

Into the Future with Border Corner Shape

The `border-corner-shape` property has been introduced as part of the Backgrounds and Borders Level 4 module and has been the subject of intense debate recently in the CSS mailing list, also spreading across the web. Lea Verou, a fierce advocate of the feature, has been leading the charge. The CSS Working Group only develops features that are deemed to be badly needed; in the case of `border-corner-shape`, some developers question whether it has legitimate use-cases, suggesting that most of these scenarios are already possible using `border-image` and other such techniques.

The property assists in achieving results that I have often seen hacked into place due to the lack of appropriate tools. I am therefore very much in support of the feature, and think it holds great potential for further creativity, too.

Lea has put together a fantastic preview application for the property (`http://leaverou.github.io/border-corner-shape/`) as well as an accompanying blog post (`http://lea.verou.me/2013/03/preview-border-corner-shape-before-implementations/`) that are both well worth your time.

The concept and syntax behind the feature are relatively simple; it accepts four keywords, with the strength of the effect determined by the `border-radius` value. These four keywords are `curve`, `bevel`, `scoop`, and `notch`, with `curve` being the obvious initial value allowing for basic rounded corners. The following code provides an example, while Figure 3-12 illustrates the effects of each `border-corner-shape` keyword value:

```
div {
    border-corner-shape: scoop;
    border-radius: 30px;
    width: 300px;
    height: 200px;
    background: blue;
}
```

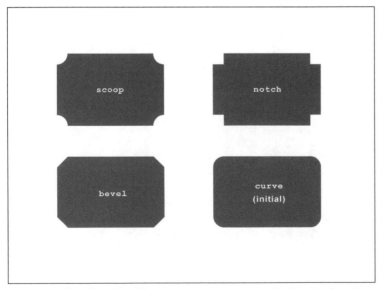

Figure 3-12 The effects of each border-corner-shape value, each with a border-radius value of 30px

I suspect that this feature will remain due to the amount of attention and publicity it has received lately, but it will probably undergo significant syntax changes before it gets picked up by the browsers.

Gradients

Gradients are *everywhere*. Yes, they're typically decorative and therefore not usually essential in terms of functionality, but they add a certain depth and aesthetic value that many would argue play a crucial part in the effectiveness of a website. Consider user interface components; it's no coincidence that buttons often use gradients to create the illusion of realism and depth because this helps to form a more "clickable" element. And if something has an effect on whether or not your button is clicked, I'd say it has a pretty strong case for its claim as a functional tool rather than being dismissed as solely a decorative feature.

The vast majority of websites feature a gradient somewhere in some form or another, no matter how subtle, and more often than not whoever built the site has gone to the effort to save a background image slice to achieve it. Sometimes, it's much more than just an image slice, though. Sometimes, it's a 960x500 pixel radial gradient that your extremely talented designer (who conveniently doesn't have the burden of having to code his designs) has kindly forced upon you.

What if I told you that you didn't have to plot the demise of your extremely talented but annoyingly code-unaware designer? What if I told you that—you know the drill by now—CSS3 has stepped in to once again make your life easier a thousand times over?

I say *easier,* but you'll have to get your head around the syntax first, which isn't the most basic in the CSS3 specification. Luckily for you, though, you're reading a book that explains it with exceptional clarity!

Linear Gradients

Linear gradients are straightforward in concept, as they simply define the merging of two or more colors along a straight line. In terms of CSS, linear gradients in their most basic form are extremely simple, but there's a lot more to get your head around to create more sophisticated outputs.

The Linear Gradient Syntax

The fairly complex syntax situation isn't helped by the fact that multiple versions have existed for this feature, with the various browsers having supported a bit of a mish-mash of these methods in the past, although they do finally seem to be conforming to the current W3C syntax (thankfully).

Kudos must go to the Webkit team for introducing CSS3 gradients way back in 2008, but their first crack at the syntax was a little intimidating, to say the least! The W3C proposed a much more simplistic syntax, which fortunately Webkit soon adapted to, along with the other major browsers.

The original Webkit syntax is long gone, but since then amendments have been made to the new syntax. However, they are still experiencing a bit of an overlap in terms of browser support, so I touch on both before proceeding to use the newest version in the examples. The following code snippet demonstrates a few examples of the old syntax:

The Old Syntax

```
background-image: linear-gradient(black, white);
background-image: linear-gradient(top left, black, white);
background-image: linear-gradient(90deg, #000 30%, #ccc 50%, #fff 70%);
```

The first example is the most basic, simply specifying a black-to-white gradient in the default direction (top to bottom). The second example explicitly states the starting point or angle of the gradient with the keywords `top left`, which can also be stated in degrees. The final example shows how things can get a little more complex with the introduction of additional colors and color stops. This example is quite simple when broken down; the first color (`#000`) is used until it reaches `30%` of the container, where it starts to merge into the second color (`#ccc`), which begins the transition into the final color (`#fff`) at `50%`, before this merging finishes at `70%`. You can see the result in Figure 3-13.

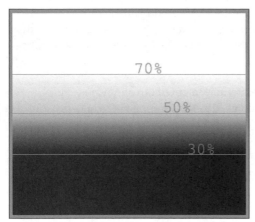

Figure 3-13 The result of the more complex third linear gradient example

The differences between the old syntax and new syntax are marginal, but it's important to be aware of them to ensure your gradients work correctly in all browsers. The following code shows how the previous examples are handled using the new syntax:

The New Syntax

```
background-image: linear-gradient(black, white);
background-image: linear-gradient(to bottom right, black, white);
background-image: linear-gradient(0deg, #000 30%, #ccc 50%, #fff 70%);
```

Can you spot the difference? I told you it was pretty minor. Instead of keywords such as `top`, `left`, `bottom`, and `right` to specify the start point of a linear gradient, you must now use `to bottom`, `to right`, `to top`, and `to left` which allow you to specify the gradient's direction.

The other notable change is the way the angles work. With the old syntax, a value of `0deg` would direct the gradient from left to right, whereas the new syntax goes from bottom to top. To make things even more complicated, the old syntax seems to move the degree values around in the opposite direction to the new syntax! For example, with its start position of left to right, the old syntax would go from bottom to top with a value of 90deg, whereas using the same value, the new syntax would direct the gradient from left to right.

Browser Support

That's a lot of information to take in, but don't get too hung up on it. Until the syntax really settles down, you just need to employ a bit of trial and error to ensure the gradient is rendering in the way you want. Alternatively, you can attempt to memorize the browser support information in Table 3-1.

Table 3-1: Linear Gradients Browser Compatibility

Browser	Syntax	Vendor Prefix
Chrome 4+	Old	`-webkit-`
Chrome 26+	New	None
Safari 4+	Old	`-webkit-`
Firefox 16+	New	None
Firefox 3.6+	Old	`-moz-`
Opera 12.1+	New	None
Opera 11.1+	Old	`-o-`
IE 10	New	None

Bear in mind that Chrome, Firefox, and Opera are backward compatible, so both the new and old syntaxes work in their current respective browser versions. So, to ensure that your gradients work in all the browsers mentioned in Table 3-1, you need a stack similar to the following:

```
/* Old Syntax for Safari and old Chrome/Firefox/Opera versions */
background-image: -moz-linear-gradient(top, #000, #fff);
background-image: -webkit-linear-gradient(top, #000, #fff);
background-image: -o-linear-gradient(top, #000, #fff);

/* New Syntax for current Chrome, Firefox, Opera and IE */
background-image: linear-gradient(to bottom, #000, #fff);
```

Linear Gradients in Action

Now that you've nailed the syntax, it's time to put that code to use. Cast your mind back to the multiple backgrounds section where I used a semi-transparent PNG to overlay the `trees.jpg` background image, creating a much more eerie-looking image. Well, now you can do away with the PNG image and make use of CSS3 gradients to do the job instead! You can take a look at the demo at `0308-linear-gradient.html`.

This is what the code looked like before:

```
body {
    background: url(gradient-overlay.png) bottom repeat-x fixed,
                url(trees.jpg) 0 0 / cover;
}
```

Now to get rid of the `gradient-overlay.png` image and replace it with a CSS gradient!

```
body {
    background: linear-gradient(to top, #000, transparent) bottom fixed,
                url(trees.jpg) 0 0 / cover;
}
```

And with that, you have a minimal number of extra bytes in your CSS, and you've managed to eliminate an entire image! Satisfying.

Radial Gradients

Whereas linear gradients travel in a straight line from one point to another, radial gradients travel outwardly from a center point forming circular shapes.

The Radial Gradients Syntax

The syntax for radial gradients is perhaps even more intimidating at first glance than its linear counterpart and has undergone similar alterations. But once again, when you manage to wrap your head around all the values, you should be able to control every aspect of your radial gradients with ease.

As I just alluded to, the radial gradient syntax was altered in a similar vein to the linear syntax. The old syntax is demonstrated with the following code examples:

The Old Syntax

```
/*
radial-gradient([position], [shape] [size], [color-stops]);
*/

background-image: radial-gradient(black, white);
background-image: radial-gradient(top left, circle, black, white);
background-image: radial-gradient(200px 300px, circle closest-side,
                  #000 30%, #ccc 50%, #fff 70%);
```

Again, in its simplest form, this syntax couldn't be easier, but as more and more control is required, the complexity of the syntax is heightened. The following list attempts to break things down:

- The first value positions the center of the gradient, abiding by the standard positioning laws, which accept numeric length values for the vertical and horizontal positioning as well as keywords such as `top left`.

- The next value determines whether the shape of the gradient should be circular or elliptical, accepting a value of either `circle` or `ellipse`.

- The size of the radial gradient is then specified using a predefined list of acceptable keywords, which have the following effects:

  - closest-side extends the gradient until it meets the nearest edge of the container. Note that the contain keyword is also accepted, which has exactly the same effect. Additionally, if the shape is specified as an ellipse, the closest-side keyword extends the gradient to both the nearest horizontal and nearest vertical edges, which effectively squashes or stretches the gradient, creating an elliptical shape.

  - farthest-side, unsurprisingly, works in the same way as the previous keyword, but extends the gradient until it reaches the edge of the container that is farthest from its center.

  - closest-corner extends the gradient until its edge reaches the nearest corner of its container.

  - farthest-corner extends the gradient until its edge reaches the corner that is farthest away from the gradient's center. You also can achieve the exact same effect using the cover keyword.

- The final aspect of radial gradients is the color values, which work exactly the same as when used with linear gradients.

Have you got all that? It's a lot to take in, but if you take a step back, you really need to understand only a couple of features additional to the linear syntax. So how does the new radial syntax differ?

The New Syntax

```
/*
radial-gradient([size] [shape] at [position], [color-stops]);
*/

background-image: radial-gradient(black, white);
background-image: radial-gradient(circle at top left, black, white);
background-image: radial-gradient(closest-side circle at 200px 300px,
                 #000 30%, #ccc 50%, #fff 70%);
background-image: radial-gradient(30em at 200px 300px, black, white);
```

What's changed then? Time for another breakdown:

- The position values are now preceded by the word at. So you describe the size and shape of the gradient and then state at which position it should be placed; for example, farthest-corner circle at 50% 10%.

- The contain and cover keywords for describing the size of the gradient have been dropped because they only duplicated the functionality achieved by closest-side and farthest-corner, respectively.

- The size of the gradient can now be declared in actual length values, such as pixels and percentages, in addition to the existing keywords. This new feature also makes the shape value (circle or ellipse) redundant if used, as if you specify a single size value (50em for example); then this applies to both the vertical and horizontal length of the gradient, ensuring a perfect circle. And if you specify two size values (such as 50em 30em), the first applies to the width of the gradient and the second to the height, ensuring an elliptical shape is formed.

You can see where the syntax has been tidied up and made slightly easier to understand. Now, how can you make use of radial gradients in the real world?

Radial Gradients in Action

Once again, I refer you back to the `trees.jpg` image, to which I'm going to apply a classic vignette effect (darkened corners) using a radial gradient. It's actually *really* easy.

```
body {
    background: radial-gradient(transparent, black 90%) fixed,
                url(trees.jpg);
    background-size: auto, cover;
}
```

But that's too easy isn't it? If you've been looking at the examples described so far on the companion website, you may have noticed I've been using some CSS filters (which are discussed in depth in the next chapter) in Chrome to make the image look a bit more pleasant. These filters are supported only in Webkit browsers at the moment, so the other browsers have to go without. Or do they?

Gradients can be used to imitate these effects to a certain extent, so I'm going to use them to enhance the vignette effect further (`0309-radial-gradient.html`):

```
body {
    background: radial-gradient(rgba(199, 161, 57, 0.2) 20%, black)
                fixed,

                radial-gradient(rgba(250, 250, 250, 0.3),
                rgba(0, 0, 0, 0.3) 90%) fixed,

                url(trees.jpg);

    background-size: auto, auto, cover;
}
```

Remember the `rgba()` function described earlier? I mentioned that you can use it to specify a color instead of the traditional hexadecimal code, and that is no different when it comes to gradients. This capability allows you to create semi-transparent gradients so you can overlay low-opacity colors over an image, for example. You can see the final result in Figure 3-14.

Figure 3-14 A vignette effect enhanced with a low-opacity brown-to-black radial gradient on top

Browser Support

Browser support differs ever so slightly from linear gradients because most browsers were a bit more hesitant in terms of supporting the radial syntax. Table 3-2 shows how each browser fares.

Table 3-2: Radial Gradients Browser Compatibility

Browser	*Syntax*	*Vendor Prefix*
Chrome 10+	Old	`-webkit-`
Chrome 26+	New	None
Safari 5.1+	Old	`-webkit-`
Firefox 16+	New	None
Firefox 3.6+	Old	`-moz-`
Opera 12.1+	New	None
Opera 11.6+	Old	`-o-`
IE 10	New	None

To ensure browser support in all the browsers shown in Table 3-2, your stack should look similar to the following code block:

```
/* Old Syntax for Safari and old Chrome/Firefox/Opera versions */
background-image: -moz-radial-gradient(top left, circle, #000, #fff);
background-image: -webkit-radial-gradient(top left, circle, #000, #fff);
background-image: -o-radial-gradient(top left, circle, #000, #fff);

/* New Syntax for current Chrome, Firefox, Opera and IE */
background-image: radial-gradient(circle at top left, #000, #fff);
```

Pushing the Limits with Gradient Patterns

This technique is an extremely clever and creative use of CSS gradients and all of the credit must go to all round CSS genius, Lea Verou, who showcased exceptional innovation by pioneering it (http://lea.verou.me/css3patterns/). Figure 3-15 demonstrates some of the patterns that can be created using *only* CSS. I know, right? How is that possible?!

Figure 3-15 Lea Verou's CSS pattern gallery

The key ingredient here is the background-size property, which was discussed earlier in the chapter. If you want to create a polka-dot pattern, for example, you could use a radial gradient to create a solid circle before scaling it down with the background-size property to form a repeating background of smaller circles! The code to achieve this is shown here and the process explained visually with Figure 3-16 (you can take a look at the demo at `0310-gradient-pattern.html`):

```
body {
    background: radial-gradient(rgba(250, 250, 250, 0.1) 10%,
                transparent 11%),

                #124a54;

    background-size: 80px 80px;
}
```

Pretty cool, right? Well, it gets better because this is the place where multiple gradients become of great use. I added an additional layer of circles identical to the first but positioned it 40px across and 40px down from the original layer to create a true polka-dot pattern:

```
body {
    background: radial-gradient(rgba(250, 250, 250, 0.1) 10%,
                transparent 11%),

                radial-gradient(rgba(250, 250, 250, 0.1) 10%,
                transparent 11%),

                #124a54;

    background-size: 80px 80px;
    background-position: 40px 40px, 0 0;
}
```

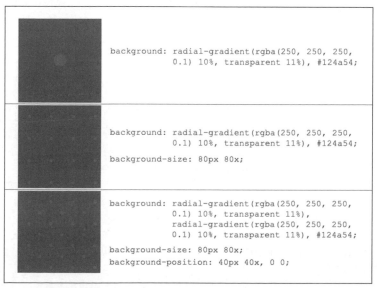

Figure 3-16 The polka-dot pattern creation process explained

With gradient patterns, you can let your imagination roam and get really creative by adding any number of additional gradient layers to form more abstract patterns. My second example (see Figure 3-17 and `0311-gradient-pattern-advanced.html`) combines several linear and radial gradients to create a diamond pattern with the addition of faint horizontal and vertical lines.

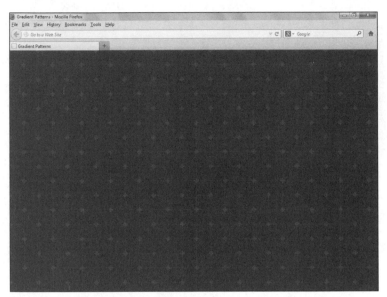

Figure 3-17 Combining multiple gradient layers to create more advanced patterns

First, create the two identical diamond layers using the same logic as the previous example and scale them down so they repeat. Note that I used the shorthand method of positioning the first gradient layer to ensure the related values are grouped together:

```
body {
    background: radial-gradient(transparent 90%, rgba(250, 250, 250, 0.1)
                91%) 40px 40px,

                radial-gradient(transparent 90%, rgba(250, 250, 250, 0.1)
                91%),

                #124a54;

    background-size: 80px 80px;
}
```

Next, to create the suitably thin and faint lines, you need a horizontal and vertical gradient for each of the two diamond layers. You can achieve this effect using just two linear gradients by filling only the first 3 percent and the middle 3 percent (between 49 and 52 percent) of the scaled-down container with the low-opacity white color and using `transparent` to fill the remainder:

```css
body {
    background: radial-gradient(transparent 90%, rgba(250, 250, 250, 0.1)
                91%) 40px 40px,

                radial-gradient(transparent 90%, rgba(250, 250, 250, 0.1)
                91%),

                linear-gradient(rgba(250, 250, 250, 0.07), transparent
                3%, transparent 49%, rgba(250, 250, 250, 0.07) 49%,
                transparent 52%),

                linear-gradient(to right, rgba(250, 250, 250, 0.07),
                transparent 3%, transparent 49%,
                rgba(250, 250, 250, 0.07) 49%, transparent 52%),

                #124a54;
    background-size: 80px 80px;
}
```

And with that you have two repeating diamond layers as well as two sets of horizontal and vertical lines, thanks to a total of four gradient layers! In an ideal world where all browsers support the latest gradient syntax, this method of creating patterns would be convenient, easier to maintain, and more flexible due to its scalable nature. However, with the number of vendor prefixes currently required to make this work in all browsers, the size of this code would dramatically increase, and its effectiveness in terms of better performance would, in turn, take a huge hit.

With that in mind, I advise that you implement this method where possible but always be conscious of the amount of code it requires. Is it really more beneficial than a simple background image? As long as you are suitably cautious, you will be fine.

Summary

Clearly, many new functionalities have been introduced in the Level 3 Backgrounds and Borders module that provide you with a finer level of control and increase the scope for creativity considerably. From simple conveniences such as multiple backgrounds and background sizing to more complex features like border images and gradients, you now have an abundance of new toys to play with!

As with the new tools you encountered in Chapter 2, some of these background and border properties are raring to hit the mainstream and considerably enhance your websites in the browsers that can handle them; others require a bit more caution and consideration to ensure you won't suffer adverse effects in terms of performance and functionality in the older browsers.

To reiterate, make sure you are using these features as progressive enhancement tools, and you will be fine. It always helps to keep one eye on the specifications and the browser support situation to stay current and to ensure you're up-to-date.

Further Reading

CSS Backgrounds and Borders Module Level 3
`http://www.w3.org/TR/css3-background/`

CSS Image Values and Replaced Content Module Level 3
`http://www.w3.org/TR/css3-images/`

Lea Verou's CSS3 Pattern Gallery
`http://lea.verou.me/css3patterns/`

Ultimate CSS3 Gradient Generator
`http://www.colorzilla.com/gradient-editor/`

Chapter 4

Into the Browser with CSS3 Filters and Blending Modes

Now this is what you've been waiting for! You've probably heard the buzz about reproducing Photoshop-like effects directly in your browser, using only CSS. The Filters module, like most CSS3 modules, is by no means finalized, but it is far enough along that the WebKit-based browsers (Chrome, Safari, and Opera 15+) have shown enough confidence to implement support.

Blending modes, on the other hand, which have been proposed as part of the Compositing and Blending specification, are much further away from being implemented by any of the browsers. The working draft is still very much in development, and considerable changes are likely to come.

Both of these specifications have their roots in SVG, originating as tools for vector graphics, but it was Mozilla's Robert O'Callahan who was among the first to recognize the potential for applying SVG effects to HTML elements using CSS (http://robert.ocallahan.org/2008/06/applying-svg-effects-to-html-content_04.html).

The CSS Working Group and the SVG Working Group have since formed the rather awesomely named FX Task Force, which focuses solely on developing features such as filters and blending modes for use in both CSS and SVG.

From this chapter, you can expect a thorough breakdown of CSS3 filters and the various effects that you can achieve through their use. The chapter finishes by briefly discussing the much younger and much more mutable blending modes feature.

CSS3 Filters

CSS filters, of course, take their name and concept from the traditional photographic filters, applying various visual effects such as sepia or blurring to alter the view of the subject. If you're a designer and regularly use graphical editing software such as Photoshop, you are probably already familiar with the concept of digital filters and recognize their use as effective image enhancing tools.

A common use case for such effects in websites is for providing visual feedback for triggered events such as hover or active states, resulting in the need for multiple states of an image. You probably know that image sprites are traditionally used to tackle this issue, allowing you to deliver different states of an image depending on the current scenario.

That practice involves applying the effects to the alternative states in a graphics editor before saving the multiple image states as part of a sprite, resulting in something horrendously inflexible and a maintenance nightmare. So you can understand why web designers often consider the introduction of such capabilities into CSS as the Holy Grail!

CSS3 proposes to transform the aforementioned process into a solitary line of code. And if your client suddenly decides she wants a particular element to be darker instead of lighter on hover? Simply delete a couple of characters in your stylesheet and the job's done.

How Do CSS Filters Work?

The beauty of CSS filters is that they're really easy to understand and use; you don't need to wrap your head around any overly complicated syntax or anything like that.

Their application is not limited to certain elements such as `img` either. You can add a filter to any old element, and everything inside it conforms to the effect, opening a whole host of possibilities. The basic syntax for the filter property is demonstrated in the following code:

```
div {
    filter: grayscale(1);
}
```

Each of the 10 CSS filter functions is discussed in the rest of this section. I continue with `grayscale()` for the first example.

You surely noticed that the images in this book are in black and white, and with many of the filters being based on color, a printed example of the effect would be redundant, so I have not included an image for every filter effect. I therefore very much recommend having the companion website (`www.wiley.com/go/ptl/css3`) open while you read this chapter, if at all possible, because it includes wonderful examples of all of the filter functions in their full glory. Start with `0401-filters.html` for some excellent illustrations of the filters discussed. I know I've mentioned that all of the demos are optimized for Chrome, but it's particularly important to note that in this case as filters are currently only supported in Chrome and Safari.

Grayscale

Many of the filter functions are self-explanatory, not least the `grayscale()` function, which predictably extracts all color from an element, creating a black-and-white output, much like the images in this book!

You can specify the value as a number or a percentage; the number scale ranges from 0 to 1. Note that the higher the value, the more the grayscale effect is applied.

```
filter: grayscale(0.56);

/* Or... */

filter: grayscale(56%);
```

Additionally, rather than declare `grayscale(1)` or `grayscale(100%)`, you can omit the parameter to apply the full effect, so `grayscale()` would produce the same result.

Brightness

The `brightness()` filter also accepts number or percentage values, where `0%` is pure black, `100%` is normal, and anything above that multiplies the effect to increase the brightness, with no pure white achievable.

The following code snippet demonstrates how to achieve the effect displayed in Figure 4-1 using both number and percentage values:

```
filter: brightness(50%);

/* Or... */

filter: brightness(.5);
```

Note that wherever a decimal value such as 0.5 or 0.34 is required, the initial 0 that precedes the decimal point is unnecessary and can be omitted. However, I continue my examples using only percentage values instead of displaying both methods each time.

Brightness

`filter: brightness(50%);`

Figure 4-1 The standard image (left) and the darkened image (right)

If the `brightness()` filter is applied without a value, it defaults to `0%`, causing the element to become solid black.

Contrast

Again, `contrast()` works with number- and percentage-based values. A value of `0%` produces an entirely solid gray image, whereas `100%` applies zero change, and anything above that multiplies the effect to increase the element's contrast. Figure 4-2 shows the effects of a low-contrast value, the code for which follows. Remember that many more examples are featured on the companion website, including color-based effects such as increased contrast.

```
filter: contrast(20%);
```

Figure 4-2 The standard image (left) and the low-contrast image (right)

As with the brightness filter, `contrast()` defaults to `100%` when applied without a value, resulting in zero change to the standard element.

Saturate

The `saturate()` function employs the same type of scale as the contrast filter, with a value of `0%` completely desaturating an element, `100%` applying no change, and anything above that increasingly saturating the image:

```
filter: saturate(300%);
```

You may have realized that a `saturate()` value of `0%` would achieve exactly the same result as the `grayscale()` filter with a value of `100%`, so between these percentage values, the filters' effects are identical, only in reverse!

As with the preceding filters, if the `saturate()` filter is applied with the parameter omitted, it defaults to `100%`, applying no change to its target.

Sepia

The `sepia()` filter is a bit of a specialist effect in that all the other filters are basic, traditional image adjustment controls, whereas this filter is a predefined effect that you might have expected to achieve only through the combined use of the other filter functions. It's a nice shortcut to have and is certainly a popular and widely used effect.

The scale of the sepia filter is similar to the `grayscale()` method in that `0%` causes zero change and `100%` produces the full effect, with everything in between specifying the strength in which the effect is partially applied. However, anything above or below this range is invalid and will apply no effect. Again, using this filter without specifying the parameter causes the value to default to `100%`, which, in this case, applies the full sepia effect:

```
filter: sepia(100%);
```

The sepia effect applies a low saturation shade of brown, and so is apparent only in color, which is showcased in the demo on the companion website.

Hue-Rotate

The `hue-rotate()` filter function works a bit differently from the others because its value takes the form of an angle rather than an amount and is specified in degrees. The reason is that in contrast to using the other filters, you're not declaring the strength of a particular effect; you're simply applying different hue values to alter the element's color. It helps to picture a typical color wheel as the appropriate hue value is located by traveling around the wheel until it reaches the specified angle:

```
filter: hue-rotate(180deg);
```

Aside from its obvious uses in terms of image adjustment, due to its rotational nature, the `hue-rotate()` function can produce some pretty cool effects when combined with animation techniques such as CSS Transitions (which are discussed in depth in Chapter 6), as the filter's journey around the color wheel to find the specified angle would effectively be animated.

If you apply the `hue-rotate()` function while omitting the parameter, the value defaults to `0deg`, causing no changes to occur.

Invert

The `invert()` filter does exactly what you expect, inverting the colors of an element. For example, in a black-and-white image, the light and dark areas swap around when inverted, as shown in Figure 4-3.

Figure 4-3 The standard image (left) and the inverted image (right)

However, just as with the other filters, the inversion effect is not required to be simply true or false; it can be applied partially using a scale of 0% to 100%, with 0% having no effect and 100% causing the targeted element to be fully inverted:

```
filter: invert(100%);
```

In this instance, you don't need to specify a value of 100% when you want to achieve a fully inverted result because this is the default value, so you can omit it from the function.

Opacity

You are no doubt familiar with the opacity property, the functionality for which is duplicated with the opacity() filter; however, the latter benefits from some browsers providing hardware acceleration for filters, allowing for better performance. The filter is also slightly more versatile, allowing for varying effects when combined with other filters, as shown in Figure 4-4 and in the demo file 0402-opacity.html. The following code demonstrates how to achieve these effects:

```
/* Example 1 */
filter: opacity(50%) drop-shadow(5px 5px 0 #000);

/* Example 2 */
filter: drop-shadow(5px 5px 0 #000) opacity(50%);
```

Figure 4-4 The varying effects that can be achieved when using the opacity() filter with other functions. Example 1 is shown on the left, Example 2 on the right.

In contrast to the property, the opacity() filter accepts percentages as well as number values, with 0% being fully transparent, 100% causing no change, and everything in between obviously achieving semitransparency of varying levels.

Drop Shadow

Wait—more duplicate functionality? Yes, the drop-shadow() filter is similar to the box-shadow and text-shadow properties, but not quite identical. You can actually achieve more effects with the drop-shadow()

filter than you can with the properties, as shown in Figure 4-5 and in the demo file `0403-drop-shadow.html`.

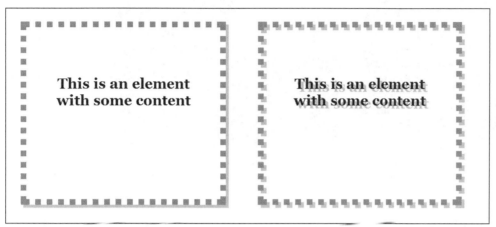

Figure 4-5 The element on the left uses box-shadow, while the element on the right uses the drop-shadow() filter with exactly the same values.

You can see that `box-shadow` applies to the outline of the element, whereas `drop-shadow` actually takes into account transparency and renders the shadows accordingly.

Fortunately, as you can see from the previous `opacity()` example, you don't have to learn any new syntax to utilize this filter because it simply uses the same as the other shadow properties:

```
/* The Syntax ---
[horizontal offset] [vertical offset] [blur radius] [color]
*/
box-shadow: 3px 3px 5px #000;
filter: drop-shadow(3px 3px 5px #000);
```

In contrast to all the other filters, the `drop-shadow()` function requires parameters to be specified and has no fallback default value.

Blur

The final filter to be discussed is the `blur()` function, which accepts a pixel-based value to specify the radius of the Gaussian blur that is applied, as shown in Figure 4-6.

```
filter: blur(3px);
```

The `blur()` filter allows you to obscure elements, which opens up a lot of possibilities additional to the obvious image adjustments use case. When applied without a value, the `blur()` filter defaults to `0px`, which results in zero change to the target element.

Figure 4-6 The standard image (left) and the blurred image (right)

Combining Filters

As I mentioned when discussing the `opacity()` function, you can combine the various filters, allowing for an endless list of considerably more advanced effects. The syntax is elementary, simply accepting space-separated functions as shown in the following example:

```
filter: grayscale() sepia() drop-shadow(8px 8px 0 #333);
```

The `grayscale()` and `sepia()` filters are applied without parameters, ensuring that the full effect is applied in each case, and an additional `drop-shadow()` effect is also used. However, the ordering of these filters is important because it can significantly affect the result achieved.

The ordering from the preceding code snippet converts the image into grayscale and *then* adds a sepia effect before applying a dark gray drop-shadow, resulting in a low saturation image with a brown tint from the sepia effect. If you declared these filters in the reverse order, the drop-shadow would be applied first, then the sepia effect, and then the grayscale filter on top of that, resulting in a completely black-and-white image.

An effective way to make use of combined filters is to use them to enhance your trigger events, such as hover effects. Consider the following example, the effects of which are shown in Figure 4-7 and in the demo file `0404-combining-filters.html`:

```
img {
    filter: brightness(50%) opacity(60%) grayscale();
}

img:hover {
    filter: brightness() opacity() grayscale(0);
}
```

Figure 4-7 The filter effects are applied to the images by default, before being removed on hover.

You can see that the effects are applied to the image by default, obscuring them slightly by making them darker and more transparent and converting them to grayscale. The filter values are then reversed on the hover state, restoring the images to full color and natural brightness when the user hovers over them. Note that the effects are obviously not displayed in their full glory when displayed without color.

Now, a final word of caution on filters. It's evident that this feature, although fairly solid, is still subject to possible change, and in the case of the `brightness()` filter, the browser vendors can sometimes get it wrong in terms of implementation. Performance can also be an issue with effects that use large blur radii, for example, but the majority of these filters have a minor impact in this regard.

There's no doubt, though, that filters will prove a wonderful addition to the CSS toolkit, allowing for faster and more efficient creativity directly in the browser. You can also look forward to the possibility of more flexibility in terms of how these filters are applied to an element, with suggestions in the specification that you should have the ability to apply filters to certain areas of an element such as the background or borders.

One last note on browser support: Chrome, Safari, and Opera 15+ are currently the only browsers to support CSS filters, as mentioned at the start of the chapter, but they require the `-webkit-` prefix, so don't forget to include it for now!

Blending Modes

If you're familiar with Photoshop, you know exactly what blending modes are and are wise to their power in terms of image adjustment tools. And you will probably be excited to learn of their inclusion in the W3C Blending and Compositing specification!

At the moment, they feel an age away from any kind of everyday, mainstream usage because the draft is much younger than some of the other elements with no browser vendor yet to take a chance in terms of implementing these new features. However, the types of effects that can be applied have only ever been associated with graphical editing software such as Photoshop, so their addition to CSS is a huge deal for many, meaning the browser vendors are likely to pick up this capability sooner rather than later—due to demand if nothing else.

What Are Blending Modes?

If you're not a designer, you might not know what blending modes are, and even if you do, you may not be aware of all the various modes and their respective effects.

In basic terms, the colors of an element (the source color) are blended into the colors of a background (the backdrop color) in different ways to create the result color. Figure 4-8 shows how an object appears when blended into a gradient background using the `overlay` blending mode.

Figure 4-8 The gradient is visible through the object due to the blending of the source and backdrop colors.

The specification includes a considerable number of proposed blending modes, listed here, the effects of which are largely color-based.

- `normal`
- `multiply`
- `screen`
- `overlay`
- `darken`
- `lighten`
- `color-dodge`

- `color-burn`
- `hard-light`
- `soft-light`
- `difference`
- `exclusion`
- `hue`
- `saturation`
- `color`
- `luminosity`

The Blending Modes Syntax

You apply the blending modes to an element using the `blend-mode` property, which accepts all the values in the preceding list. The syntax is as basic as it gets, as shown in the following code:

```
blend-mode: overlay;
```

Nice and simple, I'm sure you'll agree! This new feature comes with much more functionality than just the basic application of a blending mode to an entire element, though. Bear in mind that the following additional properties are much less solid than the standard `blend-mode` property and are subject to change at any time:

- `background-blend-mode` sets the blending mode for the background area of an element only.
- `box-shadow-blend-mode` sets the blending mode for any box-shadow values applied to an element.
- `text-shadow-blend-mode` sets the blending mode for any text-shadow values applied to an element.
- `foreground-blend-mode` applies the blending mode to an element's content against the background of the element.

The blending mode feature is evidently very versatile and looks to have the potential to be an extremely useful and widely utilized aspect of CSS.

As already mentioned, browser support is currently nonexistent because the spec is still in its youth, but this is definitely one to watch.

Summary

Filters and blending modes represent a real advancement in a styling language once associated with inadequacies, providing a new dimension to CSS that will potentially revolutionize the way users perceive and use it.

Although I think graphical editing software will always have a place in assisting the web, many are in agreement that the web has relied on it to an extent that we can no longer live without it. With the addition into CSS of so many functionalities traditionally associated with graphic editors, the web is once again becoming self-reliant, in turn maximizing efficiency.

Of course, it's early days, but keep an eye on the specifications and on the browser support situation and experiment as much as you possibly can to get the best out of these features.

Further Reading

Filter Effects 1.0
http://www.w3.org/TR/filter-effects/

Mozilla Developer Network on Filters
https://developer.mozilla.org/en-US/docs/CSS/filter

Using CSS3 Filters to Enhance Your Image Transitions
http://www.tangledindesign.com/blog/using-css3-filters-to-enhance-your-transitions/

HTML5 Rocks—Understanding CSS Filter Effects
http://www.html5rocks.com/en/tutorials/filters/understanding-css/

CSS Filter Effects Playground
http://html5-demos.appspot.com/static/css/filters/index.html

Compositing and Blending 1.0
http://www.w3.org/TR/compositing/

Introducing CSS Blending
http://www.adobe.com/devnet/html5/articles/css-blending.html

Part II

Transforms, Transitions, and Animation

Chapter 5

Introducing CSS3 2D Transforms

Transforms are an extremely powerful addition to CSS3, forming the basis of many of the jaw-dropping CSS experiments you've probably come across around the web in the past couple of years. The true potential of transforms is only fully realized when used in combination with CSS transitions (discussed in Chapter 6) or when their 3D capabilities are tapped into (Chapter 7). First, though, you need to understand how they work, starting with their most basic form—2D transforms. This chapter gives you an in-depth look at 2D transforms that will stand you in good stead when it comes to utilizing their 3D capabilities and combining them with transitions.

On their own, 2D transforms allow you to manipulate an element from its originally intended state in terms of position, size, orientation, and perspective. And they can do all that with just one line of CSS, whereas you may have previously had to rely on image replacement techniques or JavaScript to make such adjustments.

This particular area of CSS3 has received a lot of attention since its emergence and certainly appears to be one of the more fashionable features from the CSS3 specifications. The power and capabilities of transforms as well as their ease of use have pushed the imaginations of front-end developers into overdrive and have justified the excitement and attention surrounding them. It's for this reason that the Transforms module has been picked up fairly quickly by the browser vendors and has subsequently filtered its way through into relative mainstream use before many other features from the CSS3 specs.

In this chapter, I introduce the range of transform functions that afford you the capability to adjust the appearance of your elements in a 2D context in ways that were previously possible only through use of images or JavaScript. I take you through each function, showing you how to use them to reposition, skew, rotate, and scale an element from its original state, before demonstrating how to combine these techniques to further exploit this feature's functionality.

The Transform Property

If you're not familiar with CSS3 transforms, you could be forgiven for expecting an array of complex control properties considering the impressive effects that you can achieve with them. In terms of 2D transforms, though, there is just a solitary property that does the business, which is appropriately named the `transform` property.

The `transform` property accepts a number of functions, but in 2D terms, it has four main players:

- `translate()`
- `skew()`

- `rotate()`

- `scale()`

Each function (expect for `rotate()`) accepts two parameters: one for each dimension. The dimensions in a 2D environment are, of course, the horizontal x-axis and the vertical y-axis, which are addressed further as I discuss the `translate()` function.

> In addition to the four main transform functions, you also have the `matrix()` function. For every transform, there is an equivalent matrix which is significantly more complex and challenging to understand. This is why the previously listed, more human-friendly functions exist. If you've got a mind for math, however, and fancy digging deeper into the ways of the `matrix()` function and getting to grips with the mechanics behind transforms, I recommend taking a look at this article from the Opera development site: `http://dev.opera.com/articles/view/understanding-the-css-transforms-matrix/`.

Translate

What does `translate()` do? Despite the name, I can assure you that it's nothing to do with foreign languages! In short, this function actually allows you to reposition an element from its original location to somewhere else on your page by moving it along the x- and y-axes.

This vertical and horizontal repositioning can be done separately or combined into one function, as demonstrated by the following code:

```
div {
    width: 300px;
    height: 300px;
    background: blue;
    transform: translateX(100px) translateY(50px);
}

/* Or... */

div {
    width: 300px;
    height: 300px;
    background: blue;
    transform: translate(100px, 50px);
}
```

Bear in mind that if the latter example includes just one parameter, it is applied as the x-axis value, while the y-axis gets a value of 0. Figure 5-1 shows how the preceding code *translates* a blue box from its original position to a new location. You can take a closer look in the demo file `0501-translate.html` on the companion website at `www.wiley.com/go/ptl/css3`.

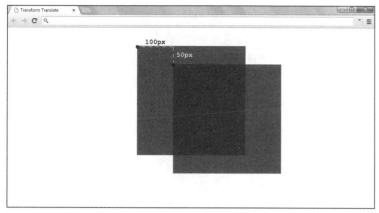

Figure 5-1 The box has moved 100px along the x-axis and 50px along the y-axis.

Wait a second. How does this differ from other, existing positioning tools such as the `position` property and the associated `top`, `left`, `right`, and `bottom` properties? For starters, the `position` property moves an element relative to a container, whereas the `translate()` method always positions an element relative to its original location.

Additionally, an element with `position: absolute;` applied becomes completely independent from the rest of the layout, causing no effect on its sibling elements. The `translate()` function, however, maintains the space originally occupied by the element, while the physically visible, translated element *does* become independent from the rest of the layout. Figure 5-2 explains these effects visually.

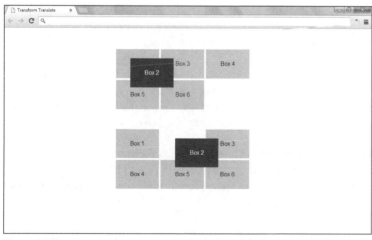

Figure 5-2 The top example uses position: absolute; and the bottom example uses translate().

The following code block shows how the examples in Figure 5-2 are achieved:

```
HTML
<article>
    <div>Box 1</div>
    <div>Box 2</div>
```

```
        <div>Box 3</div>
        <div>Box 4</div>
        <div>Box 5</div>
        <div>Box 6</div>
</article>

/* The above code is replicated exactly for the second example */
```

CSS

```
article {
    position: relative;
}

article:first-child div:nth-child(2) {
    position: absolute;
    left: 40px;
    top: 25px;
}

article:last-child div:nth-child(2) {
    transform: translate(40px, 25px);
}
```

You can see that the first example positions *box 2* relative to its container, so it is 40px in from the left and 25px down from the top of the container. Moreover, as described previously, this box then becomes completely independent from the layout, with the remaining five boxes rendering as if only five boxes were originally defined in the markup.

The second example behaves very differently, with the `translate()` function moving *box 2* to the right by 40px and down by 25px from its original position. However, the space occupied by its original location is maintained, while the visible, translated element does not occupy space in the layout.

With such contrasting behavior, the method you choose to use is obviously heavily dependent on the situation because their use cases vary. I find that `position: absolute;` tends to be more appropriate for layout solutions, whereas `translate()` comes in handy for trigger events, such as `hover` and `active` states. This is a general rule, however, and you must ensure that you consider your particular use case.

Chrome developer and front-end master Paul Irish put together an in-depth article, complete with video demonstration, on why moving elements with `translate()` is better than using `position: absolute;` and `top`/`left` in terms of both performance and output. The following quote from Paul refers to an animation using the two different methods:

> *The top/left has very large time to paint each frame, which results in a choppier transition. [...] The translate version, on the other hand, gets the element elevated onto its own layer on the GPU (called a RenderLayer). Now that it sits on its own layer, any 2D transform [...] can happen purely on the GPU which will stay extremely fast and still get us quick frame rates.*

The full article is certainly worth a look (`http://paulirish.com/2012/why-moving-elements-with-translate-is-better-than-posabs-topleft/`).

Skew

The skew() function has received the least attention of the various transform functions, simply due to a more limited range of uses. Or so is often perceived anyway—perhaps we're just not thinking creatively enough! This function certainly has its uses and when animated can produce some very impressive effects.

Note that while current implementations still support it to ensure compatibility for legacy content, the skew() function on its own has actually been deprecated, and its use should therefore be avoided. Instead, you must use the individual skewX() and skewY() functions to specify the respective x and y skew values, because when combined into the skew() function, they produce different, unexpected results.

So what does the skew transformation actually do? In short, it basically slants an element by turning it around an axis. The best way to understand how it works is to look at my example on the companion website (0502 skew-animated.html), which animates an element from its original starting position to a skewX() value of 360deg, allowing you to see how the element is affected full circle. The example really helps to provide some clarity on the possible ways an element can be skewed, so go take a look…now! I'll wait.

As you can see, because the element is turned around an axis, the function takes parameters in degree values, although you will rarely need to specify a value outside the -90deg to 90deg range. An element is skewed with increasing severity until it reaches complete flatness at the aforementioned right-angle values where the element effectively disappears. Again, this behavior is demonstrated in the animated example on the companion website. If you can't access the site right now, Figure 5-3 should go some way to illustrating how the skew function affects an element. The corresponding demo can be seen in the demo file 0503-skew.html.

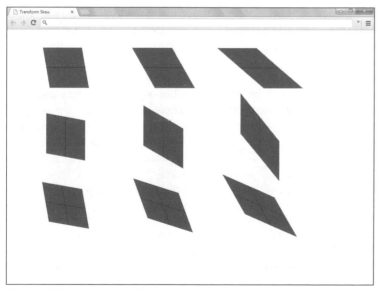

Figure 5-3 The top row skews about the x-axis with increasing severity; the middle row skews about the y-axis with increasing severity; and the bottom row skews about both axes with increasing severity.

The following code shows how each example in Figure 5-3 is achieved:

```
/* Top Row */
div:first-child  { transform: skewX(10deg); }
div:nth-child(2) { transform: skewX(30deg); }
div:nth-child(3) { transform: skewX(50deg); }

/* Middle Row */
div:nth-child(4) { transform: skewY(10deg); }
div:nth-child(5) { transform: skewY(30deg); }
div:nth-child(6) { transform: skewY(50deg); }

/* Bottom Row */
div:nth-child(7) { transform: skewX(10deg) skewY(10deg); }
div:nth-child(8) { transform: skewX(20deg) skewY(20deg); }
div:last-child   { transform: skewX(30deg) skewY(30deg); }
```

The skew transformation type has its uses in its own right in terms of altering the perspective of an element and creating more abstract shapes without having to resort to images, but as with most of the other transform functions, it really starts to shine when animated, as you will discover in Chapter 6!

Rotate

The `rotate()` function is pretty powerful and has proven popular due to a never-ending list of use cases that have been tackled in the past through use of images and/or JavaScript.

As with the skew transform, the `rotate()` function works with degree-based values, as logic would suggest of a rotational transformation. However, whereas the other 2D transform types operate horizontally and vertically along the x- and y-axes, rotation in a 2D environment involves working around the *z-axis*. Confused? It's actually rather simple and very logical. Let me explain.

The z axis typically operates in a 3D environment because this axis comes from the page toward the viewer, as if it were coming out of your screen. Now, picture an ordinary circular disc with a hole in the middle (like a CD or DVD) lying flat on your screen and imagine that this z-axis line is coming through the middle of the disc toward you. If you were to spin the disc around, it would be rotating *around* that z-axis line, but still in a 2D space. Simple!

If you're still not getting this concept, don't worry too much at this stage, as I'll pick it up again in Chapter 7.

So why has this particular transformation type caught the imagination of web designers in such a big way? The reason is largely that it exerts a certain sense of possibility and control over a design that is traditionally associated with graphical editing software that typically comes with much fewer constraints. It opens doors and it does so without any struggle, offering simple and easy-to-understand syntax and functionality in a 2D context.

A basic use case for the `rotate()` function would be to serve more abstract designs without having to resort to using an image, as demonstrated in Figure 5-4 and in the demo file `0504-rotate.html`.

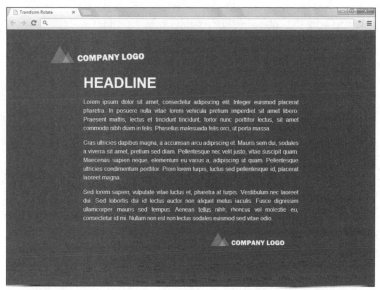

Figure 5-4 The main logo is rotated for aesthetic benefit, whereas the same image is used for the footer logo, which takes the standard orientation.

You can see that the main header logo and footer logo differ in terms of orientation; the main logo is slightly rotated to enhance the aesthetics. This difference would usually require you to save two images: one for the header and one for the footer. With the `rotate()` function, this additional image is eliminated and replaced with a tiny bit of code!

```
header .logo {
    transform: rotate(-3deg);
}
```

Another frequent use case for the `rotate()` function is to change the orientation of text, as shown in Figure 5-5.

Figure 5-5 The month text has been rotated 90 degrees counterclockwise; and the year text, 90 degrees clockwise.

In Figure 5-5, the `rotate()` function maintains the design while still ensuring that real text is delivered, as opposed to an image. It's also flexible and easy to edit; the following code shows how it's done:

HTML
```html
<time datetime="2013-02-06">
    <span>Wednesday</span>
    <span>06</span>
    <span>Feb</span>
    <span>2013</span>
</time>
```

CSS
```css
span:first-child {
    transform: rotate(-90deg);
}

span:last-child {
    transform: rotate(90deg);
}
```

This design obviously takes a lot more styling than is displayed in the preceding code, but I'm just concentrating on the `transform` property here. Head over to the companion website to explore how this example is achieved in more depth (`0505-rotate-text.html`). To reiterate, I've coded the demos to be viewed in Chrome only, to keep the code as simple as possible.

To conclude, the `rotate()` function is, as ever, much more powerful when animated, but I hope it is evident from this section that it has significant value in its own right.

Scale

Last up is the `scale()` function, which allows you to adjust the size of an element by multiplying the original dimensions by a certain amount. For example, a `scaleX()` value of 2 would transform a 200px wide element to be 400px wide. The following code explains this further:

```css
div {
    width: 200px;
    height: 100px;
    transform: scaleX(2) scaleY(2);
}
```

This code effectively gives the `div` element a `width` of `400px` and a `height` of `200px` as both the x and y dimensions have been scaled up by 2. However, you can combine the `scaleX()` and `scaleY()` functions into a single `scale()` function, where the x and y parameters are comma-separated:

```css
transform: scale(2, 2);
```

This particular example can be shortened further, because if you use the scale() function with a single parameter, it applies this value to both the x and y dimensions instead of applying a value of 0 to the omitted parameter:

```
transform: scale(2);

/* A single parameter is applied to both the x and y dimensions */
```

As you may have figured out by now, the scaling system works on the basis that a scale() value of 1 maintains the element's original dimensions, whereas any value above that scales up and any value below scales down.

You may be wondering why you would ever need to use this feature when you could use ready-made width and height properties for specifying an element's dimensions. I refer you back to the translate() section where I touched on the fact that transformed elements have absolutely no effect on their surroundings. Take a look at Figure 5-6 or the demo file 0506-scale.html.

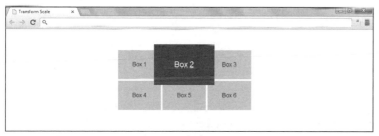

Figure 5-6 The second box is scaled up to twice its original size but has no effect on the flow of the other boxes.

You can see that *box 2* has increased in size while the remaining boxes experience no change in their position or size as if no adjustments have taken place. Now consider this effect being applied to the :hover state of the boxes.

The scale() transform function would produce drastically different results to the output achieved by using the standard width and height properties to scale up the boxes on hover. The best way to see this stark contrast is on the companion website (0507-scale-hover.html), but Figure 5-7 goes some way to illustrating the difference.

You can see that when the boxes are scaled up using the width and height properties, the flow is badly affected, pushing the other boxes down onto the next row. The scale() function, on the other hand, simply enlarges the hovered box from its center, creating the illusion that the box is popping out toward the user while ensuring the surrounding layout is in no way affected.

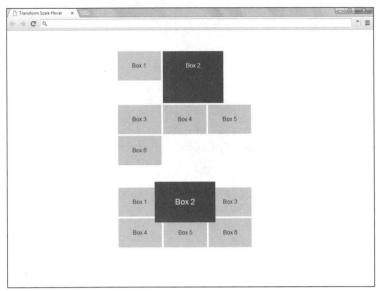

Figure 5-7 The top set of boxes shows how box 2 reacts when scaled up using the width and height properties; the bottom set of boxes resizes box 2 using the scale() transform function.

Bear in mind that if you use this technique on an image thumbnail gallery to enlarge the thumbs on hover, scaling up an image above its initial size would cause the image to pixelate. To remedy this situation, you need to save the image in its largest form; that is, the enlarged thumbnail image. Then you can scale the images *down* by default, before scaling them back up to their original size on hover. The following code illustrates further:

```
.gallery img {
    transform: scale(0.6);
}

.gallery img:hover {
    transform: scale(1);
}
```

As long as the image remains at or under its initial scale, there is no threat of the image being pixelated.

The `scale()` function becomes of increased importance when applying scaling effects on trigger events such as `:hover` states, but this function is also evidently a valid scaling tool in its own right for situations in which the standard sizing properties are not suitable.

Transform Origin

When I began discussing the `transform` property, I made the claim that it works the magic all on its own when it comes to 2D transformations. It certainly can, but there is another option should you need to make use of it: the `transform-origin` property.

You may have noticed that all the transformations featured so far operate from the center of the element. For example, the scaled examples enlarge toward you from the center, and rotated elements are rotated around the central point of the element.

The `transform-origin` property allows you to specify a different point for the transformation to be based around by using x and y parameters to state where this origin point should be. The following code block shows how this works, with the output displayed in the demo file `0508-transform-origin.html` and in Figure 5-8:

```
.boxes1 div:nth-child(2) {
    transform: scale(1.4);
    transform-origin: 50% 50%; /* This is the default central value */
}
.boxes2 div:nth-child(2) {
    transform: scale(1.4);
    transform-origin: 20% 20%;
}
.boxes3 div:nth-child(2) {
    transform: rotate(45deg);
    transform-origin: top left;
}
```

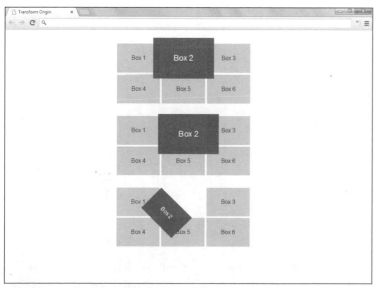

Figure 5-8 The three examples show how the origin point of the transformation has been altered.

The first example shows the default behavior, finding the central point of the element by traveling 50% across the box and 50% down so the transform-origin point is dead center. The next example shows an element that has been scaled up by the same amount as the first example, but the origin of this transformation is 20% across and 20% down.

The final example alters the origin point of a rotated element. When you apply a transform-origin value of top left, the element is rotated around the top left corner point, creating a hinge-like effect. This example makes it apparent that as well as length values, the transform-origin property also accepts the standard positional keyword values.

Combining Transforms

Just like the filter functions that were discussed in the preceding chapter, the transform functions can also be combined, forming a much broader range of achievable effects. Again, just like the filter functions, the transforms are simply space separated, as shown in the following code; the results of which are shown in Figure 5-9.

HTML
```
<article>
    <div>Box1</div>
    <div>Box2</div>
    <!-- etc. -->
</article>
```

CSS
```
article div:nth-child(3) {
    transform: translate(260px, -85px) scale(3.13);
    transform-origin: 0 0;
}
```

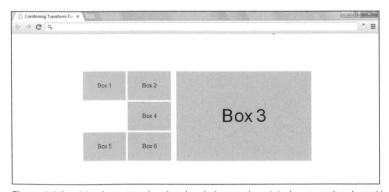

Figure 5-9 Box 3 has been translated and scaled up to show it is the currently selected box.

You can see that *Box 3* has been explicitly targeted and styled as if the user had selected it to be the currently active box, by scaling the element up to over three times its original size and by moving it to the right side of the other boxes.

That result looks great and it shows perfectly how multiple transform types can be combined to produce powerful effects, but with a bit of work, you can make this example a functioning reality using *only* CSS.

If you have a particularly good memory, you might already have an idea about what needs to be done, as you need to cast your mind all the way back to the advanced selectors discussed in Chapter 1 for the answer.

A couple of the selectors I discussed allow you to trigger events on click, including the :checked pseudo-class. Well, it's time for the encore!

With that in mind, the six buttons (one to select each box) take the form of radio check boxes ensuring only one box can be selected at any one time. This is how the markup looks now:

```
<input id="one" name="transforms" type="radio" value="1">
<label for="one">Box 1</label>

<input id="two" name="transforms" type="radio" value="2">
<label for="two">Box 2</label>
<!-- etc. -->

<article>
    <div>Box1</div>
    <div>Box2</div>
    <!- - etc. -->
</article>
```

Remember how this works? The following code shows how you can use this markup structure to target each of the boxes:

```
input[value="1"]:checked ~ article div:first-child {
    transform: translate(260px, 0) scale(3.13);
}

input[value="2"]:checked ~ article div:nth-child(2) {
    transform: translate(135px, 0) scale(3.13);
}

/* etc. */
```

Now let's dissect how this works using the first rule-set from the preceding code snippet:

- When a user clicks a radio button with a value attribute of 1, this particular radio button is targeted using the :checked pseudo-class.

- The next part of the selector targets any article elements that follow this checked radio button thanks to the general sibling combinator (~).

- The final part of the selector targets the first div inside that article element.

- This element then becomes the active box, allowing you to apply your transform functions!

Take a look at the companion website (0509-combining-transforms.html) to see the final example with full functionality.

Browser Support

The time has come to discuss that dreaded subject—browser compatibility. I realize you're probably beginning to recognize me as the bearer of bad news in that regard, but not so much with 2D transforms, you will no doubt be delighted to learn!

Such is the popularity of these new features that the browser vendors have been fairly quick to implement support for 2D transforms, not wanting to be left behind and deemed out-of-date.

> Note that I am referring to support for transforms only in a 2D context at the moment. The 3D transforms come with much more baggage, and browser support differs significantly, as you will discover in Chapter 7.

Of course, IE8 and below present the inevitable stumbling block, but otherwise there is support for 2D transforms across the board, which is exceptional considering the advanced capabilities provided by this module. Chrome, Safari, Opera, and IE9 provide support with their respective vendor prefixes (`-webkit-` and `-ms-`), while Firefox and Internet Explorer 10 provide support even for the un-prefixed `transform` property.

Summary

In this chapter, you learned that elements can be manipulated from their original states in terms of size, orientation, position, and perspective, using just a single line of code and without the need for images. I hope this has given you some idea as to their considerable potential as one of the most powerful features of CSS3; I tap into this potential in the next couple of chapters.

The CSS3 Transforms module represents an unbelievable advancement in terms of the power that CSS is able to provide as a styling language. The module results in yet another score for the web browser in terms of radically reducing the perceived reliance on images and graphical editing software to create aesthetically desirable design elements.

Browser support is undoubtedly in excellent shape and will only improve, so feel free to get those creative cogs turning and experiment with transforms to your heart's content. However, despite impressive browser support, some significant browsers (hello, IE8) still lack support, so *always* ensure graceful degradation in these browsers! I can't stress this point enough. Just be responsible.

Further Reading

CSS Transforms Specification
`http://www.w3.org/TR/css3-transforms`

Mozilla Developer Network on Transforms
`https://developer.mozilla.org/en-US/docs/CSS/transform`

Chapter 6

Bringing 2D Transforms to Life with Transitions

You no doubt grew fed up with my persistent reminders throughout the preceding chapter that the true power and versatility of CSS transforms is only really achieved when they are animated. Well, unsurprisingly, this chapter outlines how to do just that. But not with JavaScript…with pure CSS! CSS3 Transitions, to be precise.

This chapter begins by discussing transitions in great detail, describing how you can harness their full power to produce the most impressive effects. I then show you how to take 2D transforms to the next level by combining them with transition effects, addressing how each transform function can benefit. To finish, I walk you through the process of creating a fully functional scattered image gallery, using nothing but CSS3.

Introducing CSS Transitions

As with transforms, transitions are an extremely powerful addition to CSS and add a brand new dimension to its capabilities in the form of animation.

Don't confuse CSS transitions with the completely separate CSS Animation module; they are entirely different beasts. The Animation module is much more extensive, complex, and capable, and is covered in detail in Chapter 9.

So what are CSS transitions, and how do they differ from CSS animation? In short, transitions ensure that when an element changes from one state to another (such as a hover effect), this change is animated, or *transitioned*, over a set duration.

In keeping with the theme raised in the previous chapters, this tool allows you to transform lines of complex JavaScript into a single line of very readable CSS. The following code shows how you might use the popular JavaScript jQuery library to fade an element over 0.5 seconds to half of its original opacity when hovered, and back again when the hover is released.

```
$('a').hover(function(){
    $(this).stop().animate({opacity: '.5'}, 500);
}, function() {
    $(this).stop().animate({opacity: '1'}, 500);
});
```

Okay, so maybe this example is not particularly *complex,* but it certainly is long-winded, especially for such a simple effect. You have no fewer than 125 characters and 5 lines of code when formatted for readability, not to mention the fact that the code relies on the inclusion of the jQuery library itself, which *then* relies on the user having a JavaScript-enabled browser.

CSS transitions tackle this particular use case with much more grace, efficiency, and conciseness. Using the jQuery method is like standing up and walking over to your TV set to change the channel; using CSS transitions is like sitting back with your feet up using the remote control. They both achieve exactly the same result, but one requires much less time and effort. Look at the following code to see how CSS does the job:

```
a {
    transition: .5s;
}

a:hover {
    opacity: .5;
}
```

What a difference! The CSS method shaves a total of 87 characters off the jQuery method to form this gloriously simple and pleasantly readable block of code. Simple code for a simple effect—that's more like it!

This example uses the absolute bare minimum shorthand syntax to emphasize its simplicity compared to jQuery; however, four properties in total provide control over the actual transition. So let's break it down and look at the individual properties that work the wonders here.

Controlling Your Transitions

The first of these control properties is `transition-property`, which allows you to specify the individual properties to which you want to apply the transition effect. For example, you may want the `background-color` to fade from its original yellow color into blue on `:hover`, but you want your text `color` to change instantly from black to white; in other words, you want to transition the change in `background-color` but not the change in text `color`.

```
a {
    background-color: yellow;
    color: black;
    transition-property: background-color;
    /* Other transition properties */
}

a:hover {
    background-color: blue;
    color: white;
}
```

This code ensures that only the `background-color` change is animated on `:hover`. You can also specify a value of `all` for this property, which, of course, applies the transition effects to all property changes; however, this is the default value, so it can be omitted if this is the desired outcome.

It's important to note that the preceding example does not work in its current state because it lacks the one *required* transition control—the `transition-duration` property. As you might expect, this property allows you to specify the time over which the transition is played out, accepting millisecond (`ms`) or second (`s`) values:

```
transition-property: background-color;
transition-duration: 1s; /* This is the same as 1000ms */
```

This code simply causes the transition from yellow to blue `background-color` to last one second.

Now things start to get a bit more complex as I introduce the `transition-timing-function` property. I explain this aspect of transitions in depth a little further into this chapter, but in basic terms, it allows you to state how a transition accelerates and decelerates over the specified duration.

```
transition-property: background-color;
transition-duration: 1s; /* This is the same as 1000ms */
transition-timing-function: linear;
```

> The `transition-timing-function` **property accepts a predefined list of keywords that will serve your needs in most situations, but for custom effects you could also use the** `cubic-bezier()` **function, covered later in this chapter.**

This particular timing function (`linear`) ensures that the transition maintains a constant speed throughout the duration of the animation. The default value (`ease`) quickly eases the transition into full speed before easing out of the transition slightly more gradually. The other predefined keywords, which are effectively all shorthand for `cubic-bezier()` functions, are covered in the upcoming section on understanding the timing function.

The final piece in the puzzle is the `transition-delay` property, which allows you to declare a certain amount of time from the transition event being triggered to the animation actually starting. For example, a value of `0.5s` would ensure that when the element is hovered, the animation does not begin until half a second has passed:

```
transition-property: background-color;
transition-duration: 1s; /* This is the same as 1000ms */
transition-timing-function: linear;
transition-delay: .5s; /* This is the same as 500ms */
```

All very simple. But as you already know from the initial example, it gets a whole lot simpler when the properties are combined into the shorthand syntax using the `transition` property.

Understanding the Shorthand Syntax

As mentioned previously, the only required `transition` value is the duration parameter because its initial value is `0s`, which would obviously result in an immediate change and therefore no transition!

The only other rule that you must adhere to regards the ordering of the two time-based properties, `transition-duration` and `transition-delay`. You must always specify the duration first; other than that, you may position the various values as you please.

The following examples are all valid and all achieve the same outcome:

```
transition: opacity .5s linear 2s;
transition: linear .5s opacity 2s;
transition: linear opacity .5s 2s;
transition: .5s 2s opacity linear;
```

Of course, sometimes you will be thankful for the amount of control you can exercise over your transitions, but in my own experience, I have rarely found a need to use anything other than the shorthand syntax, and in the majority of cases, the default values have also sufficed (apart from the `duration` parameter, of course). This has resulted in many of my transition rules looking much like the initial example used at the start of this section:

```
transition: .4s;
```

Beautifully simple.

Understanding the Transition Property

You may have noticed that I've been adding the `transition` property to the element's default styles and not to the `:hover` rule-set, as shown in the following example:

Correct
```
a {
    background: blue;
    transition: background .5s ease-in-out;
}

a:hover {
    background: red;
}
```

Incorrect
```
a {
    background: blue;
}

a:hover {
    background: red;
    transition: background .5s ease-in-out;
}
```

The latter (incorrect example) is the result of a common misconception held by many a web designer; that is, if you want the transition to affect the `:hover` state of an element, logic would suggest that the `transition` property must be placed among the `:hover` rules.

This placement works to a certain extent in that the change from the regular state to the `:hover` state is transitioned when the element is hovered; however, when this hover is released, the element snaps back to its default styles rather than gradually reverting back. This may sometimes be the desired effect, but typically you want the `:hover` effect to transition in *and* out.

To ensure you don't fall into this trap, you need to take on a different mindset. Although this misuse of the `transition` property is understandable, it very much limits the property's capabilities. Rather than attempting to ensure that the `:hover` state is animated, you must realize that when applied properly, the `transition` property allows *all* changes to be animated.

For example, when the `transition` property is applied to the default styles, any change to the element is transitioned, from simple `:hover` states to `:focus` states, and even through use of the browser's zoom controls!

As long as you keep these consequences in mind, you should be able to avoid misuse of transitions and apply them exactly as required.

Applying Separate On and Off Transitions

Now that I have issued that warning, there are likely to be occasions on which you want different transition effects when the mouse pointer enters the element and when the pointer leaves. This is the point at which the previously described technique becomes a valid usage of transitions and not a misusage.

For example, suppose you want to change an element's `background-color` from blue to red when hovered. However, you want the initial hover transition to be fairly instant, but when the hover is released, you want the color to revert back to the original state much more gradually. The following code shows how it's done.

> Accurately describing animation in print is quite a challenge, so make sure you head over to the companion website at `www.wiley.com/go/ptl/css3` **and view demo file** `0601-on-off-transitions.html` **to get a better idea of how things are really going down.**

```
div {
    background: blue;
    transition: 5s;
}

div:hover {
    background: red;
    transition: .4s;
}
```

You can see that a secondary `transition` property has been added, but why? The initial transition for when the element is hovered has been moved to the `:hover` rule-set and has been replaced by another `transition` property that will animate the change from the hovered state back to the original state.

The resulting behavior is that when the element is hovered, the `background-color` changes from blue to red over 0.4 seconds, and when this hover is released, the red background changes back to blue over a longer duration of 5 seconds.

All nice and simple, but it can get a little more complex. Consider the following code example:

```
div {
    background: blue;
    transition: .4s;
}

div:hover {
    background: red;
    transform: rotate(360deg);
    transition: background 1s;
}
```

Not a lot's changed from the previous code, but this example produces a radically different effect, largely due to the return of the `rotate()` transform function that you grew to know and love in Chapter 5!

The initial `:hover` transition has been limited through the introduction of a `transition-property` parameter, ensuring that it animates only the `background` property, changing it from blue to red over a duration of one second. This ensures that no animation is applied to the `rotate()` function, causing it to have zero effect on the initial `:hover` action due to its value of `360deg`, which is, of course, the same as its initial value of `0deg`.

In contrast, the `transition` property on the default rule-set that affects the change from the hovered state back to the original state still has only a `duration` parameter, ensuring that all properties will be transitioned back to their original values when the mouse pointer leaves the element. Because the element was rotated 360 degrees on `:hover` (although you wouldn't know it because the rotation wasn't animated), when the mouse pointer leaves, the element rotates full circle from `360deg` back to its original value of `0deg`. And because the rotation is animated this time, the element physically performs this rotation, spinning around in a full circle! Check out `0602-on-off-transitions-complex.html` on the companion website for a demonstration.

Here's a short breakdown of the overall, final result:

- The user hovers on the element, causing the `background-color` to change from blue to red over a period of one second.
- When the mouse pointer leaves the element, the `background-color` changes back from red to blue, and the element spins 360 degrees counterclockwise over a duration of 0.4 seconds.

Understanding the Timing Function

The timing function aspect of CSS-based animations may be tedious, but understanding what it does and how it actually works is important.

As previously alluded to, the `transition-timing-function` property describes the varied acceleration of an animation; it denotes *where* the animation speeds up and slows down over the specified duration of the transition.

The `cubic-bezier()` function allows you to conjure up custom acceleration patterns, but five predefined keywords accepted by the `transition-timing-function` property are effectively shorthand for particular `cubic-bezier()` values:

- ease
- linear
- ease-in
- ease-out
- ease-in-out

The following sections walk you through the specifics of these options.

The Bézier Curve

The `cubic-bezier()` function is made up of four decimal values (on a typical scale of 0–1) that help to form a *Bézier curve*, determining where the transition accelerates and decelerates. The following code shows a typical `cubic-bezier()` function; this particular example equates to the `ease-in-out` keyword:

```
/* cubic-bezier(x, y, x, y); */

transition-timing-function: cubic-bezier(.42, 0, .58, 1);
```

As ever, the best way to understand how this code forms a Bézier curve is to see a visual representation, which is demonstrated in Figure 6-1.

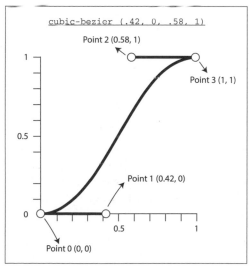

Figure 6-1 The graph shows how the coordinates are plotted to form the Bézier curve.

I expect you're scratching your head at this point—metaphorically if not literally. The first thing to understand is that a total of four points are plotted on the graph to form the curve (points 0, 1, 2, and 3), but points 0 and 3 are always 0, 0 (bottom left) and 1, 1 (top right), respectively. This leaves points 1 and 2 to be plotted using the `cubic-bezier()` function, with the first pair of numbers specifying the x- and y-coordinates for point 1, and the second pair of numbers determining the x- and y-coordinates for point 2.

So, using the preceding example and as shown in Figure 6-1, point 1 is positioned at `0.42` on the x-axis and `0` on the y-axis, while point 2 is positioned at `0.58` on the x-axis and `1` on the y-axis.

Even after an in-depth explanation, the concept of the `cubic-bezier()` function can still be hard to grasp, but it becomes a whole lot easier after you play around with the curve manually and see how the resulting animation corresponds to it.

Lea Verou has created a particularly impressive playground for creating and comparing `cubic-bezier()` **functions, located at the aptly named** `http://cubic-bezier.com`**. I strongly recommend paying a visit and having a play around on the site before proceeding with the rest of this chapter. Verou's tool makes it extremely easy to see how the timing function can dramatically affect the perceived speed of the animation. For example, the** `ease-in-out` **example I've been using starts and finishes slowly, meaning it has to cover the middle ground at a faster pace to be able to finish in the specified duration. Alternatively, the** `linear` **timing function maintains a constant speed throughout the duration, so although it is quicker off the mark, it appears slower than** `ease-in-out` **for the majority of the animation.**

Before moving onto the preset keywords and their various effects, I'm going to touch on using values outside the typical 0–1 range in `cubic-bezier()` functions. While the x-coordinates *are* limited to this range, the y-coordinates can theoretically be anything you like—even negative values!

You can use this technique to add some pretty interesting "bounce" effects to your animations. Consider the following example:

```
transition-timing-function: cubic-bezier(.32, -0.6, .68, 1.6);
```

As shown in Figure 6-2, the y-coordinate for point 1 of the curve delves to a negative value of `-0.6`, while the y-coordinate for point 2 of the curve stretches beyond the standard range to a value of `1.6`.

This code results in slight backward motion at the beginning and end of the animation, causing a bounce-like effect. Think of it like taking a couple of steps back to get a running start, and then at the end, the momentum carries you past your destination, causing you to take a couple of steps back again to ensure you do finish at the intended destination. Again, you really need to open the companion website and take a look at `0603-cubic-bezier.html` to truly understand how this works in terms of the final output.

Now, on to the keywords.

You can see a demo of the various keywords on the companion website: `0604-timing-function-keywords.html`.

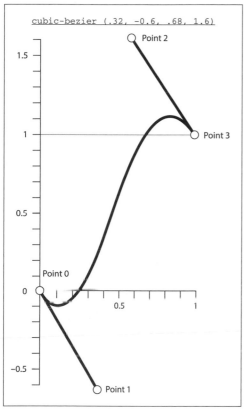

Figure 6-2 This symmetric Bézier curve stretches below and beyond the standard range of 0–1.

Ease

The ease keyword is the default value for the transition-timing-function property. As previously described, it quickly eases the animation into full speed before easing out slightly more gradually. The Bézier curve for ease is formed using the following cubic-bezier() function, which is represented visually in Figure 6-3:

```
transition-timing-function: ease;

/* The equivalent cubic-bezier() function... */

transition-timing-function: cubic-bezier(.25, .1, .25, 1);
```

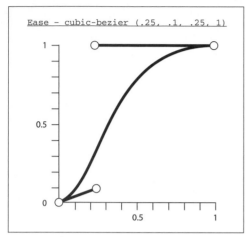

Figure 6-3 The Bézier curve for the ease keyword

Linear

I touched on the linear keyword a couple of times already, which as the name suggests, ensures that the animation maintains a constant speed throughout the duration, so no acceleration or deceleration occurs. The following code shows the equivalent cubic-bezier() function with the resultant curve shown in Figure 6-4:

```
transition-timing-function: linear;

/* The equivalent cubic-bezier() function... */

transition-timing-function: cubic-bezier(0, 0, 1, 1);
```

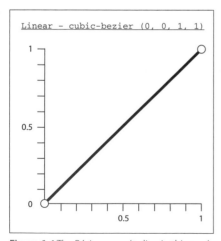

Figure 6-4 The Bézier curve (or line in this case) for the linear keyword

Ease-In

The `ease-in` keyword does just what you might expect: it eases the animation into full speed before maintaining a constant speed through to the finish of the transition. Again, the Bézier curve is shown in Figure 6-5 using the following code:

```
transition-timing-function: ease-in;

/* The equivalent cubic-bezier() function... */

transition-timing-function: cubic-bezier(.42, 0, 1, 1);
```

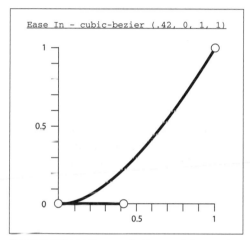

Figure 6-5 The Bézier curve for the ease-in keyword

Ease-Out

Predictably, the `ease-out` keyword does the opposite to its `ease-in` counterpart, hitting full speed right off the bat before slowing down for the finish. And again as you would expect, the Bézier curve shows the exact opposite of the previous example as if it has been rotated 180 degrees, as shown in Figure 6-6.

```
transition-timing-function: ease-out;

/* The equivalent cubic-bezier() function... */

transition-timing-function: cubic-bezier(0, 0, .58, 1);
```

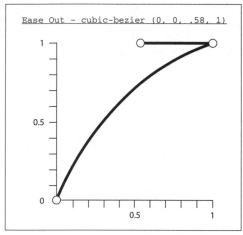

Figure 6-6 The Bézier curve for the ease-out keyword

Ease-In-Out

The final `cubic-bezier()` shorthand keyword is the `ease-in-out` value, which is basically a combination of the preceding two examples. It is similar to the default `ease` value, although this one eases in and out at the same rate, whereas the `ease` value begins with a much stronger acceleration. Figure 6-7 illustrates the equivalent Bézier curve.

```
transition-timing-function: ease-in-out;

/* The equivalent cubic-bezier() function... */

transition-timing-function: cubic-bezier(.42, 0, .58, 1);
```

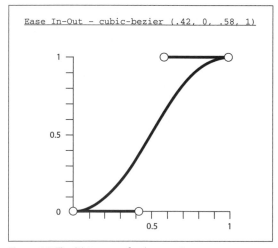

Figure 6-7 The Bézier curve for the ease-in-out keyword

Stepping Functions

Did you think you'd seen the last of CSS timing functions? You should be so lucky! As well as the Bézier curve, the timing function can also be expressed as a *stepping function*. Rather than a smooth transition, the steps() function specifies a number of, errm, steps that the animation should be divided into.

The function accepts two parameters. The first is a positive integer (decimal values are invalid here) specifying the number of steps. The second is a value of either start or end, dictating whether the state change should take place at the start or end of a step (this parameter is optional, with a default value of end). For example, if the step intervals are three seconds each, a value of start would trigger the state change at the start of the three seconds, whereas a value of end would trigger the state change *after* the three-second intervals.

To keep the math simple, consider the following example:

```
div {
    width: 300px;
    height: 300px;
    transition: 5s steps(5, start);
}

div:hover {
    transform: translate(500px, 0);
}
```

This code states that when hovered, the div moves to the right by 500px in five steps over a duration of five seconds. The result, thanks to the steps(5, start) function, is that the box moves by 100px each second. So, the box is hovered, causing it to move instantly to the 100px mark (the first move is instant due to the start parameter). After one second, it snaps to the 200px mark, and then after another second, it snaps to the 300px mark, and so on.

Figure 6-8 shows how the stepping functions translate to a graphical representation.

For a practical use case, consider a sprite image containing the frames to an animation, as shown in Figure 6-9. If you apply this image as the background to an element, you can then use background-position to move the sprite image all the way to the left and animate this change in position using a transition.

However, a typical smooth transition does not achieve the desired effect here because it simply causes each frame to slide in and out of view. Using the steps() function, though, you can bring each frame into view, step by step, which effectively plays the desired animation, frame by frame. The following code shows how it's done, but head over to the website to see it in action (0605-steps-timing-function.html).

```
div {
    width: 125px;
    height: 150px;
    background: url(images/sprite.jpg) left;
    transition: 2s steps(16);
    /* The no. of steps equals the number of frames in the sprite */
}

div:hover {
    background-position: -2000px 0;
}
```

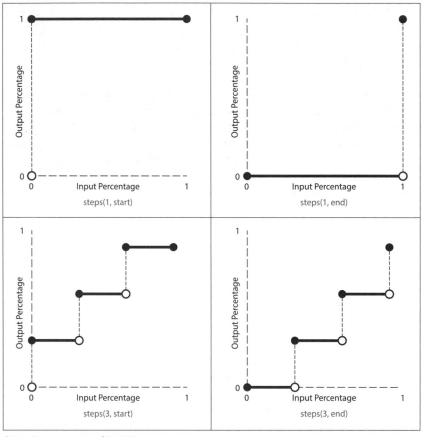

Original image courtesy of the W3C
Figure 6-8 Visual representations of the steps() function

Figure 6-9 A sprite image containing 16 frames to an animation

Before signing off on timing functions (hooray!), let's look at two shorthand keywords for the `steps()` function, demonstrated in the following code:

```
transition-timing-function: step-start;
/* is the same as... */
transition-timing-function: steps(1, start);

transition-timing-function: step-end;
/* is the same as... */
transition-timing-function: steps(1, end);
```

And with that, your understanding of CSS-based timing functions should now be rather substantial!

Browser Support for Transitions

As with Transforms, the Transitions module has been a cause of much excitement in the world of web development, which has subsequently led to the browser vendors meeting this demand fairly promptly.

Support in an experimental capacity has been available for a long time now in the more modern browsers with the use of vendor prefixes. However, such is the popularity and widespread use of CSS transitions at the current time that the vendors have shown the confidence to actually drop the prefix!

Some browsers still haven't picked up on some areas of the Transitions module yet, such as the more advanced timing functions, but in general, transitions are extremely well supported. Table 6-1 provides an overview of which browsers support transitions with and without a prefix, and Table 6-2 shows the support for timing functions.

Table 6-1: Transitions Browser Compatibility

Browser	Prefixed Support	Unprefixed Support
Chrome	4+	26+
Firefox	4+	16+
Opera	10.5+	12.1+
Safari	3.1+	Not supported
IE	N/A	10

Table 6-2: Timing Functions Browser Compatibility

Browser	Basic Support	Cubic Bézier (below and beyond 0–1 range)	Steps()
Chrome	4+	16+	8+
Firefox	4+	4+	4+
Opera	10.5+	12.1+	12.1+
Safari	3.1+	6+	5.1+
IE	10	10	10

You can see that four of the five major browsers now support unprefixed transitions, which is properly *awesome*. Moreover, the advanced timing functions have been picked up by all the browsers now too!

All in all, transitions are in excellent shape, and you can begin making use of them right away! And you will recall from the preceding chapter that transforms have reached a similar level in terms of browser compatibility, which is rather convenient because when the two technologies are combined, the results can be staggering.

Transitions in Action

Okay, enough theory—on to the exciting stuff! I already gave you a few tastes of what can be achieved with transitions, but they are capable of so much more.

To begin, cast your mind back to Chapter 3 and the section on animating multiple backgrounds. You may remember that I promised to pick up that example again in this very chapter, so here it is! Figure 6-10 provides a reminder of the effect achieved by the animation, but you can see the full works in the demo file `0606-animating-multiple-backgrounds.html`.

Figure 6-10 The process of the animation from its start position (left) to the end state (right)

Bear in mind that in the code examples, I include only the important stuff that's relevant to the animations and omit everything else. As ever, it would be beneficial if you had the live demo open throughout this section.

First, the markup couldn't be simpler, and the styling uses nothing that hasn't already been covered, as shown by the following block of code:

```
HTML
<div>
    <p>Trees</p>
</div>

CSS
div {
    background: url(cover-left.png) 0 -1px no-repeat,
                url(cover-right.png) right no-repeat,
                url(trees.jpg) 0 0 / cover;
}

p {
    font: bold 0em Arial;
}

div:hover {
    background-position: -295px -100px, 295px 100px, 0 0;
    filter: sepia(0.8); /* Don't forget vendor prefixes! */
```

```
}

div:hover p {
    font-size: 3em;
    background: rgba(250, 250, 250, 0.5);
}
```

The next step is to analyze what happens to the two elements when the div is hovered. You can see that the div uses the background-position property to move the two covering background images out of view (to reveal the trees.jpg background image) and applies a sepia filter. The p element is hidden by default due to a font-size value of 0em; however, this is increased to 3em when the div is hovered, and a semi-transparent background is added with help from the rgba() function.

So, the preceding describes the original state and the final hovered state, but these value changes need to be transitioned to create the animation. How is this effect achieved? First, you obviously need to apply a transition to the div element, as shown in the following code:

```
div {
    background: url(cover-left.png) 0  1px no-repeat,
                url(cover-right.png) right no-repeat,
                url(trees.jpg) 0 0 / cover;
    transition: 1s;
}
```

This code simply ensures that any changes to the div element will be animated, so that's half the job done! However, the transition property doesn't cascade, which means the p child will not inherit it, causing any changes to the p element to snap into effect rather than using a gradual change, which is obviously not the desired effect. You can easily remedy this situation by adding a transition onto the p element as well as the div:

```
div {
    background: url(cover-left.png) 0 -1px no-repeat,
                url(cover-right.png) right no-repeat,
                url(trees.jpg) 0 0 / cover;
    transition: 1s;
}

p {
    font: bold 0em Arial;
    transition: 1s;
}
```

Now the text is smoothly enlarged as if popping out toward the user when the div is hovered.

Almost there! This code would suffice in many situations, but in this particular example, it's not quite perfect. Granted, you have to look pretty closely, but if you do, you can see that during the transition, the p element's text and background are visible *on top of* the sliding background images that are supposed to cover up this text, which is the opposite of the illusion you're trying to achieve.

This situation creates a bit of a Catch-22; to prevent the text showing on top of the sliding cover images, it needs to be slower to transition in but much faster to transition out. For example, adding a `transition-delay` parameter would ensure that the text doesn't start to enlarge until the covers have slid out of view, which is just the ticket! But then when the hover is released, this delay is still applied to the *hover off* transition, allowing the sliding covers to almost shut before the text has even started to shrink back down.

I'm hoping you already know what's coming next by applying the logic from earlier in the chapter. The answer, of course, is to utilize the technique that allows you to apply a different transition when you hover on and off an element.

To put this technique into practice, you must move the transition controlling the *hover on* effect to sit among the p element's hovered styles, whereas you must place the transition controlling the *hover off* effect among the p element's default styles, as demonstrated in the following code:

```
p {
    font: bold 0em Arial;
    transition: .5s; /* Hover off effect */
}

div:hover p {
    font-size: 3em;
    transition: 1s .2s; /* Hover on effect */
}
```

The *hover on* transition is delayed by 0.2 seconds, allowing the sliding cover images just enough time to move out of view before the text starts enlarging. Then the *hover off* effect shrinks the text down at a doubly quick speed of 0.5 seconds, ensuring it is no longer visible by the time the sliding covers are moving back into place.

To enhance the *hover on* effect further, you could also use the `cubic-bezier()` timing function and use a value outside the 0–1 range to create a "bounced" finish to the enlarging text transition:

```
div:hover p {
    font-size: 3em;
    transition: 1s .2s cubic-bezier(.2, .4, .4, 2);
}
```

And with that, you have a functional, animated solution. If you've struggled to make sense of certain parts of the process, take another look at the demo while you walk through the code again.

Combining Transitions and 2D Transforms

Right, you're coming toward the business end of this chapter now. After all the tasters, in this section I address explicitly the combination of transitions and 2D transforms.

Transitioning Rotate

You've seen a few glimpses of the `rotate()` function being transitioned in some of the previous examples, but now it's time for a bit more of an in-depth look. If you read the preceding chapter, you should know how the `rotate()` transform operates in a 2D environment, turning around the z-axis in degree-based values.

A common way of using `rotate()` with transitions is to spin an element full circle when hovered. A value of `360deg` is, of course, exactly the same as `0deg`, so when applied to a `:hover` state without a transition, there is no visible change. However, with the simple addition of the `transition` property, this full circle journey from 0 degrees to 360 degrees becomes animated, causing the element to spin around when hovered. The code is extremely basic, as demonstrated in the following snippet:

```
div {
    width: 300px;
    height: 300px;
    background: blue;
    transition: 1s;
}

div:hover {
    transform: rotate(360deg);
}
```

For an animation that can look so impressive, this code is delightfully simple; just two lines achieve the desired result!

What else can be done by animating the `rotate()` function? The possibilities are nigh on endless if you think creatively enough; here's another example.

I touched on this use of `rotate()` in the preceding chapter, but here I show you how it works when animated. Picture an art gallery with a framed painting on the wall; unfortunately, the painting slips and ends up hanging from one corner, as shown in Figure 6-11. The scene is set. Now, I'm going to demonstrate how you can play out this frankly disastrous scenario in your browser using transforms and transitions!

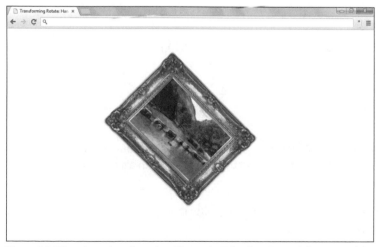

Figure 6-11 The picture has slipped and is now hanging from its top left corner only!

The `transform-origin` property comes into play here, which, in the case of `rotate()`, allows you to control where the central point of rotation is located within the element. Consider the following code, for example:

```
div {
    background: url(painting.jpg);
    transform-origin: 0 0;
    transition: 1.4s;
}

div:hover {
    transform: rotate(45deg);
}
```

Obviously, the `transition` property ensures that when the `div` is hovered, the journey from `0deg` to `45deg` is animated. Additionally, this `transform-origin value` ensures that the rotation happens about the top left corner of the element, creating the "hanging" effect that you want to achieve.

Of course, you need to look at the working demo (`0607-transforming-rotate.html`) to see the effect in all its glory, but I hope you can get the gist from this description. The outcome so far is that when the `div` is hovered, it rotates 45 degrees clockwise around its top left corner. However, the resulting animation comes to a pretty abrupt halt at this 45-degree mark, which isn't really a natural movement for a painting that has fallen from one corner.

This is the point at which our old friend `cubic-bezier()` comes into play again. By playing around with parameters outside the standard 0–1 range, you can create effects that include backward motion, which is perfect for adding the finishing touch to the hanging painting example.

To create a more realistic motion, you would ideally want the painting to swing past the "final" 45-degree mark and then swing back a little before settling to a stop on the final 45-degree spot. As previously alluded to, this effect is possible thanks to the following `cubic-bezier()` function:

```
div {
    background: url(painting.jpg);
    transform-origin: 0 0;
    transition: 1.4s cubic-bezier(.55, 2.3, .52, .52);
}

div:hover {
    transform: rotate(45deg);
}
```

You can see from the actual Bézier curve in Figure 6-12 that this timing function causes the animation to run beyond the intended finishing spot before going back on itself and then finishing with a slight touch of forward motion to finally land on the intended spot.

I told you those timing functions may appear tedious, but, boy, are they nifty little tools!

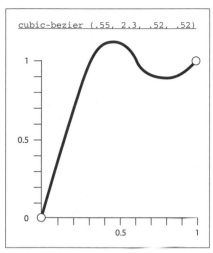

Figure 6-12 The Bézier curve that creates the swinging motion

To give this example a final bit of polish, I applied a different transition for when the hover is released, which causes the painting to slide back into place at a much slower pace because the original swinging motion isn't so natural going the other way. The following snippet shows how the final code should look:

```
div {
    background: url(painting.jpg);
    transform-origin: 0 0;
    transition: 1.4s; /* Hover Off */
}

div:hover {
    transform: rotate(45deg);
    transition: 1.4s cubic-bezier(.55, 2.3, .52, .52); /* Hover On */
}
```

Transitioning Translate

The `translate()` transform function probably isn't as impressive as `rotate()` in a 2D environment because it is essentially a positioning tool, which is, of course, not a drastically innovative feature. However, as I described in depth in the preceding chapter, this function certainly has its benefits—namely, that it is translated in relation to its original position and that the translated element becomes independent of its surroundings.

To illustrate this function, I describe how to create a rolling ball, which is undeniably simple (`0608-transitioning-translate.html`). You can, of course, use an image, but I used some other CSS3 features that have already been discussed to create a ball-like shape:

```
div {
    width: 200px;
```

```
    height: 200px;
    border-radius: 50%;
    background: radial-gradient(40% 40%, #acd9fc 5%, #0090ff 50%,
                #002f53 90%);
}
```

The `border-radius` value of `50%` ensures that the `div` always takes the form of a perfect circle, providing the `width` and `height` values are the same. I also used a radial gradient to make the circle appear slightly more spherical, in turn, adding a touch more realism and depth.

The ball is not quite done there, though! A real, spherical ball casts a shadow, so this one should too. Your first thought would probably be to use the `box-shadow` property, but it has one major drawback in this particular instance. The ball will be made to roll with help from the `rotate()` function, which will cause the entire element to spin around in a circle, including the shadow that is supposed to be cast on the ground!

To address this issue, I simply added another div element adjacent to the ball to act as the shadow, which you can target using the adjacent sibling combinator, from all the way back in Chapter 1.

HTML
```
<div></div> <!-- Ball -->
<div></div> <!-- Shadow -->
```

CSS
```
div {
    width: 200px;
    height: 200px;
    border-radius: 50%;
    background: radial-gradient(40% 40%, #acd9fc 5%, #0090ff 50%,
                #002f53 90%);
    transition: 3s;
}

div + div {
    width: 200px;
    height: 40px;
    background: radial-gradient(#000 5%, #666 30%, transparent 70%);
    border-radius: 50%;
    transition: 3s;
}
```

Bear in mind that I omitted some of the less relevant positional properties for brevity; you can view the omitted lines by looking at the full source code in the demo.

The shadow is formed using another radial gradient that sits just below the ball, and because it's a sibling of the ball element rather than a child, it can be subject to a completely different animation. You can see the final ball, complete with shadow and ready for rolling, in Figure 6-13.

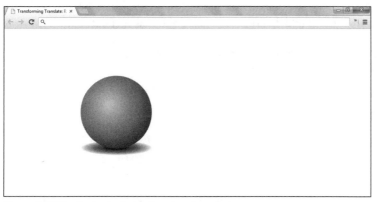

Figure 6-13 The final, spherical ball ready to be rolled

Right, then, let's get the ball rolling (quite literally) in terms of animation. You can see from the preceding code block that I added a transition property to both the ball and shadow, which share a duration parameter of three seconds. Now you just need to specify what to do with these elements when the ball is hovered:

```
div:hover {
    transform: translate(300px) rotate(360deg);
}

div:hover + div {
    transform: translate(300px);
}
```

You'll be pleased to see that nothing too complicated has happened here. Remember that when only one parameter is given to the translate() function, this is applied to the x-axis value while the y-axis receives a value of 0, so can be omitted in this case. The result in this example is that the ball and shadow are both moved, or *translated*, 300 pixels to the right.

The transition property obviously animates this movement, causing the ball to effectively slide across the page; but that's not quite rolling, is it? The final part of the puzzle is a simple (and fairly obvious) addition and comes in the form of the rotate() function, which, with a value of 360deg, rotates the ball full circle during the translation, causing it to appear as if it is rolling across the screen.

Note that the ordering of these transforms is important here because if they were swapped around, you would get very different results. When an element is rotated, *everything* about the element is rotated, including its coordinate system. For example, if an element is rotated 90 degrees clockwise, a margin-top value would affect the right side margin, a margin-right value would affect the bottom margin, and so on. Because in this example, the translate() function is specified first, it is moved according to the element's original bearings.

So there it is: a rolling ball animation in which the shapes, the shading, and the actual animation are all achieved using only CSS!

For my next trick, I'll be playing around with balloons and helium! No, seriously. I won't be making you any fancy animals or anything, but I will be showing you how to add "helium" to a balloon to make it float to the sky.

First things first; you need to create the balloon, which again I have done using only CSS:

```
div {
    border-radius: 60% 60% 55% 55%;
    width: 150px;
    height: 210px;
    background: radial-gradient(40% 20%, #acd9fc 10%, #0090ff 50%,
            #002f53 90%);
}
```

I also used the same technique as the previous example to create the shadow for the balloon, and I used a *pseudo-element* (which I discuss in depth in Chapter 13), to create the small triangle.

The concept is that the user must hover over the balloon to "add helium" and make the balloon float up. Because the animation moves the object in an upward direction, it is easier to translate the element by default and then have it return to its true position on hover, as shown in the following block of code:

```
div {
    border-radius: 60% 60% 55% 55%;
    width: 150px;
    height: 210px;
    background: radial-gradient(40% 20%, #acd9fc 10%, #0090ff 50%,
            #002f53 90%);
    transform: translate(0, 300px) rotate(-50deg);
    transition: 2s cubic-bezier(.65, 2, .03, .32);
}

div:hover {
    transform: translate(0) rotate(0deg);
}
```

You can see that, by default, the balloon is moved down by 300 pixels and rotated slightly. Then, when the element is hovered, it returns (or floats) back up to its true position. The floating illusion all comes down to finding the right `transition` parameters; for example, I again made use of the `cubic-bezier()` function to create a soft bounce when the balloon hits the ceiling, adding to the realism. Figure 6-14 shows the start and end points of the transition, but as always, you should really head over to the companion website (`0609-transforming-translate-balloon.html`) if you want to see the full effect and to analyze the complete code.

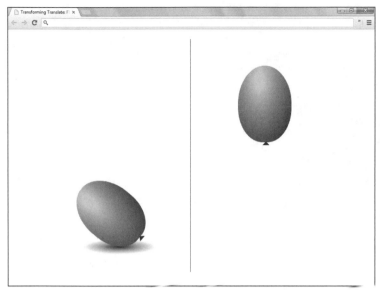

Figure 6-14 The balloon sits on the floor to start (left), then when hovered, it floats up to the ceiling (right).

Transitioning Scale

The scale() function provides an ideal way of applying subtle enhancements to elements, particularly thumbnail image galleries. Even Google Images was scaling its image results up on hover to provide that additional, satisfying teaser before clicking through to the full image.

As ever, this effect is ridiculously easy to implement too. Just remember that you should ensure your images are saved at the largest size you want them to appear on your website:

```
.gallery img {
    transition: .4s;
}

.gallery img:hover {
    transform: scale(2);
}
```

This code causes the image to smoothly enlarge from the image's center when hovered, without affecting any of its siblings or surrounding layout. Figure 6-15 shows the thumbnail gallery with one of the images enlarged on hover, while the working example can be seen in demo 0610-transitioning-scale.html.

Figure 6-15 The second image enlarged on hover using the scale() transform function

You can, of course, get much more creative with the `scale()` function, but this is a great practical use case. Try combining it with the `rotate()` function as in the previous examples to further enhance the hover effect. This addition would cause the images to also rotate full circle during the scaling when hovered:

```
.gallery img {
    transition: .4s;
}

.gallery img:hover {
    transform: scale(2) rotate(360deg);
}
```

Transitioning Skew

The `skew()` function is probably the most limited of the transform types, certainly according to my creative mind and the use of transforms that I've seen around the web. However, the transition property breathes new life into the `skew()` function, allowing some pretty cool effects. Consider the following code, the result of which is suggested by Figure 6-16.

```
div {
    transform: skewX(-20deg) skewY(-30deg);
    transition: .5s;
}

div:hover {
    transform: skewX(20deg) skewY(30deg);
}
```

Don't forget that unlike the other transform functions, the x and y parameters cannot be combined into a single `skew()` function because it calculates the values incorrectly. Instead, they must be specified separately using the `skewX()` and `skewY()` functions.

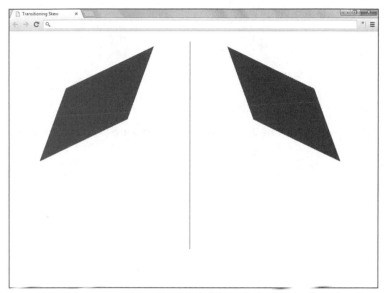

Figure 6-16 The element is skewed by default (left); and when hovered, this skew is reversed (right).

The preceding code skews the `div` to the right by default, as shown in Figure 6-16, before reversing the skew on hover. This code doesn't look or sound particularly interesting in print, but in action (`0611-transitioning-skew.html`) it produces a pretty impressive effect, creating the illusion that the element is almost liquefied or elastic.

Creating a Scattered Image Gallery

By now you should have a pretty solid grasp on both 2D transforms and transitions and the kinds of effects that you can create when they're combined. So, to finish the chapter, I'm going to combine multiple 2D transforms with transitions to create a scattered image gallery (`0612-scattered-gallery.html`) —a practical use case for the real world.

The first step is to mark up the gallery as you normally would do. You'll have to excuse my generically named images and nondescript `alt` attributes:

```
<ul class="gal">
    <li>
        <img src="1.jpg" alt="Landscape 1">
    </li>
    <li>
        <img src="2.jpg" alt="Landscape 2">
    </li>
    <li>
        <img src="3.jpg" alt="Landscape 3">
    </li>
    <li>
        <img src="4.jpg" alt="Landscape 4">
    </li>
```

```
    <li>
        <img src="5.jpg" alt="Landscape 5">
    </li>
    <li>
        <img src="6.jpg" alt="Landscape 6">
    </li>
</ul>
```

Next, you need to turn that list into a grid. I simply applied some floats and margins to create two rows of three images, as shown in Figure 6-17.

```
.gal {
    width: 620px;
    padding: 10px;
    float: left;
    list-style: none;
}

.gal li {
    width: 200px;
    margin: 0 10px 10px 0;
    float: left;
}

.gal li:nth-child(3n) {
    margin-right: 0;
}

.gal li:nth-last-child(-n+3) {
    margin-bottom: 0;
}

.gal img {
    max-width: 100%;
    float: left;
}
```

This is all pretty basic layout stuff, but one or two parts could use some clarification, so let's break it down a bit:

- The ul container is 640px wide in total, with a 10px padding all around on top of a 620px width value.

- The li elements are floated left so that they sit next to each other, and a 10px margin value is added to their right and bottom margins.

- To refresh your memory of Chapter 1, I used an nth-child() selector to remove the margin-right values from every third list item and used a negative n number to select the last three list items and remove their bottom margins.

- After you take the padding and margins into account, 600 pixels are left in the container for the li elements, with three in each row; 600 divided by 3 is 200, hence the width value.

- The actual img elements are then given a max-width value of 100%, ensuring that they are shrunk down to fit into the 200px wide list item containers.

Figure 6-17: The gallery is organized into a nice, evenly spaced grid.

Notice from Figure 6-17 that I also added a Polaroid film effect to the images simply by applying some borders. I also used the box-sizing property with a value of border-box to ensure that the border widths are included in the overall width so the grid doesn't break.

```css
.gal img {
    border: 8px solid #fff;
    border-bottom-width: 30px;
    box-sizing: border-box;
    box-shadow: 1px 1px 5px rgba(0, 0, 0, 0.5);
}
```

To ensure the border is visible, I added a subtle drop shadow too.

Okay, now you have a nicely structured gallery. It's time to apply some progressive enhancement and start scattering those images!

This rather tedious bit ensures this technique is limited to smaller galleries with a relatively low number of images. I selected the images individually to apply custom transforms to each and allow the scattering to appear as random as possible:

```css
.gal li:nth-child(1) img {
    transform: translate(-10px, 20px) rotate(-10deg);
}

.gal li:nth-child(2) img {
    transform: translate(-20px, 70px) rotate(10deg);
```

```
}

/* etc. */
```

After applying that logic to the other four images, you will have six randomly scattered images that should look something like Figure 6-18.

Figure 6-18 The images have been individually transformed to appear scattered.

Almost there! Now you want the images to enlarge when hovered, so this is where the `scale()` transform function comes into play. Remember that because the images have already been shrunk down to fit inside the 200px wide `li` elements, you are safe to scale the image *up* as long as you don't surpass the image's original dimensions:

```
.gal img:hover {
    transform: scale(2);
}
```

This code also returns the `rotate()` and `translate()` values back to their original parameters, creating a hover effect that you can see in Figure 6-19. The final point to address is that the images don't automatically appear on top when enlarged on hover, causing some ugly overlapping; however, you can easily fix this issue using the good old `z-index` method:

```
.gal img {
    position: relative; /* This is required for z-index to work */
}

.gal img:hover {
    z-index: 1;
}
```

Figure 6-19 The final scattered gallery with the first image enlarged on hover

That's all there is to it! Relatively simple code, aside from the tedious positioning of each image, that creates a pretty cool output. The best thing about this method is that as long as you code the grid properly, it degrades really gracefully in browsers that don't support transforms because the images simply revert to their original positions in the grid. Refer to Figure 6-17 to see how this gallery would appear in IE9, for example.

Summary

This chapter has taken 2D transforms to the next level, showing you just how useful they can be when combined with transitions. The resulting effects are subtle yet satisfying, and are achieved with a minimal amount of code. The various transition properties provide versatility, allowing for almost any kind of transition effect, from simple easing effects to complex `cubic-bezier()` functions.

I hope this chapter has outlined the limitless potential held by a partnership of transforms and transitions in terms of providing a bare-bones and simple method of implementing animation and movement in a web page.

These two modules, together with the CSS Animation module, represent a major revolution in the capabilities of CSS, allowing things that were previously implemented using JavaScript or Flash.

Remember, though, when it comes to use in production sites, use wisely and *always* apply a mindset of progressive enhancement to ensure that functionality is never compromised. Outside production sites, I recommend experimenting as much as possible; there are always new and creative ways to use these features that nobody has thought of yet!

Further Reading

CSS Transitions Specification
`http://www.w3.org/TR/css3-transitions/`

Lea Verou's Bézier Curve Generator
`http://cubic-bezier.com/`

Mozilla Developer Network on Timing Functions
`https://developer.mozilla.org/en-US/docs/CSS/timing-function`

Chapter 7

A New Dimension with 3D Transforms

In the last couple of chapters, you read about the capabilities of CSS transforms in a 2D environment, and you were, in all likelihood, suitably impressed. However, the CSS3 Transforms specification has quite literally another dimension—3D transforms. And if you were impressed by 2D transforms, you'll be blown away by the power and capability of their 3D counterpart.

By the end of this chapter, you will see the web differently. No longer will you see it as a flat canvas on which to paint your picture and move things up and down or left to right. Suddenly, the browser becomes a legitimate platform in which to challenge the limitations of your flat screen and its 2D nature by creating genuine, web-based 3D environments using nothing but HTML and CSS.

In this chapter I walk you through the basics of the 3D transform properties, which can be difficult to understand without concise explanation. You also learn how three of the four transform types you've become so familiar with operate in a 3D environment. You finish by creating an actual 3D cube and moving it around in a 3D space!

> Only three of the four transform types can operate in a 3D environment: `rotate`, `translate`, and `scale`. This, of course, means that the `skew()` function is limited to 2D transformations.

Like many of the CSS3 modules, the 3D aspect of the transforms module can appear rather intimidating at first glance, but as always, after you have some detailed explanation and manage to wrap your head around it, there's really not a lot to it. So get ready to dive in…

What Are 3D Transforms?

In short, 3D transforms enable you to manipulate an element in a 3D environment, allowing you to create the illusion of true depth and distance.

I already explained in detail about how transforms operate along the x- and y-axes in a 2D environment, but with 3D transforms comes the introduction of the z-axis, providing a whole new dimension to work in. Figure 7-1 shows how the z-axis forms the third dimension.

> Recall that the `rotate()` function is the exception to the rule in that it uses the z-axis in a 2D environment, and the x- and y- axes in a 3D context. I explain more on this concept further into the chapter.

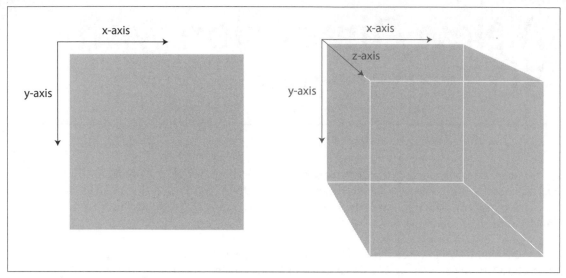

Figure 7-1 The square on the left shows the x- and y-axes in a 2D environment, and the cube on the right shows the x- and y-axes with the addition of the z-axis in a 3D environment.

So, as logic would suggest, the respective transform functions simply require an additional parameter for the z-axis to access this 3D environment (apart from `rotate()` of course). If you're thinking this description all seems a bit too simple and a bit too good to be true, you're right; this is the reason 3D transforms come with a few additional properties that allow you to form exactly the type of 3D space you want.

It's All About Perspective

Three-dimensional transforms require a bit more preparation and assistance from other properties than their 2D counterparts. To illustrate why, I need to introduce the concept of 3D rotation.

In this example, you rotate an element about the x-axis, which, of course, runs horizontally. This means that the element effectively flips vertically *around* the horizontal axis. If you simply apply the `rotateX()` function to the element on its own, your result would look something like Figure 7-2.

```
div {
    width: 300px;
    height: 300px;
    transform: rotateX(45deg);
}
```

Clearly, applying a 3D transform alone does not suffice. The element *is* rotated around its x-axis, but this transformation still takes place in a 2D context because the 3D environment hasn't been formed yet. So how do you create this 3D environment?

Figure 7-2 The element appears narrower, but there is nothing that suggests it is subject to a 3D transformation.

The Perspective Property

To create the 3D context, you need to specify a *viewing perspective*, which adds the necessary depth. You achieve this effect using the predictably named `perspective` property, which basically sets the perspective of the 3D environment by stating the assumed position of the viewer. It accepts pixel-based length values, which denote the viewer's distance from the canvas along the z-axis.

```
.container {
    perspective: 500px;
}

.container div {
    width: 300px;
    height: 300px;
    transform: rotateX(45deg);
}
```

The preceding code sets the perspective of the 3D environment based on the viewer being 500px away from the screen (or 500px along the z-axis).

If you're struggling with the concept of perspective, it basically implies distance by making smaller those things that are supposed to be farther away, and making bigger those things that are supposed to be closer. Figure 7-3 shows this logic in action and is the result of the preceding code block. For a closer look, check out the demo file `0701-perspective.html` from the companion website at `www.wiley.com/go/ptl/css3`.

Notice that the `perspective` property is actually applied to the parent of the transformed element, ensuring that all its children operate in the same 3D space with the same perspective. However, if you're interested only in applying the 3D transformation to a single element, you can do just that, but the perspective value must be applied differently, as shown by the following code:

```
.container div {
    width: 300px;
    height: 300px;
    transform: perspective(500px) rotateX(45deg);
}
```

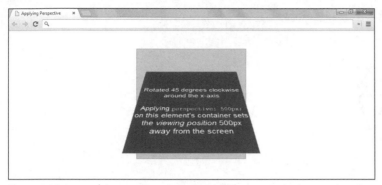

Figure 7-3 Perspective has now been added to the scene, ensuring that sizes have been altered to imply varying distance.

As you can see, the `perspective` value is applied to the actual element in the form of a functional notation. You must understand, though, that this is by no means a shorthand solution to applying perspective because it produces radically different results from using the `perspective` *property* on the container, especially when the transformed element has siblings that are also subject to 3D transformations. Figure 7-4 illustrates the difference between applying the `perspective()` function to individual elements and applying the `perspective` property to the container. You can also take a closer look at the code in the demo file `0702-perspective().html`.

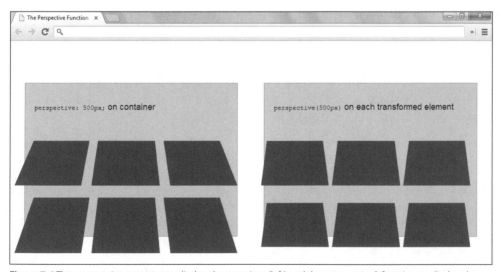

Figure 7-4 The perspective property applied to the container (left) and the perspective() function applied to the individual elements (right)

When it comes to rotation, remember that an element's entire coordinate system is rotated, which means that the elements in the preceding figures have a z-axis that is effectively pointing away from the screen at a 45-degree angle rather than pointing directly toward you. With this fact in mind, look at how the `perspective` property works with 3D translation, which isn't subject to any confusion caused by a rotated z-axis:

```
.container div {
    width: 300px;
    height: 300px;
```

```
    transform: translateZ(100px);
}
```

If you try to move an element `100px` along the z-axis without specifying a `perspective` value, absolutely zero change to the element is visible. As with the previous rotation example, the transformation *is* carried out, moving the element `100px` along the z-axis, but because there is no perspective to measure distance, this movement is not apparent. Figure 7-5 demonstrates why this happens.

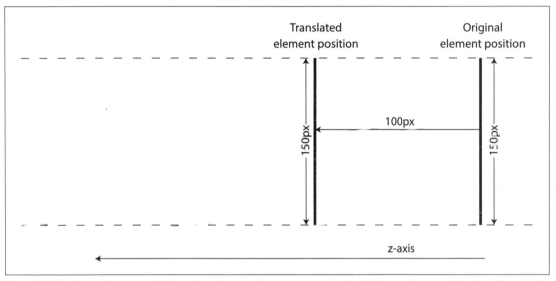

Figure 7-5 The element has moved 100px along the z-axis, but you can see no physical change because of the lack of perspective.

As you now know, you must add a `perspective` value to the container element to create a 3D perspective that will be shared by all its children:

```
.container {
    perspective: 500px;
}

.container div {
    width: 300px;
    height: 300px;
    transform: translateZ(100px);
}
```

This example moves the `div` `100px` along the z-axis *toward* the viewer's position (set by the `perspective` property), and because the element is moved closer to the viewer, it effectively becomes larger. The demo (`0703-translatez.html`) and Figure 7-6 should illustrate this process further.

Remember that the `translateZ()` function and the `perspective` property operate along the same axis, with the latter specifying the viewer's position. When you consider the preceding example, this means that the viewer is `500px` away from the screen, along the z-axis. So, if the element is translated `500px` or more along the z-axis, it suddenly becomes invisible because the element is effectively translated *behind* the viewer's position, as Figure 7-7 demonstrates.

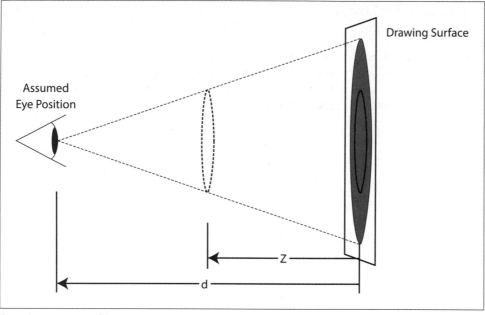

Original image courtesy of the W3C

Figure 7-6 The element appears larger as it is moved along the z-axis toward the viewer's position, which is specified by the perspective property (defined by **d** in this figure).

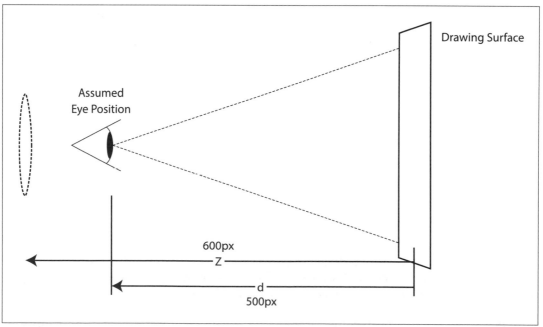

Figure 7-7 The perspective property sets the viewing position at 500px from the screen, whereas the element has been translated 600px from the screen and so sits "behind the viewer."

Perspective Origin

The perspective tool has a sister property that affords you even more control over your 3D environment: the perspective-origin property.

This feature basically allows you to state the angle of perspective by setting the *vanishing point* of your 3D space. The vanishing point of the element is specified using the standard positioning values, accepting pixel- and percentage-based units as well as the positional keywords (top, right, bottom, left, center).

This property works similarly to the way in which the transform-origin property works and shares the same default value of 50% 50%, which equates to center.

The following code block shows how different perspective-origin values can affect the viewing angle with a perspective value of 500px. The result is shown with Figure 7-8 and you can explore the code in more depth in the demo file 0704-perspective-origin.html.

HTML
```
<div class="container">
    <div></div>
</div>

<!-- The above markup is duplicated two more times -->
```

CSS
```
.container {
    perspective: 500px;
}

.container div {
    transform: rotateX(45deg);
}

.container:first-child {
    perspective-origin: 0 0; /* top left */
}

.container:nth-child(2) {
    perspective-origin: 50% 0; /* top center */
}

.container:last-child {
    perspective-origin: 100% 0; /* top right */
}
```

Again, just like the perspective property, the perspective-origin property is placed on the parent container rather than the actual element undergoing the transformation, as you can see in Figure 7-8; however, the perspective-origin property can be applied *only* to the parent.

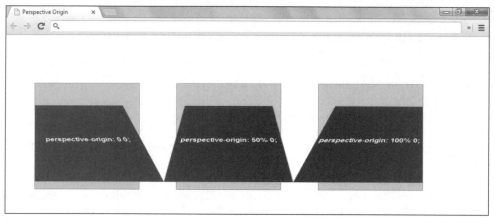

Figure 7-8 Three examples showing how the perspective-origin property affects the viewing angle

Maintaining Perspective

It's time to address an example that requires *slightly* more substantial markup in that the transformed element now has children. Consider the following code:

HTML
```html
<div class="container">
    <div class="child">
        <div class="grandchild">
        </div>
    </div>
</div>
```

CSS
```css
.container {
    perspective: 300px;
}

.child {
    transform: rotateX(45deg);
}

.grandchild {
    transform: rotate(20deg); /* 2D rotation */
}
```

If you apply the logic that has already been discussed, the main `.container` element forms the 3D space using the `perspective` property, allowing the `.child` element to be transformed in this 3D space.

Now that `.child` is rotated, everything about that element, including its children, is also subject to the same rotation and operates in relation to the rotated canvas and coordinate system of the `.child`. So *everything* that happens within that `.child` element happens at a 45-degree angle (on the x-axis), as shown in Figure 7-9.

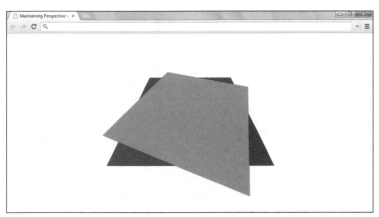

Figure 7-9 Even though the .grandchild element is only subject to a 2D rotation, it still is at a 45-degree angle (on the x-axis) due to its rotated parent.

So what's the issue? The problems arise when you want to apply 3D transformations to the `.grandchild` element in the same 3D space as its parent. So, you can amend the final part of the preceding code example to alter the transformation of the `.grandchild` element from a simple 2D rotation to a 3D rotation around the x-axis (see the demo file `0705-preserve-3d.html`). Figure 7-10 shows the result of this change.

```
.grandchild {
    transform: rotateX(20deg); /* 3D rotation */
}
```

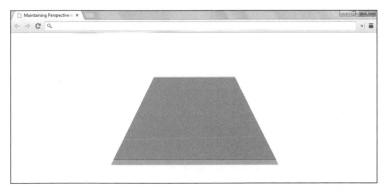

Figure 7-10 The .grandchild element is rotated around the x-axis, but no 3D effect occurs due to the lack of perspective.

Ah. You've seen this before, right? The `.grandchild` element's 3D rotation is rendered in a 2D context, but why?

It's important to note that the `perspective` property *isn't* inherited, so although the `.grandchild` element is at a 45-degree angle on the x-axis, this position is solely due to the transformation of its parent. This means that it doesn't have its own `perspective` value to work from and is separate from the `.child` element's 3D rendering context.

So how *do* you make the `.grandchild` element part of its parent's 3D rendering context?

Enter the `transform-style` property. This handy tool basically allows you to specify whether elements should operate in a 2D or 3D context. Its default value is `flat`, which explains the lack of 3D context in Figure 7-10!

The `transform-style` property has one other value, `preserve-3d`, which is what works the magic for you here.

The initial `perspective` value is applied to `.container` (the `.child` element's parent) to make its children operate in a 3D environment. However, as you just learned, the `perspective` property applies only to direct children, causing the `.grandchild` element to function without any 3D perspective.

To remedy this situation and force the `.grandchild` element to work with the same perspective and in the same 3D rendering context as its parent, you simply need to add the `preserve-3d` value to its parent, as shown in the following code:

```
.container {
    perspective: 300px;
}

.child {
    transform: rotateX(45deg);
    transform-style: preserve-3d;
}

.grandchild {
    transform: rotateX(20deg); /* 3D rotation */
}
```

Finally, the `.grandchild` element now operates in the same 3D rendering context as its parent thanks to `preserve-3d` (see Figure 7-11).

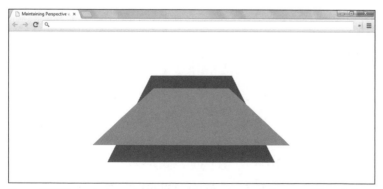

Figure 7-11 The nested .grandchild element now operates in the same 3D rendering context as its parent.

If you want to apply 3D transformations to any additional nested elements, you have to extend this 3D rendering context further by again applying the `preserve-3d` value to all elements that contain an element subject to 3D transformation.

Backface Visibility

The final part of the 3D transforms puzzle affords you yet another ounce of control over your 3D transformations. The `backface-visibility` property is simple in its application and doesn't suffer from any complex issues like the `perspective` and `preserve-3d` features.

When elements are operating in a 3D environment, their appearance is not limited to only their front face because you can rotate and manipulate them to view them from any angle. For example, if you were to flip an element by 180 degrees on the y-axis, you would effectively be looking at the back face of the element, as shown in Figure 7-12.

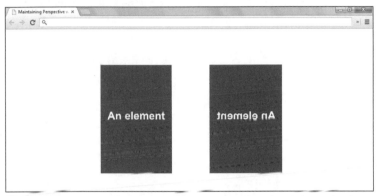

Figure 7-12 The element in its normal state, showing its front face (left) and the element after being rotated 180 degrees on the y-axis to show its back face (right)

Predictably, the `backface-visibility` property allows you to specify whether or not the back face of the element should be visible if it comes to face the viewer. Its default value is, of course, `visible` as is evident in the preceding figure. To counter the default behavior and ensure the back face of an element is not visible when given the opportunity, you simply use the value `hidden`:

```
div {
    transform: rotateX(180deg);
    backface-visibility: hidden;
}
```

For a more practical use case for this property, let's run with the playing card example that is briefly touched on in the specification (`0706-playing-card.html`). First, you must consider the markup:

```
<div class="container">
    <figure class="card">
        <img class="back" src="back.jpg" alt="Back Face">
        <img class="front" src="q-hearts.jpg" alt="Queen of Hearts">
    </figure>
</div>
```

Let's break this down a bit:

- You need a `.container` element to set the `perspective` value on so it can form the 3D environment in which its children operate.

- The `.card` element is subject to 3D transformation and also holds the front and back card face images (which also are transformed).

- The two images (the front and back of the playing card) are positioned and transformed so they sit on top of each other but are facing away from each other, effectively ensuring that they combine as one to form one playing card.

With all that in mind, take a look at what the CSS does with this markup, applying only the logic learned so far from the previous sections in this chapter:

```
.container {
    perspective: 700px;
}

.card {
    transition: 2s;
    transform-style: preserve-3d;
}

.card img {
    position: absolute;
}

.card .front {
    transform: rotateY(-180deg);
}
```

Okay, time for another breakdown:

- The `perspective` is applied to the `.container` to create a 3D rendering context.

- Because you have nested elements that are to be three-dimensionally transformed, the 3D rendering context must be extended to the `.card` element using the `preserve-3d` value of `transform-style`.

- The two images are set to `position: absolute;` so they sit on top of each other.

- The `.front` image (the face of the playing card) is then flipped around on the y-axis so it is facing away from the viewer, meaning that the image's *back* face is showing to the viewer.

This is the point at which you start to encounter some issues with your playing card. Because the `.front img` element is specified last in the markup, it appears on top of the `.back img` element, which is not the desired effect because the card needs to be facing down by default so you can't see which card it is.

However, because the .front element is flipped around, it is the *back* of the image that you can see, almost as if the image were made from glass, allowing you to see through the back of it, as shown in Figure 7-13.

Figure 7-13 With the code used so far, the flipped .front image sits on top.

Surely, you can guess what's coming next to rescue the situation! Because the back face of the flipped .front image is facing the viewer, you can simply use the backface-visibility property to ensure that when the image is flipped, it is no longer visible:

```
.card img {
    position: absolute;
    backface-visibility: hidden;
}

.card:hover {
    transform: rotateY(180deg);
}
```

Now, the back of the playing card is visible to the viewer by default as desired, with the front of the card sitting underneath and flipped 180 degrees. The final, whole playing card is formed.

Now you need to flip the playing card, which is the .card element that contains the two faces of the card. As illustrated in the preceding code, all you need to do is rotate the .card element on hover by 180 degrees on the y-axis. And because the .front image has already been subjected to the same transformation, this rotates it back to its true position. Figure 7-14 shows the process of the :hover animation (which is, of course, caused by the transition property added to the .card element earlier).

Figure 7-14 The animation process of the playing card being flipped over on :hover to reveal its face value (from left to right)

Moving on to More Transform Properties

Before I discuss the various 3D transformation types covered in this section, here's a quick summary of what's been covered so far in terms of the various properties and values that control your 3D environment and transformations:

- The `perspective` property allows you to set a 3D rendering context by placing it on the container of transformed elements.

- The `transform-style` property allows you to extend this 3D rendering context to nested transformed elements using the `preserve-3d` value.

- The `perspective-origin` property enables you to set the vanishing point of your 3D environment—that is, the point in the horizon at which all elements would disappear into the distance if the perspective was intense enough.

- The `backface-visibility` property allows you to specify whether or not the back side of an element should be visible when rotated in 3D space.

Of course, the one essential ingredient that is absent from this list is the actual `transform` property, which accepts a variety of 3D-based transform functions, all of which are displayed in the following list and are addressed in the upcoming sections:

- `rotateX()`

- `rotateY()`

- `rotate3d()`

- `translateZ()`

- `translate3d()`
- `scaleZ()`
- `scale3d()`

Rotating in a 3D Environment

You've already seen a lot of 3D rotation in the initial examples, but there is actually a lot more to this type of transform than what has been covered already.

If you think back to Chapter 5, you might recall the reason why the `rotate()` function uses the z-axis in a 2D context and the x- and y-axes in a 3D context, which is in complete contrast to how the other transform types operate.

By now, you know that the z-axis provides access to the third dimension as it protrudes out of your screen toward you, the viewer. However, the `rotate()` function uses this axis to turn elements around in a *2D* context. Figure 7-15 should illustrate this point more clearly.

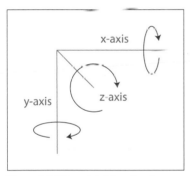

Figure 7-15 The rotate() function turns elements around the z-axis in a 2D context and uses the x- and y-axes for 3D rotation.

As you can see, the x-axis, which runs horizontally across your screen, is used to flip the element vertically in a 3D environment. The y-axis runs vertically and therefore flips an element *horizontally* in a 3D context.

You can, of course, combine these 3D rotation functions as shown in the following code, with the result demonstrated in the demo `0707-rotate-x-rotate-y.html` and in Figure 7-16:

```
.card {
    transform: rotateX(180deg) rotateY(180deg);
}
```

You can see that the element is rotated twice—first around the x-axis and then around the y-axis, effectively flipping the card vertically and then horizontally. However, this method isn't all that flexible and is limited in terms of the effects that you can produce, most notably when used with transitions, because the animation makes the fact that two separate functions are applied much more apparent (see the demo file `0708-rotate3d.html`).

The card is flipped vertically, then flipped horizontally, so two separate rotations are carried out in a single transform.

Figure 7-16 The element is rotated 180 degrees around the x-axis and then 180 degrees around the y-axis.

A much more versatile alternative, which also comes with the added benefit of being hardware accelerated, is the `rotate3d()` function. Contrary to what you may first think, this function is *not* a shorthand option for specifying the individual rotations around the three axes; it actually allows you to specify a custom axis in your 3D space, around which you can rotate your element. The `rotate3d()` function follows this format:

```
/* rotate3d(x, y, z, angle); */
```

To explain, the x, y, and z parameters are vector coordinates (accepting number-based values) that combine to specify the direction vector, denoting the axis of rotation. After this axis is formed using the first three values, the final parameter states the angle at which the element should be rotated around this axis.

To further demonstrate this concept, look at the following snippets of code:

```
rotate3d(1, 0, 0, 180deg);
/* This is equivalent to... */
rotateX(180deg);

rotate3d(0, 1, 0, 180deg);
/*This is equivalent to... */
rotateY(180deg);

rotate3d(0, 0, 1, 180deg);
/*This is equivalent to... */
rotateZ(180deg);
```

With the preceding code examples in mind, you may think that to produce the effect achieved by combining `rotateX(180deg)` and `rotateY(180deg)` as in the initial example, you would need to do the following:

```
rotate3d(1, 1, 0, 180deg);
```

However, this is the point at which you realize the power of the `rotate3d()` function because it actually produces the outcome shown in Figure 7-17. You can see the full, animated example in the demo file `0709-rotate3d-2.html`.

Figure 7-17 This effect is very different to that achieved by combining the rotateX() and rotateY() functions.

The final, transformed element is so different because the `rotate3d()` function combines those x and y parameters to form a single axis of rotation, whereas the `rotateX()` and `rotateY()` functions are carried out separately, one after the other.

This method boasts impressive versatility, affording you the ability to create interesting custom axes around which to rotate, as shown with the following snippet:

```
rotate3d(3, 10, 6, 180deg);
```

Remember that the axis of rotation is much more apparent when the transformation is animated, so head over to the companion website and compare demos `0707-rotate-x-rotate-y.html` and `0708-rotate3d.html` to truly understand the difference. Demo `0709-rotate3d-2.html` shows an additional option for another effect.

Translating in a 3D Environment

You can be thankful that 3D translation is much simpler than 3D rotation! The x- and y-axes are used to move an element horizontally or vertically in a 2D context, whereas the z-axis is used to move an element "closer" to the viewer.

Although 3D transforms are pretty powerful, their power obviously does not extend to allowing an element to physically break out of your screen and approach you along the z-axis! Translation along the z-axis is therefore effected through the illusion created by the perspective value, which effectively scales the element up as it moves closer and closer to the viewing position.

The concept is clearly a simple one, not least when compared with 3D rotation—a theme that is continued with the `translate3d()` function. In this case, the `translate3d()` function *is* a shorthand method for combining the `translateX()`, `translateY()`, and `translateZ()` functions together. Consider the following code example:

```
transform: translateX(100px) translateY(50px) translateZ(200px);

/* This is the same as... */

transform: translate3d(100px, 50px, 200px);
```

As you can see, the format is simple, with the function requiring three length-based parameters, one each for the x, y, and z translation values. The only unusual thing to note here is that the z parameter cannot be a percentage value. If you think about it, the reasoning for this is obvious: percentage values for the x and y parameters would specify a portion of the total width and height of the container, whereas there is no total *depth* value for the z parameter to base a percentage value on.

The result of the previous code example is shown in Figure 7-18, and you can see the working, animated example in demo file `0710-translate3d.html`.

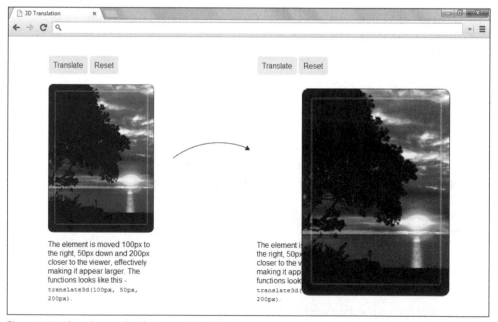

Figure 7-18 When the translate button is clicked, the original element (left) is moved 100px to the right, 50px down, and 200px closer to the viewer, effectively making it appear larger (right).

This particular example is based on a `perspective` value of `500px`, which basically says that the viewer is `500px` away from the screen. This value directly influences the effect of the translation on the z-axis, because if the viewing position were set to `1000px` away from the screen, the z-based translation of `200px` would produce a much less intense transformation, even though the translation values haven't changed.

Again, the `translate3d()` function is more efficient than specifying each individual transform function because it benefits from being hardware accelerated for improved performance.

Scaling in a 3D Environment

Just when you thought things were getting a little more relaxed, 3D scaling comes along to up the complexity factor once again! Of course, the 2D-based `scaleX()` and `scaleY()` properties are far from difficult to comprehend as they adjust the size of an element's width and height, respectively. However, the `scaleZ()` function, which opens up the third dimension, requires much more understanding because elements obviously don't have a depth value to scale up or down.

Therefore, the `scaleZ()` function comes into play only when you're working with a 3D *space* rather than with a 3D element. So, although you would normally apply your transformations to a particular element, you must apply the `scaleZ()` function to this element's *container* so as to transform the actual 3D space. For example, if you were to arrange a series of elements using 3D transformations to form a 3D shape (such as a cube), applying `scaleZ()` to the *container* would then effectively scale the cube along the z-axis.

The way this function actually operates is similar to the `translateZ()` and `perspective` tools in that it actually pushes your element closer to the viewer, in turn intensifying the perspective effect.

To understand how you would apply the `scaleZ()` function, look at the following code example:

```
HTML
<div class="container">
    <div class="child">
        <div class="grandchild">
        </div>
    </div>
</div>
```

```
CSS
.container {
    perspective: 500px;
}

.child {
    transform-style: preserve-3d;
    transform: scaleZ(2);
}

.grandchild {
    transform: rotate3d(2, 3, 2, 180deg);
}
```

In this example, the `rotate3d()` function is used to rotate the `.grandchild` element; the `scaleZ()` function is then applied to this element's container to move the entire 3D space closer to the viewer, as shown in Figure 7-19. The demo (`0711-scalez.html`) might make this a little clearer.

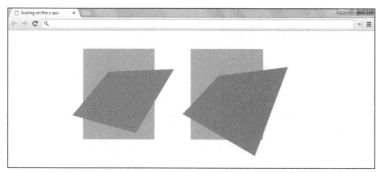

Figure 7-19 The left element has been rotated as normal, whereas the example on the right also has the scaleZ() function applied to its container.

As with the previous 3D transformation types, 3D scaling also has a `scale3d()` function, which, again, is simply a shorthand method for combining multiple scaling values:

```
transform: scaleX(2) scaleY(1) scaleZ(3);

/* This is the same as... */

transform: scale3d(2, 1, 3);
```

> Remember that a scale() value of 1 causes no transformation to occur, while anything above that scales up and anything below scales down.

Creating a Cube Using 3D Transforms

There's been a lot of information to take in so far, and it can become a bit tiresome just reading how this does that and that does this. However, now you get to combine and apply what you've learned to create an actual 3D shape, rather than just moving 2D objects around a 3D space.

The particular 3D shape on the agenda is a simple cube, which can be seen in all its glory in the working demo (`0712-3d-cube.html`). The first point to address is that a cube obviously consists of six faces, so you need an element for each. Take a look at the markup that will be transformed to form your cube:

```
<div class="container">
    <figure class="cube">
        <div class="front">Front</div>
        <div class="left">Left</div>
        <div class="right">Right</div>
        <div class="top">Top</div>
```

```
            <div class="bottom">Bottom</div>
            <div class="back">Back</div>
        </figure>
    </div>
```

I would argue that the preceding markup is fairly modest considering the impressive visual effect that will ultimately be achieved, especially when put up against the HTML structure of certain sliders and carousels.

If you looked at the live demo `0712-3d-cube.html`, you could be forgiven for feeling slightly intimidated and overwhelmed because the effects on show usually require complex JavaScript or Flash capability. The CSS method, though, is far from complex when you apply the logic you soaked up from the previous sections in this chapter.

The first task is to add some perspective to the `.container` element, and because the `perspective` property applies only to direct children, you also need to use the `preserve-3d` tool on the `.cube` element to ensure the cube faces are transformed in the same 3D rendering context:

```
.container {
    width: 300px;
    height: 300px;
    perspective: 1100px;
}

.cube {
    width: 300px;
    height: 300px;
    position: relative;
    transform-style: preserve-3d;
}
```

You don't want the cube to be distorted too much, so the viewing position (`perspective`) is set much farther away from the screen (`1100px` to be exact) to lessen the intensity of the 3D effect.

Now you can start styling the faces and manipulating their positioning and orientation so that they sit in the correct places to form the cube:

```
.cube div {
    width: 300px;
    height: 300px;
    background: rgba(0, 0, 0, .8);
    position: absolute;
}
```

Before you continue, you need to be aware that the preceding styles, notably the `position: absolute;` rule, are applied to each cube face, ensuring that they all lay on top of each other and can all be positioned from the same starting point. Now for the fun stuff!

```
.front    { transform: translateZ(150px); }
.left     { transform: rotateY(-90deg) translateZ(150px); }
.right    { transform: rotateY(90deg) translateZ(150px); }
.top      { transform: rotateX(90deg) translateZ(150px); }
.bottom   { transform: rotateX(-90deg) translateZ(150px); }
.back     { transform: rotateY(180deg) translateZ(150px); }
```

That's all there is to it! This code is simple to grasp, but I'll break it down for some clarification. Each face is rotated so that it faces the appropriate direction; for example, the cube's left face is rotated 90 degrees counterclockwise around the vertical y-axis so it is facing to the left. The next part of the transformation may be confusing you at the moment, because every face has exactly the same `translateZ()` value despite the faces ending up in very different places.

This is the point at which the ordering of the transform functions becomes extremely important. I mentioned previously that when an element is rotated, its entire coordinate system is rotated with it; for example, when the left side is rotated 90 degrees counterclockwise to face the left, the z-axis (which usually points outwardly toward you) also now points toward the left. This means that when translated along the z-axis, this element now moves in that leftward direction. The same rule applies to all the other cube faces, so when the right side is rotated to face toward the right, that element's z-axis also points rightward!

Now you should have an image that resembles Figure 7-20. This is a genuine 3D model, but the illusion of depth is lacking somewhat due to the viewing angle.

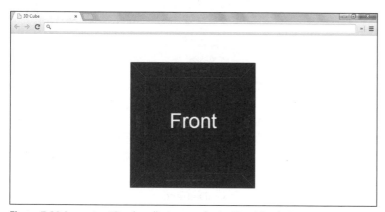

Figure 7-20 A genuine 3D cube, albeit a very flat-looking 3D cube!

To address the lack of depth, you need to adjust the viewing angle of the cube so that the sense of flatness is eradicated. I hope you remember that the tool for the job is the `perspective-origin` property:

```
.container {
    width: 300px;
    height: 300px;
    perspective: 1100px;
    perspective-origin: -50% -50%;
}
```

This rule simply sets the vanishing point of the 3D space above and to the left of the cube, going some way toward enhancing the 3D effect, as shown with Figure 7-21.

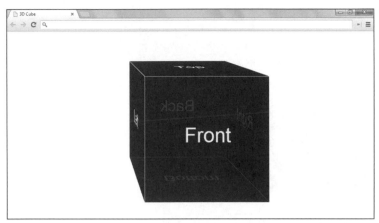

Figure 7-21 The cube has gained some more depth thanks to an adjusted vanishing point set by the perspective-origin property.

That's pretty cool, but it's not as overwhelmingly impressive as I may have claimed earlier. But don't worry—there's more to come!

Animating the Cube with Transitions

The "wow" factor is introduced when transitions are added into the equation, as you can see in the live demo (0713-animated-3d-cube.html). Before I move on to that discussion, though, I need to address the issue of scaling. Whenever anything is scaled or translated along the z-axis, an element's size is adjusted so that it appears closer to the viewer. However, the size adjustment works just like a rasterized image; in other words, an element's contents start to pixelate increasingly as it is moved further along the z-axis. Think of it as if *the viewer* is somewhat far-sighted, so the element becomes increasingly out of focus as it moves closer to the viewer's position.

This is an issue with the cube example because the front face is translated 150px closer to the viewer along the z-axis, therefore causing some pixelation within this .front element.

> **The translation is necessary because without it, the front face would sit in the middle of the cube rather than at the front.**

To address this situation, you need to ensure that nothing moves toward the viewer from its original position on the z-axis. Wait a second—didn't I just say that this is a necessity? Yes, it is, but there is an easy fix. To cancel out the 150px translation of the .front element along the z-axis, you simply apply the reverse of this translation (-150px) to the entire .cube element. Figure 7-22 shows how this simple line of code makes the vital difference:

```
.cube {
    /* Other styles */
    transform: translateZ(-150px);
}
```

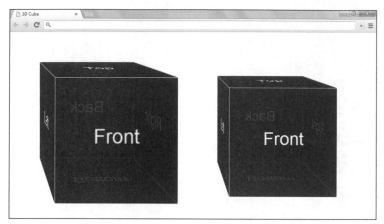

Figure 7-22 The left cube's front face is 150px closer to the viewer than it should be, causing pixelation. On the right, the whole cube element is shifted 150px further back to cancel out the original translation.

Now, as promised—some animation! The vital ingredient is, of course, the `transition` property, which simply needs to be applied to the `.cube` element, as this is what you will be animating:

```
.cube {
    /* Other styles */
    transition: 1s;
}
```

This code ensures that any changes to the `.cube` element will be transitioned. You can use the check box technique employed a couple of times in previous chapters to bring each face to the front of the cube. So start with the navigation:

```
<input id="front" name="transforms" type="radio" value="front">
<label for="front">Front</label>

<input id="left" name="transforms" type="radio" value="left">
<label for="left">Left</label>

<!-- etc. -->
```

With a button for each of the six faces, now you can target each face after its corresponding button is clicked and apply the appropriate transformations:

```
input[value="front"]:checked ~ .container .cube {
    transform: translateZ(-150px) rotateY(0);
}

input[value="left"]:checked ~ .container .cube {
    transform: translateZ(-150px) rotateY(90deg);
}

input[value="right"]:checked ~ .container .cube {
    transform: translateZ(-150px) rotateY(-90deg);
}
```

```
input[value="top"]:checked ~ .container .cube {
    transform: translateZ(-150px) rotateX(-90deg);
}

input[value="bottom"]:checked ~ .container .cube {
    transform: translateZ(-150px) rotateX(90deg);
}

input[value="back"]:checked ~ .container .cube {
    transform: translateZ(-150px) rotateY(180deg);
}
```

To refresh your memory, the preceding selectors work by first selecting an `input` element that has a certain `value` attribute and is checked by the user. The general sibling combinator (~) then selects any elements with a class of `.container` that follow this checked `input` element, before finally selecting the `.cube` element within that container.

So, when the Left button is clicked, you can apply the appropriate rotation to bring the cube's left face to the front; in this case, the cube is simply rotated 90 degrees clockwise around the vertical y axis, ensuring the left face is now at the front of the cube. Remember, though, if you were to apply only the `rotateY(90deg)` function, this would overwrite the `translateZ(-150px)` that is on the default state of the `.cube` element, so you must redeclare it!

And that's all there is to it! I hope you're feeling pleasantly surprised at the simple transformations required to make this happen, especially considering the impressive visuals that result.

Examining Browser Support for 3D Transforms

You could be forgiven for thinking that if a browser supports 2D transforms, it must support 3D transforms too; after all, it's still the same `transform` property—heck, it's just an extra X, Y, or Z on the end of the functions! If you want to create a true 3D environment, though, support is also required for the sister properties, most notably the `perspective` property.

Unfortunately, these additional functions and extra properties ensure that the 3D aspect of CSS transforms form a very different-looking compatibility table compared to the 2D version. However, it's not all doom and gloom as we've seen great progress recently, with 3D transforms finally breaking free from the Safari-only tag they had been frustratingly limited to for such a long period.

Although late to the 3D party, Firefox made the bold step of removing the vendor prefix for all the transform properties, making it the only browser to currently offer complete, unprefixed support for both 2D and 3D transforms.

As transforms were a Webkit innovation, Safari was the first to offer complete support, although it has yet to drop the prefix. Chrome has also supported the full package for a relatively long time now, but again, it still requires the `-webkit-` prefix.

Opera recently ditched its Presto rendering engine in favor of WebKit and now also offers support for 3D transforms with the `-webkit-` prefix. You may have noticed that IE10 has been fairing rather well so far in terms of browser support, and with 3D transforms, the story is no different, offering unprefixed support! However (there's always a catch with IE), IE10 currently lacks support for the `preserve-3d` value of the `transform-style` property, preventing the possibility of nested 3D transforms and thus severely limiting their capabilities. Table 7-1 shows the full picture in terms of browser support for 3D transforms.

Table 7-1: 3D Transforms Browser Compatibility

Browser	Prefixed Support	Un-prefixed Support
Chrome	12+	Not supported
Firefox	10+	16+
Opera	15+ (`-webkit-`)	Not supported
Safari	4+	Not supported
IE	Not supported	10 (no support for `preserve-3d`)

Summary

This chapter has quite literally added a new dimension to CSS, demonstrating how to use each of the transform functions in a 3D environment as well as how to establish a 3D context by adding perspective. The playing card example illustrated how to perform simple flips and introduced the concept of a reverse side to your elements! However, it was the cube example that really demonstrated the true power of 3D dimensions, while the animated version added the "wow" factor.

For me, 3D transforms hold the most potential of all the new features that have been introduced with CSS3. The power they possess and the doors they open are limitless, as shown by the countless mind-blowing experiments that have popped up (quite literally!) all around the web. Experimenting is awesome; it's the best way to learn, if you ask me, but remember that CSS is not Flash or JavaScript and it's not trying to be. It may be able to achieve some of the same effects, which is *really* cool, but if you want to create a genuine, comprehensive 3D environment, use something that was made to do that. CSS is for styling HTML content, and 3D transforms have a major part to play in this context, too.

Further Reading

CSS3 Transforms Specification
`http://www.w3.org/TR/css3-transforms`

Mozilla Developer Network on the Transform Function
`https://developer.mozilla.org/en-US/docs/CSS/transform-function`

Understanding CSS3 Transforms
`http://www.eleqtriq.com/2010/05/understanding-css-3d-transforms/`

Insightful Stack Overflow Thread on the scaleZ() Function
`http://stackoverflow.com/questions/7819802/what-does-the-scalez-css-transform-function-do`

Chapter 8
Getting Animated

Transitions are great for simple, trigger-based animation between two states, but they obviously don't provide a solution for true frame-based animation. Fortunately, CSS-based animation doesn't stop with transitions; it gets a whole lot more exciting than that! I mentioned the completely separate CSS Animations module a couple of times in the preceding few chapters, alluding to its impressive capabilities and suggesting that it belongs alongside the more powerful tools that CSS3 has to offer. I hope this chapter will serve to justify those claims.

As I touched on in the preceding chapters, transitions are effectively limited to two frames, a start and an end, with the change between these states occurring gradually. CSS Animations, on the other hand, introduces keyframes into the equation, allowing you to add any number of state changes to animate between.

This module is big news for CSS and finally provides an extremely author-friendly method of applying both simple and complex animation, without having to rely on JavaScript and Flash as you have done for so long. This reliance has been particularly frustrating when the desired effect is a simple one, often resulting in the feeling that it's not worth the effort. Thankfully, you now have a solution that requires a number of bytes appropriate to the outcome.

This chapter discusses the intricacies of CSS Animations, breaking down the module and discussing the various controls in depth. I then show how you can use this feature today to apply subtle effects that function within the laws of progressive enhancement, before finishing with something a little more substantial and complex: a functioning, automated slider.

Introducing CSS3 Animation

You now know that animations in CSS3 work with keyframes, but how do you go about creating these keyframes? You actually define them completely separate to the element you want to apply them to, as this allows the frames to be called on any number of times and utilized by any number of elements. For example, if you have 10 elements that you want to animate in exactly the same way, you still need to define the keyframes only once. Okay, so how do you define these frames?

Defining Keyframes

The key ingredient (pun intended!) in CSS based animation that affords you the ability to create any number of keyframes is the aptly named @keyframes rule, within which your state changes are defined.

The @keyframes rule uses percentages to specify the position at which each frame sits on a linear scale, allowing for the frames to be used with multiple durations. For example, the same set of keyframes can be used on two elements, one of which is animated over a 10-second period and the other over a 20-second period; this means that a frame positioned at 50% would be effective at the 5-second mark on the first element and the 10-second mark on the second element.

You probably want to know how the @keyframes rule is structured in the CSS. The following code snippet obliges:

```css
@keyframes my-first-animation {

    0% {
        /* Styles */
    }

    25% {
        /* Styles */
    }

    50% {
        /* Styles */
    }

    75% {
        /* Styles */
    }

    100% {
        /* Styles */
    }

}
```

Really simple stuff! The preceding example includes five keyframes, within which you can then specify styles as if applying them to a standard element selector. Another point to note is that the 0% and 100% keyframes can also be specified using the keywords from and to, respectively, as indicated here:

```css
@keyframes my-first-animation {

    from {
        /* Styles */
    }

    to {
        /* Styles */
    }

}
```

However, if your from and to styles are the same as the element's default styles (which they very often are), you can omit them completely because these keyframes are automatically constructed based on the element's original state. This makes it possible to define simple animations with just a single keyframe:

```css
@keyframes my-first-animation {

    50% {
        /* Styles */
```

```
        }

    }
```

The text immediately following the @keyframes rule defines the name of your animation, which you use to reference these keyframes later and actually apply them to an element.

Applying the Animation

Now you have a complete set of keyframes that, together, form your animation. So how do you use this animation? At this point, the array of animation properties comes in, allowing you to call the keyframes and apply them to an element.

Only two properties are *required* when applying an animation: animation-name and animation-duration. The former must match the name you specified in the @keyframes rule-set exactly, and the latter works just like the transition-duration property, accepting second- and millisecond-based values:

```
div {
    animation-name: my-first-animation;
    animation-duration: 5s;
}
```

As is usually the case, you can combine all the animation properties (the rest of which I get to later) into one shorthand animation property as shown here:

```
div {
    animation: my-first-animation 5s;
}
```

That's really all there is to it! You define your keyframes and then apply those keyframes to an element where you can control the animation using the various animation properties.

Further Control

As already mentioned, several additional properties (eight in total) provide you with further control over your animations. I start with the ones you are already fairly familiar with, thanks to their transition-based equivalents discussed in Chapter 6.

The first additional control property to be addressed sees the return of the timing function. The animation-timing-function property allows you to define where the animation accelerates and decelerates over the specified duration. If the section discussing timing functions in depth in Chapter 6 didn't put you to sleep, you should recall that the acceptable values are as follows:

- ease
- linear
- ease-in
- ease-out

- `ease-in-out`
- `cubic-bezier()`
- `steps()`

The default value is `ease`, so if this effect is sufficient, you can safely omit this property. When your animation requires something a little different, the following code shows the property in use:

```
animation-name: my-first-animation;
animation-duration: 10s;
animation-timing-function: ease-in;
```

> An important point to note here is that the `animation-timing-function` **property applies the timing function to each keyframe,** *not* **the entire animation. So a value of** `ease-in` **would cause the animation to ease into full flow at each keyframe. You also can apply the property on a keyframe within the** `@keyframes` **rule-set that specifies the timing function for that particular keyframe alone.**

Another property you are familiar with is `animation-delay`, which also acts just like the transition version, allowing you to specify a length of time to pass before the animation begins to play:

```
animation-name: my-first-animation;
animation-duration: 10s;
animation-timing-function: ease-in;
animation-delay: 2s;
```

Next up is the `animation-iteration-count` property, which allows you to specify the number of times that the animation should loop. It accepts number-based values as well as the `infinite` keyword, which obviously causes the animation to loop continuously.

```
animation-name: my-first-animation;
animation-duration: 10s;
animation-timing-function: ease-in;
animation-delay: 2s;
animation-iteration-count: 2;
```

Some expect the initial value for this property to be `infinite`, but it is in fact 1; so if you want your animation to play out more than once, you must specify this property.

This property also accepts decimal values; for example, a value of 1.5 would play the animation through in full once and then get to the halfway point of the next iteration. However, if this halfway point is different from the element's original state, when finished, it snaps back to the original state rather than remaining at the animation's finishing point.

Another new property is `animation-direction`. The default value is `normal`, which plays the animation from start to finish as you would expect. The other acceptable values are as follows:

- `reverse` plays the animation backward, from the end point to the start point.

- `alternate` applies only when the animation has an iteration-count of `2` or more, as it plays the animation forward and then backward and so on.

- `alternate-reverse` does exactly the same as the preceding value except that it plays the animation backward initially and then forward and so on.

As you can see from the following snippet, the application of `animation-direction` couldn't be simpler:

```
animation-name: my-first-animation;
animation-duration: 10s;
animation-timing-function: ease-in;
animation-delay: 2s;
animation-iteration-count: 2;
animation-direction: alternate;
```

The next animation control property is `animation-play-state`, which you will probably rarely need to use, but it could come in handy in some situations. It basically states whether the animation should play or not and accepts two values; the default value is `running` and the other is `paused`. At face value, it looks like a completely pointless feature, but if you consider that you could use the `paused` value on trigger events such as on a `:hover` state, this property suddenly becomes a valid tool:

```
div:hover {
    animation-play-state: paused;
}
```

The final animation property is the `animation-fill-mode` tool. Earlier I mentioned that if your animation doesn't finish in the same place as it starts, it snaps back to its original position on completion. This property addresses that issue and accepts the following values:

- `none` is the initial value; if your element's styles are different from the default styles at `0%` and `100%`, the animation snaps from the original state to the `0%` state when the animation starts (if a delay was specified) and snaps from `100%` to the original state when it finishes.

- `forwards` ensures that your element maintains the styles specified in the last encountered keyframe after the animation finishes. This last keyframe is usually `100%`, but when the `animation-direction` value is `reverse`, the last keyframe would be `0%`, so these styles would be maintained in that case.

- `backwards` applies if you have specified an `animation-delay` value because it ensures the styles from the first keyframe are applied immediately, even before the animation has begun.

- `both` applies the rules from the previous two values.

Again, the `animation-fill-mode` tool is a bit of a niche control, but it could be vital in situations in which the element needs to maintain the styles from the end of the animation:

```
animation-name: my-first-animation;
animation-duration: 10s;
```

```
animation-timing-function: ease-in;
animation-delay: 2s;
animation-iteration-count: 2;
animation-direction: alternate;
animation-fill-mode: both;
```

And with that, you have a full stack of animation control properties (excluding `animation-play-state`, which would generally be applied on a triggered state). That's a lot of bytes, though, contradicting what is supposed to be one of the main selling points of CSS animation. However, to reiterate my earlier point, you can combine them all into one shorthand animation property, as the following code snippet demonstrates:

```
animation: my-first-animation 10s ease-in 2s 2 alternate both;
```

As with the shorthand `transition` property, the `animation` property is lenient in terms of ordering, with the exception of the time-based values. Again, when both the duration and delay values are specified, the first is always the duration and the second denotes the delay.

Looking at CSS3 Animations in Action

Of course, the best way to really soak up all this information is to apply it to a working example. This section starts off with a basic demo (`0801-moving-box.html`, available from the companion website at `www.wiley.com/go/ptl/css3`), which moves a box around its container, traveling from the top left corner, to the bottom left, then the bottom right, and then the top right before finishing back in its original top left position—all while changing colors, too!

You start with the markup and the styles that define the box's original state:

HTML
```
<div class="container">
    <div class="box"></div>
</div>
```

CSS
```
.container {
    width: 700px;
    height: 400px;
    border: 2px dashed #ccc;
    position: relative;
}

.box {
    width: 100px;
    height: 100px;
    background: blue;
    position: absolute;
}
```

The code is elementary so far, simply positioning a blue square at the top left of its container, the result of which is shown in Figure 8-1.

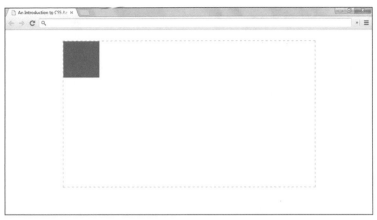

Figure 8-1 The blue box is positioned at the top left of its container, which has a dashed gray border.

Now that you have a blue box, you need to animate it in the way described previously, moving it around the container from corner to corner. Sounds as though you need some keyframes!

```
@keyframes corners {

    25% {
        top: 300px;
        left: 0;
        background: red;
    }

    50% {
        top: 300px;
        left: 600px;
        background: green;
    }

    75% {
        top: 0;
        left: 600px;
        background: yellow;
    }
}
```

As you can see, this code defines three keyframes, with each one changing the color of the box and positioning it in a different corner of the container. The change between these keyframes is then animated!

This code actually has five frames in total, but remember that when the styling for the `0%` and `100%` keyframes is the same as the element's default styles, you can omit these frames.

Again, I urge you to open the working demo to fully understand the animation that is formed by these frames, but Figure 8-2 should go some way to explaining the box's path.

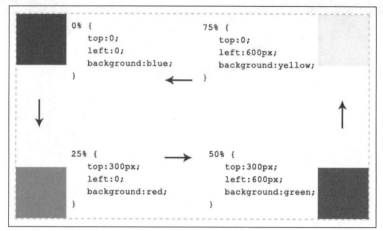

Figure 8-2 The box's path as it travels around the container and changes color from blue to red to green to yellow and then back to the original blue

Now that you have the keyframes for your animation, you can apply it to your box:

```
.box {
    width: 100px;
    height: 100px;
    background: blue;
    position: absolute;
    animation-name: corners;
    animation-duration: 10s;
    animation-iteration-count: infinite;
}

/* Remember, these animation properties can be condensed into a single
shorthand property... */

animation: corners 10s infinite;
```

As stated previously, the two required properties are `animation-name`, which must correspond with the name specified in the `@keyframes` rule-set, and `animation-duration`, which obviously specifies how long the animation should last. I also added an additional control into the equation in the form of the `animation-iteration-count` property, using a value of `infinite` to ensure the animation loops indefinitely.

So, the `.box` element uses the set of keyframes under the name `corners`, applying them over a period of 10 seconds and ensuring the frames are repeated continuously.

Now, to illustrate the abstracted nature of keyframes and the subsequent benefit, the next example demonstrates how you can apply the same set of keyframes to a different element to create a very different effect, thanks to the various animation controls. Start by adding another element, `.circle`, inside the container:

```
HTML
<div class="container">
    <div class="box"></div>
```

```
        <div class="circle"></div>
    </div>
```

CSS
```
.circle {
    width: 100px;
    height: 100px;
    background: blue;
    position: absolute;
    border-radius: 50%;
}
```

The new .circle element is identical to the original .box element, with the exception of an additional border-radius property, which, with a value of 50%, ensures the element takes the shape of a circle.

Now look at how the animation properties can utilize the same keyframes in a very different manner:

```
.circle {
    width: 100px;
    height: 100px;
    background: blue;
    position: absolute;
    border-radius: 50%;
    animation-name: corners;
    animation-duration: 5s;
    animation-iteration-count: infinite;
    animation-direction: alternate-reverse;
    animation-timing-function: cubic-bezier(.4, -.6, .6, 1.6);
}

/* I'm using the individual properties for clarity, but in production, you
should always use the shorthand animation property... */

animation: corners 5s infinite alternate-reverse
           cubic-bezier(.4, -.6, .6, 1.6);
```

As promised, the keyframes remain untouched, but I used some more animation controls that use these frames rather differently. Let's break this down and see how these additional controls actually affect the output:

- First, the duration is only 5 seconds, half that of the .box element's animation-duration value.

- The next big change is the alternate-reverse value of the animation-direction property, which plays the animation backward initially and then forward, before alternating between the two for the rest of the iterations.

- The final addition is a cubic-bezier() timing function, allowing the formation of a custom Bézier curve. The coordinates used create an effect that causes the .circle element to appear as if the momentum carries it beyond the container's boundaries.

On paper, these changes don't sound all that drastic, but the visuals are really quite different when you consider that exactly the same keyframes have been used. This is more evident in the working example (0802-reusing-keyframes.html), although Figure 8-3 goes some way toward representing the new animation.

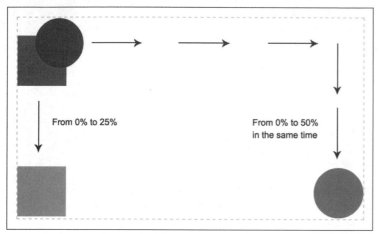

Figure 8-3 The circle plays the animation backward first and travels at twice the speed of the box.

I hope you're now pretty comfortable with the concept of animation in CSS, including the `@keyframes` rule-set and the application of these frames using the `animation` property. Now it's time to look at some more practical examples that have found a place in real-life production websites today!

Adding Progressive Enhancement with Subtle Animation

CSS animation is obviously versatile and powerful, but a more practical usage involves applying subtle enhancements to elements with small-scale, unobtrusive effects. The perfect example of this concept is provided with a wonderful little plugin developed by fast-rising web star Dan Eden.

Dan's collection of beautifully understated entrance and exit animations (`http://daneden.me/animate/`) allow you to add the final niceties to your designs, while ensuring absolutely zero risk of adverse effects in noncompatible browsers.

The actual plugin, `animate.css`, contains the keyframes for a vast range of cool effects and applies each of them to a class, such as `.fadeIn`, for example. You can then add the class to an element in your HTML markup, which in this example causes the element to fade in when the page loads. Of course, they're not all subtle and understated—some of them are very loud and scream for the user's attention, which can often be just what you're looking for.

> **A word of warning: apply great caution when using these attention-grabbing effects on your designs. Their simplicity and ease of application are a luxury in an area of web design that has relied on Flash and JavaScript for a long time now, which can make it very easy to lose your sense of judgment and get carried away.**

Overuse these effects and you will be dangerously close to those disgracefully tacky PowerPoint presentations that featured text and images flying in from every available angle! But if you use the right effects in the right places, you will be on the right side of the very thin line that separates the perfectly enhanced from the embarrassingly overdone.

I liken the use of these effects to applying cosmetics: get it right and your beauty is enhanced; too much and people start to question your taste. You need to find the balance.

Anyway, enough theory! It's time to dive into the `animate.css` file and see how things function under the hood. Head over to the Animate.css website to see these effects in action.

Fade In Effects

Let's start with a simple example to get the ball rolling. It's extremely basic in that it requires just one property alteration and one keyframe to work, although Dan has included two keyframes for clarity:

```
@keyframes fadeIn {

    0% {
        opacity: 0;
    }

    100% {
        opacity: 1;
    }

}
```

Because the original state of the element already has full opacity, you don't need to declare it again on the `100%` keyframe, so you can omit that portion with no difference in the outcome, leaving you with the following code:

```
@keyframes fadeIn {

    0% {
        opacity: 0;
    }

}
```

You then apply these keyframes to the class selector `.fadeIn`, allowing that class to be reused several times throughout your HTML:

```
.fadeIn {
    animation: fadeIn 1s;
}
```

This effect couldn't be more understated, but its effectiveness doesn't reflect its modesty because it provides the perfect enhancement to the initial loading of your elements.

To further enhance this animation and to achieve the `fadeInDown` effect from `animate.css`, you can use the `translate()` transform function to shift the element up at the `0%` keyframe before bringing it back down to its original position in the `100%` keyframe:

```
@keyframes fadeInDown {

    0% {
        opacity: 0;
        transform: translateY(-20px);
    }

}

.fadeInDown {
    animation: fadeInDown 1s;
}
```

To reiterate, you can omit the `100%` keyframe because it is the same as the default styling.

With those foundations set, you should start to realize the possible effects that can be achieved as you bring the various transform functions into the mix. For example, consider the following code, which demonstrates how to create the effect that Dan has labeled *Lightspeed:*

```
@keyframes lightSpeedIn {

    0% {
        opacity: 0;
        transform: translateX(100%) skewX(-30deg)
    }

    60% {
        opacity: 1;
        transform: translateX(-20%) skewX(30deg)
    }

    80% {
        transform: translateX(0) skewX(-15deg)
    }

}

.lightSpeedIn {
    animation: lightSpeedIn 1s;
}
```

In this *Lightspeed* effect, the element speeds in from the right and then appears as though it is skidding to a stop before finally resting in its true position. The `translateX()` function is used to move the element to the right to start the animation. Then it travels back toward its original position, where the `skewX()` function is used to create the illusion that the element is slamming on the breaks in an effort to battle the momentum and come to a stop. Again, I urge you to open the `animate.css` home page, where you can see all these effects in action.

Attention Seekers

Dan has appropriately labeled as *attention seekers* some of the more interesting effects that are showcased in `animate.css`, which gives you a clear indication when you should use them. Don't whack them on every element in your page because they're cool and exciting; apply them considerately to elements that *will* benefit from the added effort to grab the user's attention.

You probably recognize some of the effects; one common use case is to aid form validation because blank required fields and other errors physically shake at you to let you know your form completion skills are inadequate.

I think these types of enhancements are extremely beneficial. I know that I have scrolled through forms looking for that required field I missed, thinking "Well, where the hell is it then?!" An animation provides a subtle visual aid that can help you pinpoint errors immediately and ensure a smoother process.

Shake

Now look at how to achieve this shaking effect, which you can experience on Dan's site. The manipulation of the element introduces nothing new, but the actual structure of the keyframes shows how you can maximize efficiency when you would otherwise be forced to repeat yourself:

```css
@keyframes shake {

    10%, 30%, 50%, 70%, 90% {
        transform: translateX(-10px);
    }

    20%, 40%, 60%, 80% {
        transform: translateX(10px);
    }

}

.shake {
    animation: shake 1s;
}
```

As you can see, several keyframes here share the same line of code. Rather than add unnecessary bytes by repeating yourself, you can simply group the keyframe percentages together in exactly the same way as you would with standard selectors. Much more efficient and compact than writing out the code for all nine keyframes!

In terms of the actual effect, as I noted previously, nothing here is particularly new because the `translateX()` function is used to shift the element from left to right several times, creating the desired shaking effect.

Wobble

Another funky effect from the `animate.css` library is the wobble effect (see the demo file `0803-wobble.html`). It is basically a further enhanced version of the previous shaking effect. However, the enhancement comes through the addition of the `rotate()` function:

```
@keyframes wobble {

    15% {
        transform: translateX(-25%) rotate(-5deg);
    }

    30% {
        transform: translateX(20%) rotate(3deg);
    }

    45% {
        transform: translateX(-15%) rotate(-3deg);
    }

    60% {
        transform: translateX(10%) rotate(2deg);
    }

    75% {
        transform: translateX(-5%) rotate(-1deg);
    }

}

.wobble {
    animation: wobble 1s;
}
```

As the preceding code suggests, the element is moved and swung from left to right several times with decreasing intensity until the element is all wobbled out! Figure 8-4 shows the element's position at each of the seven keyframes (including the `0%` and `100%` frames omitted from the code).

These subtle enhancements make great use of CSS3 animation and can be used today without fear of losing any vital functionality in older browsers. The desired goal is obviously for all browsers to provide full support for CSS-based animation, which will ultimately allow it to realize its full potential, but in the meantime, you can experiment and push the limits of CSS animation in the browsers that allow it.

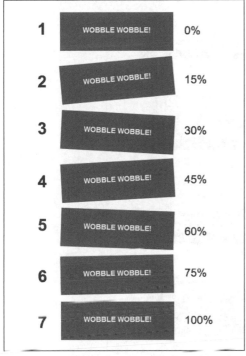

Figure 8-4 The element's position at each keyframe, bearing in mind that the change from one keyframe to another is obviously animated

Combining Animations

In the following example, you see how to combine animations to create a fun, attention-seeking runner for your website. For the desired outcome, look at the demo (0804-combining-animations.html), but Figure 8-5 gives you an idea of the animation that will be formed.

In this example, you begin by creating a four-image slide show before adding a short swinging animation as a preface. Once the runner has swung into place, you will fade its content into view and make a call to action cry for attention.

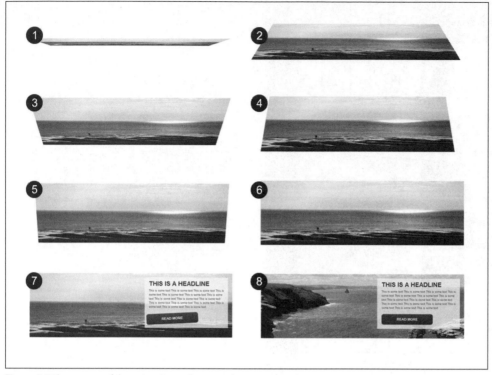

Figure 8-5 The process of the animation to be created

Forming the Structure

The first step is to form the structure for the runner, which unfortunately requires an extra containing `div` to provide perspective for the runner's 3D movements:

HTML
```html
<div class="container">
    <section class="runner">
        <!-- Runner content -->
    </section>
</div>
```

CSS
```css
.container {
    width: 960px;
    height: 300px;
    perspective: 1100px;
}

.runner {
    width: 100%;
    height: 100%;
    background: url(01.jpg);
}
```

As you can see, the runner's container element sets the `width` and `height` and applies some `perspective`, ensuring that its children will operate in a 3D space. The actual `.runner` element then fills the space of its container and applies a background image, as can be seen in Figure 8-6.

Figure 8-6 The current state of the runner after applying the preceding code

Creating an Animated Slide Show

The next step is to adjust the background image so that it becomes a fading slide show, which, of course, requires some keyframes:

```
@keyframes slideshow {
    20% { background: url(01.jpg); }
    25%, 45% { background: url(02.jpg); }
    50%, 70% { background: url(03.jpg); }
    75%, 95% { background: url(04.jpg); }
}
```

The keyframes are based on a fading slide show consisting of four images, each of which is visible for four seconds before fading into the next. The time taken to fade from one image to another is one second; so from that, you should be able to work out the total length of the slide show animation.

Four images are visible for four seconds each, which totals 16 seconds. Then four additional fade transitions last one second apiece, so if you add those to your original total, you have a grand total animation length of 20 seconds.

With this in mind, each second would be 5 percent of the total 20-second duration, so each 1-second fade transition is 5 percent and each 4-second view is 20 percent of the total duration. If you're still struggling, Figure 8-7 provides further, visual clarification.

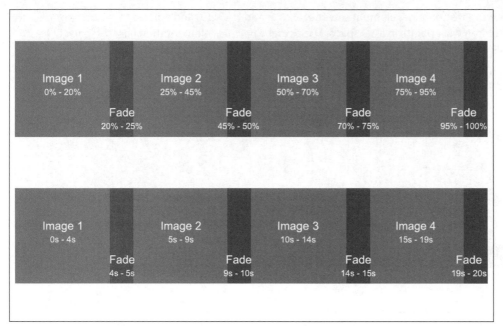

Figure 8-7 The timeline of the animation in percentages (top) and seconds (bottom)

The `0%` keyframe is the same as the element's default state, so you can omit it from the rule-set. However, you don't want the first background image to start fading into the second background image straight away, so you need to redeclare this default style at the 20% mark (after four seconds) to ensure no fading takes place until that point. Then, between 20% and 25% (one second), the first background image is faded into the second, with this logic repeated throughout the rest of the keyframes.

Nothing to it, really! Now, you simply need to apply this animation to the `.runner` element:

```
.runner {
    width: 100%;
    height: 100%;
    background: url(01.jpg);
    animation: slideshow 20s infinite 2s;
}
```

To confirm, the animation is to last 20 seconds and will loop infinitely. Also notice that I added a 2-second delay, which is to allow for an additional animation that will be carried out before this one, which brings you to the second step of this tutorial.

Creating a Swinging Animation

This next animation is slightly more ambitious but certainly no more complex because some 3D transformations are applied to the `.runner` element to create the illusion that it is swinging toward you on entry.

Before going any further, you need to make a slight adjustment to the 3D space to create the desired effect. Recall that the default `transform-origin` value, that is, the point about which the transformations are performed, is at the center of the element. This would not create the desired swinging effect, but rather a turning or spinning illusion around the element's center, so you must later alter this value so the `transform-origin` point sits at the top. The following code shows how to make this change, and Figure 8-8 provides further explanation:

```
.runner {
    width: 100%;
    height: 100%;
    background: url(01.jpg);
    animation: slideshow 20s infinite 2s;
    transform-origin-y: 0;
}
```

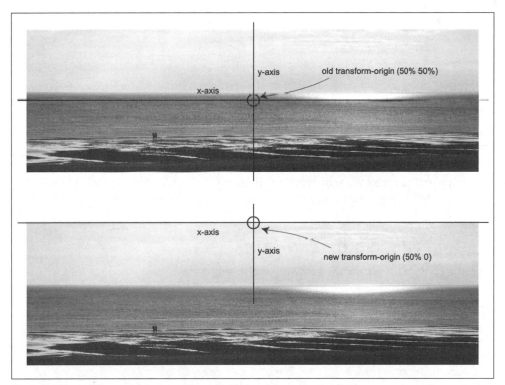

Figure 8-8 The transform-origin point on the y-axis has been moved to sit at the top.

With that step done, you next define the keyframes for the swinging animation:

```
@keyframes swing {
    0%  { transform: rotateX(-90deg); }
    30% { transform: rotateX(50deg); }
    50% { transform: rotateX(-40deg); }
    70% { transform: rotateX(20deg); }
    90% { transform: rotateX(-10deg); }
}
```

What's happened here? Because the `transform-origin` point has been moved, the x-axis now sits at the top of the element and so acts like a hinge for the rotations. The start point of the animation sees the `.runner` element pushed out to `-90deg` about the x-axis. Remove yourself from the virtual world for a moment and picture an actual, real-life swing that you'd find in a children's park. Now, imagine there's no one on the swing and you go up to it and push it back as far as it will go, ready to release. *This* is the start point of your animation, with the following keyframes creating the subsequent swinging motion from the time when the swing is let go.

After the swing is let go (metaphorically speaking), the `.runner` element then swings out toward the user (`50deg` around the x-axis) before swinging back and forth with decreasing intensity until finally settling in its true position.

Next, you need to apply this animation to the `.runner` element, which, of course, already uses keyframes from the slide show animation. You can be thankful that this is easily done, because multiple animations on a single element are simply comma-separated, much like applying multiple transitions:

```
.runner {
    width: 100%;
    height: 100%;
    background: url(01.jpg);
    animation: slideshow 20s infinite 2s, swing 3s ease-in-out;
    transform-origin-y: 0;
}
```

As the preceding code demonstrates, the swing animation lasts three seconds. I adjusted the timing function from the default value of `ease` to ensure that each keyframe eases in and out, to emulate a real-life swinging motion as closely as possible.

Introducing Content with Subtle Animation

The final step is to add some content to your `.runner`, which is also subject to some light animation:

```
<div class="container">
    <section class="runner">
        <div>
            <p>This is a Headline</p>
            <p>This is some text [etc.]</p>
            <a class="cta" href="#">Read More</a>
        </div>
    </section>
</div>
```

With a bit of styling that's not really relevant here, the runner now looks something like Figure 8-9.

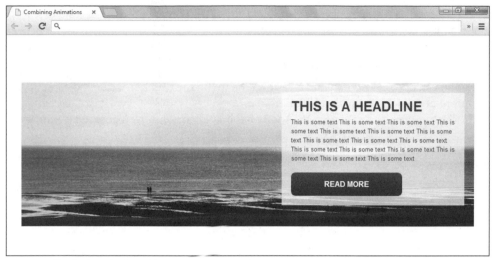

Figure 8-9 The final result after adding some content to the runner

However, you will find that this doesn't look great as the text goes in and out of focus as its container swings back and forth. To remedy this situation, you can fade in the text *after* the initial swinging animation finishes:

```
@keyframes fadeInDown {
    0% {
        opacity: 0;
        transform: translateY(-20px);
    }
}

.runner div {
    /* Other styles */
    animation: fadeInDown 1s 2.5s backwards;
}
```

I discussed the `fadeInDown` effect previously, although this time I applied the keyframes slightly differently. First, a 2.5-second delay occurs, allowing for the earlier animations, and I hope you recall what the `backwards` value relates to. It is, of course, the `animation-fill-mode` property, which is necessary due to the fact that this animation has a `0%` keyframe that differs to its default styles and also has a slight delay.

If this `backwards` parameter were not present, the `div` would be visible during the 2.5-second delay and then the `opacity: 0;` property would kick in only at the `0%` keyframe when the animation begins, which obviously isn't the desired effect. The `backwards` value of `animation-fill-mode` ensures that the `0%` keyframe comes into effect immediately, even throughout the animation's delay period.

As a reminder, the `forwards` value of `animation-fill-mode` would ensure the `100%` keyframe stays in effect *after* the animation finishes, and the `both` value applies the behavior of both the `backwards` and `forwards` values.

The result of these keyframes and the way they have been applied is that the content `div` would wait for the initial swing animation to almost complete and then fade into view.

Seeking Attention with Loud Animation

Right, almost there! Now you can add *one more* animation—this time to the call to action inside the content `div`. Remember those attention-seeking animation effects from `animate.css`? Well, if you want anything on your page to grab the user's attention, it's a call to action! Another animation means—you guessed it—more keyframes!

```
@keyframes wobble {
    15% { transform: translateX(-10%) rotate(-5deg); }
    30% { transform: translateX(5%) rotate(3deg); }
    45% { transform: translateX(-5%) rotate(-3deg); }
    60% { transform: translateX(3%) rotate(2deg); }
    75% { transform: translateX(-2%) rotate(-1deg); }
}

.runner div .cta {
    animation: wobble .75s 3.5s;
}
```

This code creates the wobble effect from Dan's plugin, although slightly modified to make the effect a tiny bit more subtle. It's also slightly quicker and obviously has a delay to allow the other animations to complete before it tries to grab the user's attention.

And that's the finished product! Head back to the companion website and take a look through the code and the final outcome in the demo file `0804-combining-animations.html` to ensure you fully understand all the code for this example.

Examining Browser Support for CSS Animation

It's time to address that dreaded subject: browser support. However, as with transforms and transitions, CSS animations are extremely well supported considering their power and capability.

They have support across the board in the current major browser versions, with Firefox recently opting to drop the vendor prefix, while IE10 has picked them straight up without a prefix. Chrome, Safari, and Opera also have support, but all currently rely on the `-webkit-` prefix. Table 8-1 shows the full picture.

Table 8-1: CSS Animations Browser Compatibility

Browser	Prefixed Support	Unprefixed Support
Chrome	4+	Not supported
Firefox	5+	16+
Opera	12 (-o-) 15+ (`-webkit-`)	12.1 (Former Presto engine)
Safari	4+	Not supported
IE	Not supported	10

Until very recently, it was a huge chore to implement CSS animation while ensuring support across the board because both the `@keyframe` rule-sets and the `animation` properties had to be repeated several times (one of each for `-moz-`, `-webkit-`, `-o-`, and an unprefixed version), resulting in a ghastly number of additional bytes.

You can be thankful that with Firefox now employing a fast release cycle, the previous versions that required the prefix are quickly becoming obsolete, making the inclusion of a `@-moz-keyframes` rule-set and a `-moz-animation` property fairly redundant. The same applies to Opera, suggesting that you really need to include only two versions of the keyframes and animation rules: one with the `-webkit-` prefix and one without.

Summary

To reiterate my earlier plea, you should apply animations like makeup: use the right amount to subtly and suitably enhance, but not so much as to appear tacky or classless.

Also remember that CSS is a styling language and is not really appropriate for hugely complex animations outside experimentation. Think about what you're doing; If it is a subtle enhancement, go ahead and start typing out those keyframes! If you want something more complex, are you sure the effect wouldn't be more suited to JavaScript or Flash? Just consider the situation at hand and apply common sense.

Additionally, the keyframes can soon take up a significant portion of your stylesheet, especially if you're creating two or three animations. Therefore, even though only one vendor prefix (`-webkit-`) is required, you are still doubling what can be a large number of bytes. In theory, one of the main advantages of CSS-based animations is their simplicity and compactness, but when this compact code is doubled, it paints a different picture, so always consider the situation and think about whether CSS animation is actually the best tool for the job.

Further Reading

CSS Animations Specification
`http://www.w3.org/TR/css3-animations`

Dan Eden's animate.css plugin
`http://daneden.me/animate/`

Part III

Getting to Grips with New Layout Tools

Chapter 9

Creating a Multicolumn Layout

As has been evident throughout the previous chapters in this book, CSS has made major advancements in almost every area, comprehensively tackling each and every issue, both big and small. There is one area, however, that CSS has been rather slow to master. Most of you are painfully aware that the area I am alluding to is, of course, layout.

This chapter begins by addressing why previous and current layout solutions do not fit the bill, before introducing each of the new layout modules proposed in CSS3. One of these new modules is Multi-column Layout, which I discuss in depth in this chapter, with the others to be addressed in the following chapters.

The Multi-column Layout module provides a method of defining columns in the stylesheet, allowing your content to flow into these columns dynamically, without the need to touch your markup. I describe how to create a multicolumn layout using the various new properties on offer, which provide control over the size and number of columns as well as spanning elements and decorative rules to separate the columns.

The Evolution of Layout Tools

CSS has famously always lacked a true layout mechanism, with web designers slowly innovating and finding new ways to utilize the tools available for creating complex and maintainable layouts.

The first website that I ever created (calling it a website is generous indeed) used *frames* to form the layout: a sidebar frame, a header frame, and a frame for the content. While easy to implement, frames came with a number of crucial flaws, most notably the fact that each frame operated independently as if each were a different window, causing the URL displayed in the address bar to go unchanged when links were clicked. This, in turn, prevented users from bookmarking the content they were looking at and left users lost; basically, frames were a usability nightmare.

It wasn't long before developers realized that there was more to layout than frames and that you could do much more with an HTML table than simply fill it with data. Obviously, you now live by the law that tables should only ever be used for tabular data (and rightfully so), but back then, using tables for layout was quite an innovative, albeit extremely nonsemantic use of existing tools to create much more advanced layouts.

Nested tables and spacer GIFs allowed front-end developers to hack together a grid, within which they could place the various elements of their web page, and with a bit of foresight, they could create all kinds of abstract layouts. Although tables did the job for a while, they were never going to succeed as a layout tool due to their rigid nature, inflexibility, and inefficiency, not to mention the fact that they are not and were never intended to be used as a solution for layout.

Table-based layout enjoyed the spotlight for longer than it should have, but when CSS-based layout techniques eventually worked their way into the mainstream, it was like a breath of fresh air for web developers everywhere. Finally, layout and content could be truly separated, ensuring the semantics of the markup and the accessibility of the content are not compromised. Today's floated layouts, often assisted by a sprinkling of the `position` property, are a million miles ahead of their predecessors and continue to prove an adequate solution for laying out web pages. However, current options also suffer from many flaws and limitations.

Basic aspects of layout such as vertical centering; flexible, equal-height elements; columns; and the re-ordering of content for presentational purposes are currently all either impossible or have to be hacked together. Basically, there are a lot of holes to be filled and tools to be sharpened when it comes to CSS-based layout techniques. You can be thankful that CSS3 has introduced a whole range of new layout modules that aim to address these issues.

What's New in Layout Solutions?

Okay, so you know that previous and current layout solutions are barely up to the task and that a number of additional solutions have been proposed in CSS3, but what exactly are these new-fangled layout mechanisms that are supposed to be solving all your layout woes?

There are actually *five* new layout modules of varying levels of maturity and stability, with some still very much in their youth and subject to change:

- **Multi-column Layout**—The oldest and most stable of the new layout modules, Multi-Column Layout is finally gaining some support from the browser vendors, affording you the capability to arrange your content into columns that flow into each other, completely independent of the document's markup! I cover this module in great detail in this chapter.

- **Flexible Box Layout**—This is one of the more comprehensive layout modules that has the potential to truly revolutionize the way you structure your web pages with CSS. Chapter 10 discusses Flexbox in depth, detailing how to use each of the new properties it proposes to create a highly flexible page layout.

- **Grid Layout**—Proposed by Microsoft, the Grid Layout module allows you to form a grid before placing the elements of your design into the various rows and columns that the grid has formed. The concept shares some similarities with HTML tables in the way that the rows and columns combine to create cells, but this obviously all happens completely independently in the CSS, ensuring the markup isn't compromised. Chapter 11 explains this module further.

- **Regions**—An exciting new layout technique put forward by Adobe, the Regions module allows for truly complex, magazine-like layouts enabling text to flow between several elements anywhere on the page.

- **Exclusions**—Also an Adobe innovation, the Exclusions module enables you to control the way your text wraps and flows around objects like never before, allowing you to create custom shapes around which your text must flow. I go into much more depth about the impressive Regions and Exclusions modules in Chapter 11.

As you can see, although several new layout-based modules are available, they all address different concerns and in most cases can work together rather than act as alternative solutions to the same problem.

As previously stated, the Multi-column Layout module is the most mature from the preceding list and also boasts the most browser support in addition to being the least complex, so it seems like a good place to start your exploration into the new layout mechanisms.

Introducing Multi-column Layout

Laying out text in multiple columns obviously has its roots in print, particularly newspapers, which have used this technique to present lots of text-based information in compact and readable formats. So widespread was its use in print long before the rise of the web, it defies belief that browser support for the use of this technique on the web is only just emerging.

Despite the difference in nature between print and web mediums, such an elementary form of layout should be an easily accessible option for developers—and now (or very soon at least), it is!

Many a column-based layout has been hacked together using various techniques, but now there is a legitimate method of dividing your text into columns that flow into each other without any modification of the markup. Exciting stuff, I'm sure you will agree—so let's get to it!

New Multicolumn Properties

With a new module comes a brand new set of properties and values to wrap your head around. Sounds daunting, but the multicolumn properties are fairly friendly and straightforward.

First, I discuss the new properties that allow you to define your columns, before addressing the more niche controls afforded to you by the Multi-column Layout module.

Defining Your Columns

First to address is the `column-width` property, which accepts any standard, length-based value. It is applied to the container element, and presto! The contents of this element are then arranged into columns at the specified width. Look at the following code example, the result of which is shown in Figure 9-1:

```
HTML
<article class="container">
    <p>Lorem ipsum...</p>
    <p>Donec tincidunt...</p>
    <p>Etiam eu elit...</p>
    <!-- Further paragraphs -->
</article>

CSS
.container {
    width: 600px;
    column-width: 180px;
}
```

Just a single, solitary property does the job! Doesn't get much easier than that, does it?

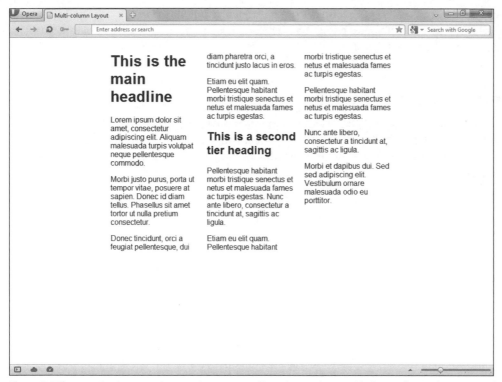

Figure 9-1 The container's content has now been arranged into three columns with the text flowing between each of them.

However, although on the surface this property is as straightforward as they come, there is a little more to it. Despite setting the `column-width` to a value of `180px`, the preceding example actually renders the resulting columns slightly wider. The reason is that the `column-width` property actually sets the *optimal* width of the columns rather than applying an explicit width, allowing the columns to grow into the available space if any exists.

In the preceding example, there is a slight remainder of space, so the columns expand to a width of `189px`, which is the closest to the optimal width they can go while ensuring that they fill all the space available.

> You may be wondering why the three columns don't expand to a width of `200px` if the containing element is `600px` wide. The reason they only go up to `189px` is to account for the *column gap*, which you can set explicitly, but the user-agent also sets a default value (the specification suggests this default UA value should be `1em`). More on this later.

An alternative to applying a length-based `column-width` value comes in the form of the `column-count` property, which accepts integer values. Rather than setting an optimal width, this property sets an optimal number of columns, with the actual computed column widths calculated depending on the space available. Consider the following example:

```
.container {
    width: 600px;
    column-count: 4;
}
```

This code ensures that the container is split into four equal-width columns, with the width of these columns depending on the width of the container. To explain further, what is a 600px wide container divided by four columns? The answer is, of course, 150px; but allowing for the column gaps, each column actually computes to a maximum possible width of 138px in this particular example, as shown in Figure 9-2.

Figure 9-2 The container is split into four columns, the widths of which are dependent on the space available.

If the width of the container were increased, the columns would also then expand to ensure that four equal-width columns still fill the available space, as Figure 9-3 demonstrates:

```
.container {
    width: 900px;
    column-count: 4;
}
```

In addition to the two properties described previously, a shorthand `columns` property also allows you to set both the `column-width` and `column-count` values. However, as the specification suggests, you rarely need to specify both a width and a count value; one or the other generally suffices.

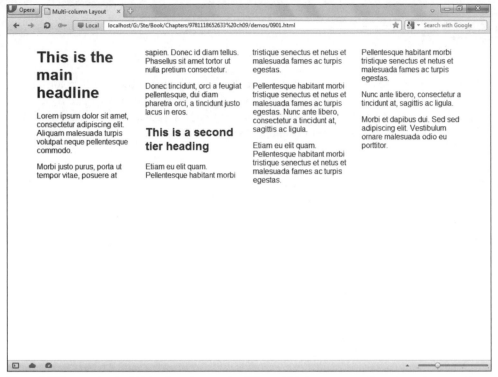

Figure 9-3 The container's width has been increased to 900px, which, in turn, causes the columns to expand to maintain the column count while filling the available space.

You can omit either parameter from the `columns` property, though, allowing you to basically use it as a shorthand method of specifying *either* the `column-width` or `column-count` value, as shown in the following code. Remember, the integer value specifies the optimal `column-count`, whereas the length-based value sets the optimal `column-width`.

```
/* Valid, but nonsensical usage... */
columns: 3 180px;

/* You can omit either parameter, which makes much more sense... */
columns: 3; /* Same as column-count: 3; */
columns: 180px; /* Same as column-width: 180px; */
```

Next up is the `column-gap` property, which I touched on already. As I stated previously, the initial value is set by the browser and is `1em` if adhering to the advice in the spec. This default spacing often suffices, but if you want more control over the column gutters, you can simply use the `column-gap` property with a length-based value.

However, much like padding, this value eats into your column widths as you saw with the initial examples, so you must take the gaps into account when determining your column width values. Another point to bear in mind is that the column gaps are only placed between columns that have content, so a three-column layout would have two column gutters, as shown in Figure 9-4.

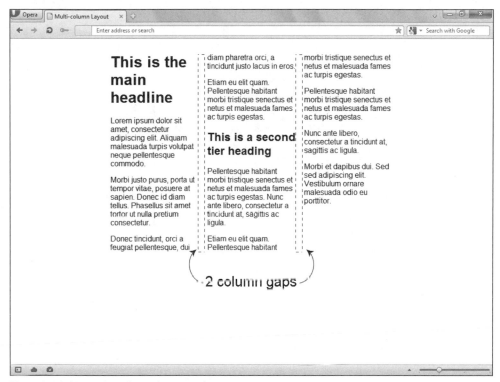

Figure 9-4 A three-column layout has two column gaps.

Consider how these gaps could affect your column-based layout. If your container is 600px wide and you specify a `column-width` value of `180px`, you have three columns totaling 540 pixels in width. This then leaves you with 60 pixels to use for the two gutters. So, a `column-gap` value of `30px` would be fine, whereas any value above `30px` would ensure the total width of the columns and gutters exceeds that of the container, forcing the three-column layout to become a two-column layout. The following code and Figure 9-5 explain further:

```
.container {
    width: 600px;
    column-width: 180px;
    column-gap: 30px;
}
```

Figure 9-6 demonstrates how a `column-gap` value above `30px` would ensure that the total column and gutter width would be too great to accommodate a three-column layout because it would be wider than the container. The layout would then transform into a two-column layout, expanding the width of the columns in the process to fill the available space.

```
.container {
    width: 600px;
    column-width: 180px;
    column-gap: 31px;
}
```

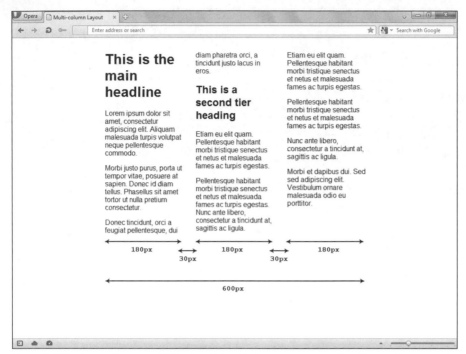

Figure 9-5 The three columns total 540px in width, with the two gutters totaling 60px, making a grand total of 600px—the exact width of the container.

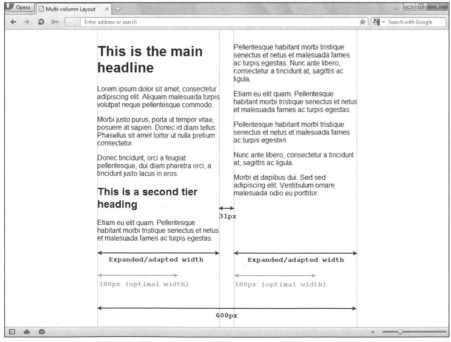

Figure 9-6 The layout adapts to fill the available space, using the column-width value as a basis only, while ensuring column gaps are exactly 31px.

Another new property from the Multi-column Layout module is the `column-rule` property, which allows you to add a decorative touch to your columns. It is actually a shorthand property for the `column-rule-width`, `column-rule-style`, and `column-rule-color` properties, similar to the way in which the border property works. The big difference with `column-rule` is that it doesn't take up any physical space, so it does not eat away at your column widths in the same way that the `column-gap` property does.

The `column-rule` property basically adds a vertical rule in the center of your column gaps, between all columns that contain content. Figure 9-7 illustrates this effect, and the following code shows how it's achieved:

```
.container {
    width: 600px;
    column-width: 180px;
    column-gap: 30px;
    column-rule-width: 2px;
    column-rule-style: dotted;
    column-rule-color: #ccc;
}

/* This should of course be shortened to... */

.container {
    width: 600px;
    column-width: 180px;
    column-gap: 30px;
    column-rule: 2px dotted #ccc;
}
```

Figure 9-7 The column rule is placed in the center of the column gap and does not occupy any physical space.

Providing you with even further control is the `column-span` property, which enables you to target elements—typically headings, quotations, and other similar elements—that you want to stretch across all your columns. Figure 9-8 demonstrates the difference between standard headings and spanning headings; notice that spanning elements create a break in the content, ensuring that in this example, the text reflows to fill the columns above the second spanning head before filling the columns below. Also note that currently, this property is limited to a value of either `all` or `none` (the default value).

```
h1, h2 {
    column-span: all;
}
```

The next property to address is the `column-fill` property. The default value is `balance`, which distributes the content across the columns as equally as possible to avoid a partially full, short final column. The other acceptable value (`auto`) fills the columns sequentially, which *could* result in a final column that contains much less content than the others. However, the `auto` value takes effect only if the container's height is constrained; otherwise, the columns are always balanced.

Figure 9-8 The headings break up the content by spanning across all the columns.

Figure 9-9 shows how multiple columns with a constrained height render using the default `balance` value of `column-fill`.

```
.container {
    width: 600px;
    height: 500px;
    columns: 4;
}
```

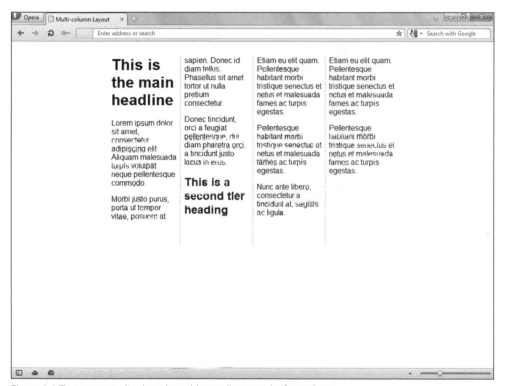

Figure 9-9 The content is distributed roughly equally across the four columns.

Because the container has a `height` value applied to it, you can utilize the `auto` value of `column-fill` here. Figure 9-10 shows how this rule ensures that the content flows sequentially throughout the four columns.

```
.container {
    width: 600px;
    height: 500px;
    columns: 4;
    column-fill: auto;
}
```

Figure 9-10 The fourth column is now only partially filled as the content flows sequentially from one column to the next.

When you consider that it takes just the one property to transform a body of text into a column-based layout, you might be a little surprised to learn all these additional properties that afford you even further control. And there are still more to come!

Handling Column Breaks

The last few properties to be discussed allow you to control where column and page breaks occur, or where they should be avoided, in your layout.

The `break-before` and `break-after` properties are applied to an element within a multicolumn layout and determine whether or not breaks should occur before and after this element, as well as the type of break that should or should not occur. Both of these properties accept the same values, detailed in the following list:

- `auto` is the default value and applies neither a break nor the avoidance of a break before or after the targeted element.

- `always` ensures that a page break is always forced before or after the targeted element.

- `avoid` ensures that any type of break is avoided before or after the targeted element.

- `left` forces one or two page breaks before or after the targeted element to ensure that the next page is formatted as a left page.

- `right` forces one or two page breaks before or after the targeted element to ensure that the next page is formatted as a right page.

- ▨ `page` ensures that a page break is forced before or after the targeted element.

- ▨ `column` ensures that a column break is forced before or after the targeted element.

- ▨ `avoid-page` ensures that page breaks are always avoided before or after the targeted element.

- ▨ `avoid-column` ensures that column breaks are always avoided before or after the targeted element.

Take a look at how a couple of these values can be used to affect your column-based layout. Consider a scenario within which you want to place a column break before all `h2` elements so that they always start a new column. The `break-before` property makes this extremely easy to achieve:

```
h2 {
    break-before: column;
}
```

Told you it was easy! Now a column break occurs before each `h2` element in your multicolumn layout, as shown in Figure 9-11.

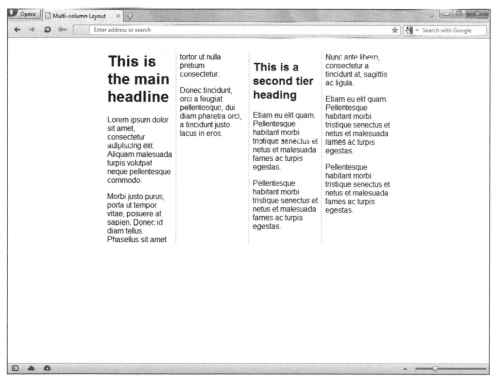

Figure 9-11 Each h2 element starts a new column through use of the break-before property.

Now imagine that you've added a `blockquote` element, which sits awkwardly at the bottom of a column. You decide that you always want text to surround quotations so you want to ensure that column breaks are avoided before and after all `blockquote` elements. Again, achieving this effect is a cinch, but this time you must use the `break-after` property as well:

```
blockquote {
    break-before: avoid-column;
    break-after: avoid-column;
}
```

As desired, all `blockquote` elements now appear as an island between blocks of text (see Figure 9-12), because column breaks are always avoided immediately before and after each occurrence of this element.

The final property to be introduced from the Multi-column Layout module is the `break-inside` property. As you would imagine, it is similar to the two properties discussed previously, but it accepts a smaller range of possible values. They are `auto`, `avoid`, `avoid-page`, and `avoid-column`.

The `break-inside` property allows you to control column breaks *within* elements. A typical example would involve the avoidance of column breaks in the middle of paragraphs. I'm sure you've grasped the concept of the break properties by now, but the following code should clarify, with the result shown in Figure 9-13:

```
p {
    break-inside: avoid-column;
}
```

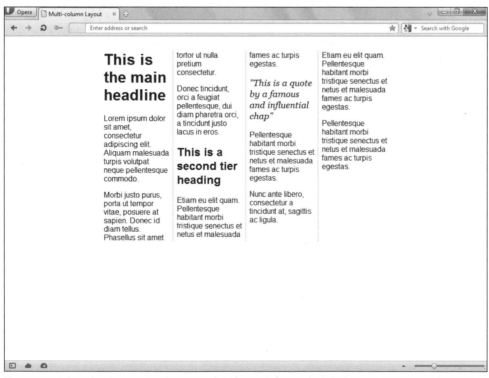

Figure 9-12 Column breaks are avoided immediately before and after blockquote elements, ensuring they are always surrounded by body text.

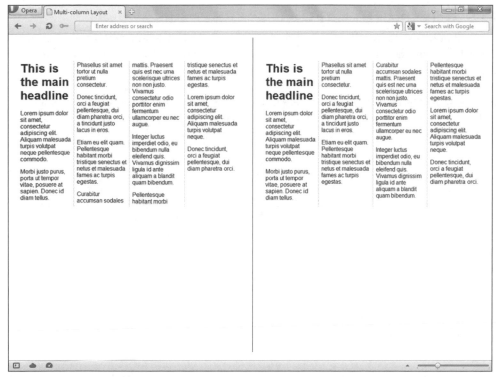

Figure 9-13 By default, column breaks can occur within paragraphs (left), but the break-inside property helps to prevent this from happening (right).

Limitations

I really like the simplicity of the Multi-column Layout module. All it takes is one property and you have a basic, flowing, column-based layout! However, I can easily see how some developers may label it as *too* simplistic with not nearly enough scope for customization.

Of course, the columns are defined purely with CSS, so you don't have any physical HTML elements to target, meaning you cannot style each column individually, but only as a uniform collective. That is, you can't give your three-column layout three different widths or three different font families.

However, the specification seems to acknowledge these limitations and the possible need for columns of varying styles, as it states:

> *Future specifications may add more functionality. For example, columns of different widths and different backgrounds may be supported.*

The spec gives hope of a more powerful column-based layout tool, but for the time being, you have a perfectly functional and delightfully simple method of restructuring your content into flexible columns.

You're now well educated on everything this module has to offer, so let's apply these new properties to build a real-life example of a multiple-column layout.

Creating a Multicolumn Layout

Thanks to the ease of use that this layout mechanism boasts, this section is fairly brief and aims to clarify all the explanations featured so far in the chapter while illustrating how you can use this module to create beautiful, column-based layouts.

To begin, Figure 9-14 shows the final result of this exercise: a multicolumn layout that makes use of several of the control properties discussed in the previous section to form an aesthetically desirable, compact, and readable collection of text, in a layout typically associated with print-based media.

> I built the demo (0901-multi-column-layout.html) in Opera 12.1 as it (along with IE10) was the only browser to support the entire Multi-column Layout module without a prefix. However, since Opera's switch to the WebKit rendering engine, it now requires the `-webkit-` prefix (from version 15) and lacks support for the column break properties. It's worth noting, though, that all of the latest browser releases can cope with this particular example with their respective vendor prefixes. I have applied only the `-webkit-` prefix in this case, so the demo will work in Chrome, Safari, or Opera.

Start with the markup. Remember you don't need to alter your HTML to rearrange your content into columns, so this portion of the code will remain almost entirely untouched from here.

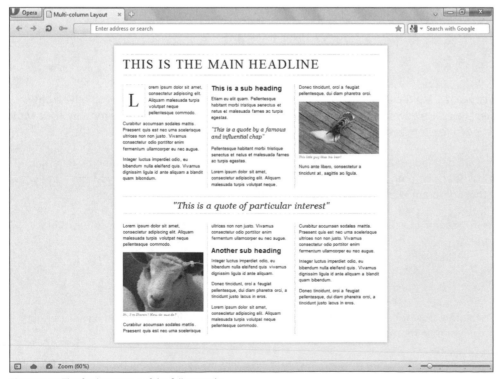

Figure 9-14 The final outcome of the full example

It would be rather pointless to take up the next few pages with the dummy text that fills these columns, so the following code has been edited down for brevity. It includes the main points of interest and indicates a section of body text with a single paragraph element. You can see the full source code in the online demo.

```html
<article class="container">
    <h1>This is the Main Headline</h1>
    <p>Paragraphs</p>

    <h2>This is a sub heading</h2>
    <p>Paragraphs</p>

    <blockquote>This is a quote by...</blockquote>

    <p>Paragraphs</p>

    <figure>
        <img src="thirsty-wasp.jpg" alt="Thirsty Wasp">
        <figcaption>This little guy likes his beer!</figcaption>
    </figure>

    <p>Paragraphs</p>

    <blockquote>This is a quote of particular interest</blockquote>

    <p>Paragraphs</p>

    <figure>
        <img src="sharon-sheep.jpg" alt="Sharon the Sheep">
        <figcaption>Hi, I'm Sharon! How do ewe do?</figcaption>
    </figure>

    <p>Paragraphs</p>

    <h2>Another sub heading</h2>
    <p>Paragraphs</p>
</article>
```

After some basic styling that doesn't warrant much attention in this chapter, the content is starting to look presentable (see Figure 9-15). However, the linear display of the content together with the outrageous line length don't really invite readers or ensure they engage with the content.

Time to bring in the columns! As you already know, the initial implementation couldn't be easier:

```css
.container {
    /* Other styles */
    columns: 3; /* Shorthand of column-count: 3; */
    column-gap: 1.8em;
    column-rule: 2px dotted #ccc;
}
```

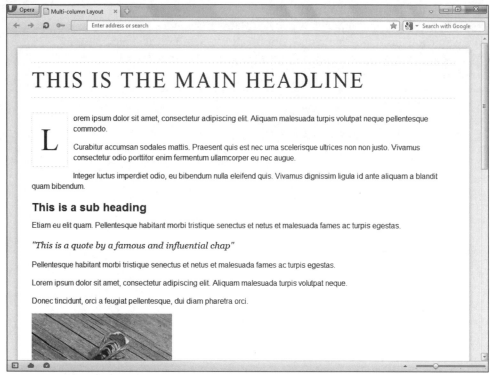

Figure 9-15 The content before being restructured into columns

And just like that, all the content is arranged into three columns, tastefully separated with subtle dividing lines, as shown in Figure 9-16.

The aesthetics of the layout have already improved significantly, but some areas still require some attention to establish a clearer structure and improve the user experience. For example, on most displays, the current organization of the content would force users to scroll down to the bottom of a column, before having to scroll back up to continue reading at the top of the following column. This is obviously not an ideal scenario and is not likely to maintain the readers' attention.

You will probably recall from the final outcome that the main strategy here is to break up the columns and establish a more solid structure through spanning elements. The first example of this is the main headline, which spans across all three columns at the top of the layout structure. Then, to prevent the columns growing to an uncomfortable length, I decided to highlight a particularly interesting quote by also spanning it across all three columns, which then serves to break the content into more readable sections:

```
h1 {
    /* Other styles */
    column-span: all;
}

blockquote.important {
    /* Other styles */
    column-span: all;
}
```

Figure 9-16 All the content has now been rearranged into three columns.

As is apparent from the preceding code, I decided to use the class named `.important` for all `blockquote` elements that should stand out in the content. Figure 9-17 shows these spanning elements in action, but this layout appears to have caused other issues.

The issue that has now surfaced is that the image sits at the bottom of the second column, while its caption has been pushed out to the top of the third column. At this point, the break properties come into play, providing you with the necessary control over where column breaks are allowed to occur in your layout.

The `img` and `figcaption` elements both sit inside a `figure` container element, so the `break-inside` property is the most appropriate tool in this particular example:

```
figure {
    /* Other styles */
    break-inside: avoid;
}
```

This code prevents any kind of break occurring within this `figure` element, ensuring that the image and its caption are never separated.

Figure 9-17 The main headline and the important quotation now span across all three columns.

While the matter of column breaks is on the agenda, it would be wise to address where these breaks should be allowed to occur generally in your column-based layout. For example, it's unlikely that you would ever want column breaks to occur immediately after any headings because this arrangement would leave them stuck at the foot of a column—hardly the place for a heading! Therefore, you can safely define the following break rule:

```
h1, h2, h3, h4, h5, h6 {
    break-after: avoid;
}
```

With all that in mind and with a couple of additional niceties, you now have a layout that organizes large amounts of text into compact and readable columns. And all it took was a few additional properties! Refer back to Figure 9-14 for a reminder of the final product or take a look at the live demo (`0901-multi-column-layout.html`) on the companion website at `www.wiley.com/go./ptl/css3`.

Examining Browser Support for Multi-column Layout

As mentioned earlier in the chapter, the Multi-column Layout is the oldest and most stable of all the new CSS3 layout modules and so boasts much more impressive support among the major browsers.

Internet Explorer 10 offers complete, unprefixed support for the entire range of properties, whereas the prefixed support offered by Firefox, Chrome, Safari, and Opera is a little patchier. Table 9-1 provides a full breakdown of the current browser compatibility situation.

Table 9-1: CSS Multicolumn Layout Browser Compatibility

Browser	Supported Versions	Nonsupported Properties

Chrome	4+ (prefixed)	`break-before`
		`break-after`
		`break-inside`
		`column-fill`

Firefox	2+ (prefixed)	`break-before`
		`break-after`
		`break-inside`
		`column-fill`
		`column-span`

Opera	15+ (`-webkit-` prefix)	`break-before`
		`break-after`
		`break-inside`
		`column-fill`

Safari	3.1+ (prefixed)	`break-before`
		`break-after`
		`break-inside`
		`column-fill`

IE	10	N/A

As I said, it's patchy. However, the most important properties are supported across the board, and the break properties just provide additional control that you don't always need. Add to that the fact that columns usually degrade very gracefully, as noncompatible browsers simply ignore the properties and render the content linearly as normal.

With this information in mind, you should find it fairly safe to go ahead and use multiple columns now. Just bear in mind that currently, you need to use the `-moz-` and `-webkit-` prefixes for each property in addition to the unprefixed versions.

Summary

The Multi-column Layout mechanism is delightfully easy to implement, leaving your markup completely untouched. It's also fairly well supported across the board, and when it fails, it simply falls back to the standard, single-column layout. As someone who has hacked together inflexible columns of text in the past, I feel this module is a breath of fresh air and long overdue.

It's important to remember, however, that web design has spent the best part of 20 years trying to break free of the constraints set by print-based media to embrace the freedom and flexible nature that web-based platforms offer. So use columns wisely and don't get sucked back into the quest to replicate print!

Further Reading

CSS Multi-column Layout Specification

`http://www.w3.org/TR/css3-multicol/`

CSS3 Multicolumn Generator

`http://www.aaronlumsden.com/multicol/`

Introducing the CSS3 Multi-Column Module

`http://alistapart.com/article/css3multicolumn`

Chapter 10
Flexible Box Layout

At this point, things get really interesting. The Flexible Box Layout module, or *Flexbox*, is along with Grid Layout the most comprehensive of the new layout modules, offering an entirely new layout mode designed for assembling more complex web pages and applications.

Having said that, most of the layout concepts that CSS currently struggles with are far from complex; they're actually extremely basic demands, such as vertical centering, for example, that have traditionally relied on substantial yet fragile hacks to be achieved.

Well, at long last, Flexbox provides trivial solutions that reflect the elementary nature of these concepts, in addition to tackling the more challenging aspects of layout such as flexibility and distribution of space.

For me, this is one of the most exciting modules of all that CSS3 has to offer. The upcoming Regions and Exclusions modules will probably win the "wow factor" awards, but Flexbox addresses many everyday issues and genuinely has the potential to truly revolutionize the way you lay out your web pages.

At a time when the industry is adapting to the shift away from fixed-width layouts and responding to the realization that the web has no bounds, the introduction of Flexbox is a timely addition, and couldn't be more appropriate for the direction the web is heading.

I won't sugarcoat it: This module can be daunting and comes across as pretty complex at first glance, but I can assure you that once you've wrapped your head around the concept, everything will click into place and you will love these new tools. The main reason for its perceived complexity is its unfamiliarity because it introduces brand new ideas and methods of forming layout, requiring a new way of thinking about this fundamental aspect of web design.

This chapter looks at what exactly Flexbox is and what it is capable of before going through each of the new properties and values that have been proposed throughout this substantial module. I then finish by applying this new toolset to a real-life example.

What Is Flexbox?

Okay, so what exactly is this Flexible Box Layout, and what's so great about it?

The basic model of this layout mechanism involves a *flex container*, the contents of which are known as *flex items*. These flex items play by very different rules in comparison to nonflex elements and are afforded many more capabilities.

The fundamental functionality of a flex item is its capability to "flex" its sizes—that is, to adjust the width or height according to the available space. Flex items can also flex their size based on a proportion of the available space, as specified by you; I tackle this topic in depth later in the chapter.

Another impressive capability boasted by flex items involves visual order and direction. In basic terms, the flex layout model allows you to display your flex items in any order or direction you want, completely independent of the actual source so as not to compromise accessibility.

Finally, the Flexbox model provides you with the alignment control you've always dreamed of! Equal widths and spacing, equal height columns, vertical alignment, and much more that you've no doubt been forced to hack together in the past!

Okay, enough theory; let's get to the good stuff!

New Flexbox Properties

The Flexbox module is fairly substantial, and it has a lot of new properties and values to examine. Once you open your mind to these new ideas, you'll happily rely on Flexbox to solve many of your layout challenges.

Establishing the Flex Formatting Context

Although this module proposes many new properties, some of the new functionalities have found a place with existing properties, notably the `display` property. The Flexbox module proposes two new values for `display`, which enable you to transform an element into a flex container at either the block or inline level:

- `display: flex;` specifies a block-level flex container.
- `display: inline-flex;` specifies an inline flex container.

When applied to an element, these display values establish a new flex formatting context for their contents, which now become flex items. Consider the following code example:

```html
HTML
<section class="container">

    <div class="bucket">
        <h2>Heading One</h2>
        <img src="an-image.jpg" alt="An image">
        <p><!-- 4 lines of text --></p>
    </div>

    <div class="bucket">
        <h2>Heading Two</h2>
        <img src="an-image.jpg" alt="An image">
        <p><!-- 3 lines of text --></p>
    </div>

    <div class="bucket">
        <h2>Heading Three</h2>
        <img src="an-image.jpg" alt="An image">
        <p><!-- 2 lines of text --></p>
    </div>

</section>
```

```css
CSS
.container {
    width: 960px;
    margin: 50px auto;
    background: #eee;
    display: flex;
}

.bucket {
    background: #ccc;
    padding: 20px;
    border: 1px solid #666;
    width: 250px;
}
```

In this example you have three buckets, each with a heading, an image, and varying amounts of descriptive text.

The container has some basic styling applied to it. In addition to the `display: flex;` rule that transforms it into a *flex container*. This code establishes a flex formatting context, ensuring that the contents of this flex container (the `.bucket` elements) become *flex items*.

To get a nice row of equally sized buckets, you would generally have to float the buckets, give them a horribly inflexible and explicit `height` value, as well as clear the float to prevent the container from collapsing. What a mess! As you can see from the preceding code example, though, all that's required here is a `display` value of `flex` on the container to achieve the aforementioned row of equally sized buckets—not to mention enabling the potential for so much more Flexbox functionality (potential that I show you how to fulfill shortly).

The code from this example results in the output illustrated in Figure 10-1.

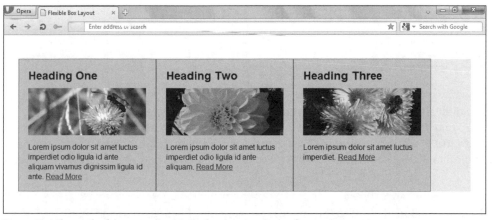

Figure 10-1 The result of the preceding block of code, using display: flex; on the container

You can see that the buckets appear as if they are floated to the left, the container is not collapsed, and all the buckets are of equal heights, despite containing different amounts of content. That's right—flexible, equal-height columns are a thing now! And they are evidently outrageously simple to implement.

That's a fair amount of functionality already, and all I've done is use a single new value of the pleasantly familiar `display` property. So far, so very, very easy.

Examining Direction, Flow, and Visual Ordering

Before I describe how Flexbox can address the aesthetic concerns of the layout shown in Figure 10-1, I'm going to explain the concept of direction and flow in a flex formatting context.

The reason that the previous example effortlessly displayed the buckets in a row as if they'd been floated involves the `flex-direction` property. It enables you to control the directional flow of your flex items in terms of whether they should display rightward, leftward, downward, or even upward!

The default value for the `flex-direction` property is `row`, which, assuming a Western writing mode, renders the flex items from left to right as you saw in the previous example, therefore imitating the behavior of a floated layout. The other values of `flex-direction` give you an idea of just how easily you can alter the visual flow and order of your content using Flexbox. The following explanations all assume a Western writing mode (left to right, top to bottom):

- `row` is, as previously stated, the initial value and directs the flow from left to right.

- `row-reverse` directs the flow from right to left.

- `column` directs the flow of items vertically from top to bottom.

- `column-reverse` directs the flow of items vertically from bottom to top.

This property is applied to the flex container as shown in the following code snippet, with the result displayed in Figure 10-2:

```
.container {
    width: 960px;
    margin: 0 auto;
    background: #eee;
    display: flex;
    flex-direction: row-reverse;
}
```

The next new tool to be discussed is the `flex-wrap` property, which, predictably, enables you to control how your flex items wrap onto multiple lines. The default behavior is actually that of the `nowrap` value, which prevents the flex items from wrapping onto multiple lines. Instead, the flex items adjust their widths to ensure that they all fit on a single line. Figure 10-3 shows how the row of buckets reacts when a few more are added.

Note that I added a `width` value of `100%` to the images to ensure they become fluid and not fixed, because otherwise the buckets wouldn't be able to shrink smaller than the image widths. I also ensured all buckets have the same amount of content for now for simplicity.

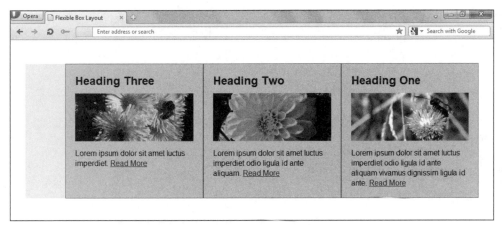

Figure 10-2 The direction of the buckets now flows from right to left.

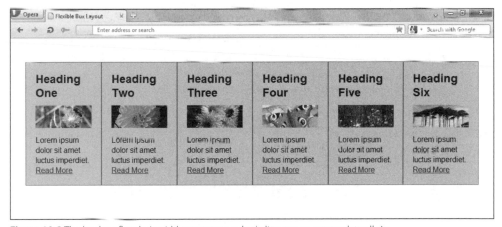

Figure 10-3 The buckets flex their widths to ensure a single line can accommodate all six.

It's important to note that flex items can only shrink to a certain extent, at which point they simply start to overflow the container unless you specify that they are allowed to wrap onto multiple lines. The extent to which they can shrink is based on a brand new `min-width` value that is automatically given to flex items. This new value (`auto`) enables elements to shrink their width to their minimum content size (the length of their longest word or fixed-size element, which is the word *Heading* in this example). Figure 10-4 demonstrates how far the buckets can shrink.

You can use two other `flex-wrap` values in addition to the default `nowrap` value, which are as follows:

- `wrap` simply allows the flex items to flow onto multiple lines within the flex container.

- `wrap-reverse` also allows flex items to flow onto multiple lines, but in the opposite direction; for example, whereas `wrap` pushes flex items onto a new row below, `wrap-reverse` pushes items onto a new row *above.*

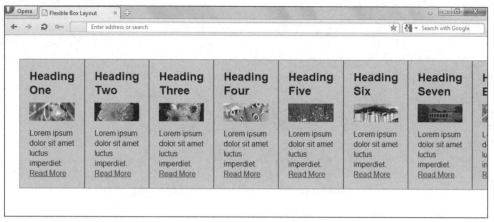

Figure 10-4 This image shows how far the buckets can shrink while making sure they can still accommodate their content; the extra buckets overflow the container.

The `flex-wrap` property is applied to the flex container, as shown in the following code, with Figure 10-5 demonstrating how the flex items wrap when using the `wrap-reverse` value:

```
.container {
    width: 960px;
    margin: 0 auto;
    background: #eee;
    display: flex;
    flex-wrap: wrap-reverse;
}
```

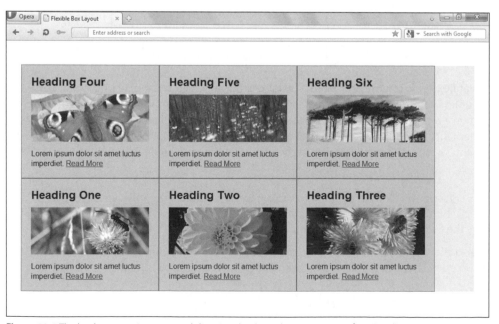

Figure 10-5 The buckets wrap in an upward direction thanks to the wrap-reverse functionality.

Now seems like an appropriate time to touch on the `flex-flow` property, which is actually a shorthand method of specifying the `flex-direction` and `flex-wrap` values (the two properties discussed previously). The syntax is lenient, because the two parameters can be specified in any order and either can be omitted.

If I add a height to the buckets container, you can see how the buckets render with a direction value of `column` and a wrap value of `wrap-reverse`. You can see the result in Figure 10-6.

```css
.container {
    width: 960px;
    margin: 0 auto;
    background: #eee;
    display: flex;
    height: 500px;
    flex-flow: column wrap-reverse;
}
```

Figure 10-6 The buckets render vertically and wrap in the reverse direction from right to left.

As is apparent from the preceding explanations, these tools grant you impressive control over the order and direction of your flex items, but another property affords you an even greater level of control in terms of visual order.

The appropriately named `order` property enables you to explicitly specify in which order your flex items should be rendered. This property works in a similar way to the concept of `z-index` as it accepts integer-based values, but instead of defining a layered stacking context, it determines where your flex items appear in the directional flow of elements.

All flex items have an initial `order` value of 0, and when flex items share the same `order` value, they are simply rendered in source order, which is, of course, the default behavior.

To better understand how this works, consider a linear scale of numbers that define the order of your flex items. By default, all the flex items are positioned at 0 on the scale and so are rendered in source order. You can then move your items up or down the scale to determine their place in the visual order. Take a look at the following code and see how this defines the visual order of your elements in Figure 10-7:

```css
.item1 {
    order: 1;
}

.item2 {
    order: -2;
}

/* No change to .item3 */

.item4 {
    order: 2;
}

.item5 {
    order: -1;
}
```

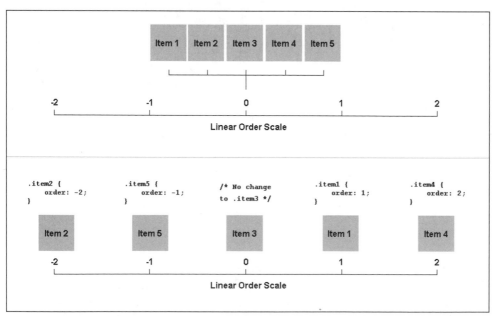

Figure 10-7 The original order (top) has been amended according to the flex item's individual order values, creating a new visual order (bottom).

The beauty of this ordering method is that it operates completely independently from the actual content, ensuring that your markup can still be structured as appropriately as possible so as not to compromise on accessibility. Let's revisit the buckets example to demonstrate this usage.

The markup of each bucket is structured logically, with a heading first, followed by an image and a link. Perhaps your design would deem it more appropriate for the *image* to appear first, followed by the heading and link; generally, you would make the compromise and simply swap these elements around in the markup, but that makes much less sense in terms of content structure. And when you start messing with content structure to satisfy visual desires, your website's accessibility will inevitably take a hit, causing those who use screen readers or other assistive technology to suffer.

With Flexbox, this issue is eradicated because it offers an exceptional level of control over the visual order, without any modification to the source output. Top stuff.

Controlling Alignment

The next big issue to address is that of alignment—such a fundamental aspect of layout, but one that CSS developers have long struggled with. Now, however, Flexbox puts forward several new methods of aligning your elements both horizontally and—at long, long last—vertically!

The first alignment tool to be discussed is the `justify-content` property, which deals with horizontal alignment (unless you're working with a vertical writing mode or if your `flex-direction` value is column). The acceptable values for this property are detailed in the following list, with a visual representation of each illustrated in Figure 10-8.

> Note that my explanations of the `justify-content` values assume a Western writing mode and a default `flex-direction` value of `row`, which ensures the directional flow of the flex items is from left to right and top to bottom. I explain why this matters a little later.

- `flex-start` is the default value and aligns the flex items to the left of the container.
- `flex-end` aligns the items to the right of the container.
- `center` aligns the items in the center of the container.
- `space-between` aligns the first item to the left edge and the last item to the right edge before distributing the remaining space evenly between the other items.
- `space-around` produces the same behavior as the preceding rule but the first and last items aren't pushed right to their respective edges; the space is also distributed *around* them too.

> The reason these values have names such as `flex-start` and `flex-end` rather than `flex-left` and `flex-right` is that the effect relies wholly on how the directional flow of the items has been defined. For example, if a `flex-direction` value of `column-reverse` has been applied, the directional flow of the document would go from bottom to top, so `flex-start` would actually align the content to the bottom of the container.

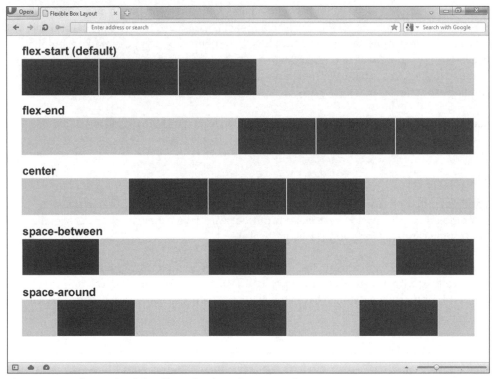

Figure 10-8 Visual examples of the effects of each justify-content value

Next up is the `align-items` property, which allows you to control the alignment of your flex items in relation to each other. As an example, cast your mind back to the first iteration of the buckets example, where simply applying `display: flex;` to the container ensured that all the flex items were of equal heights and lined up with each other perfectly. That behavior was due to the initial value of the `align-items` property (`stretch`), which ensures that all items in a single row adjust their height to line up with the item containing the most content (as you saw in Figure 10-1).

The other values of `align-items` are detailed in the following list, with a visual representation of what each value does illustrated in Figure 10-9. Again, these explanations assume a Western writing mode and a directional flow that goes from left to right, top to bottom:

- `stretch` is the default value, as stated previously, which stretches all flex items until they align with each other.

- `flex-start` produces a more familiar effect, with each item's height determined by the amount of content it contains.

- `flex-end` does the same as the preceding rule, but pushes the items to the bottom of the container.

- `center` distributes any remaining space above and below each item equally, therefore vertically centering each item!

- `baseline` aligns all items by their respective baselines (established by their content), which could be at different positions within each item.

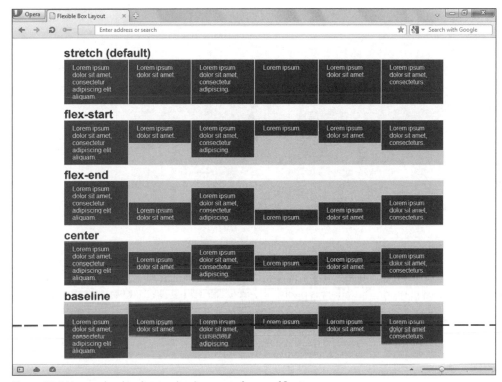

Figure 10-9 How each value dictates the alignment of a row of flex items

Let's just take a minute to soak in the satisfaction of achieving vertical centering so trivially! Feels good, doesn't it? The following code shows how this might be applied, with Figure 10-10 demonstrating its effect on the buckets example.

```
.container {
    width: 960px;
    margin: 0 auto;
    background: #eee;
    display: flex;
    justify-content: space-between;
    align-items: center;
}
```

As you can see, the `align-items` property is applied to the container to generally align the items it contains; however, another property provides an even greater level of control over alignment as it is applied directly to a flex item, allowing you to specify how each individual item should be aligned. This additional tool is the `align-self` property, which works in exactly the same way as `align-items` with precisely the same set of values; the telling difference is that it's applied to individual flex items.

Figure 10-10 The buckets that had available space beneath them are now vertically centered!

For example, consider that your flex items take the default `stretch` behavior of `align-items`, ensuring all items are of equal heights. However, you decide that you want one of the items to sit at the bottom of the container and be only as tall as its content. This effect is pleasantly trivial to achieve in that you simply target the individual item you want to behave differently; Figure 10-11 shows how the following code would render:

```
.bucket:last-child {
    /* other styles */
    align-self: flex-end;
}
```

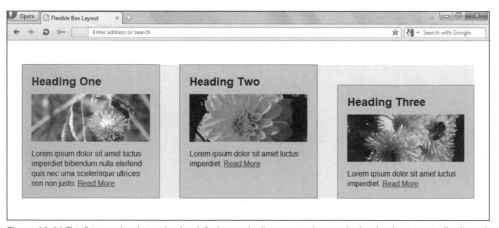

Figure 10-11 The first two buckets take the default stretch alignment, whereas the last bucket is vertically aligned to the bottom of the container.

Are you suitably impressed with Flexbox's comprehensive range of alignment functionality? Well, there's even more to come!

The final alignment property, `align-content`, allows you to control the alignment of multiline flex containers—that is, flex items that have been allowed to wrap onto multiple rows. It works in much the same way as `justify-content`, only on the opposing axis.

Its initial value is `stretch`, which ensures that the items on each row adjust their height to fill the container's vertical space (again, assuming a Western writing mode and a default `flex-direction` value of `row`). The following details all the acceptable values of `align-content`, with Figure 10-12 demonstrating how each of these values affects a multiple-row Flexbox layout:

- `stretch` is the initial value, which flexes the height of the items to fill the height of the container.

- `flex-start` aligns the multiple rows to the top of the container, rendering all the available space beneath these rows.

- `flex-end` aligns the multiple rows to the bottom of the container, rendering all the available space above these rows.

- `center` distributes the available space evenly above and beneath the multiple rows, therefore vertically centering them.

- `space-between` aligns the first row to the top edge of the container and the last row to the bottom of the container, before distributing any available space evenly between the other rows.

- `space-around` behaves the same as the preceding rule, although some of the available space is distributed before the first row and after the last row, ensuring they aren't aligned with the top and bottom edges of the container.

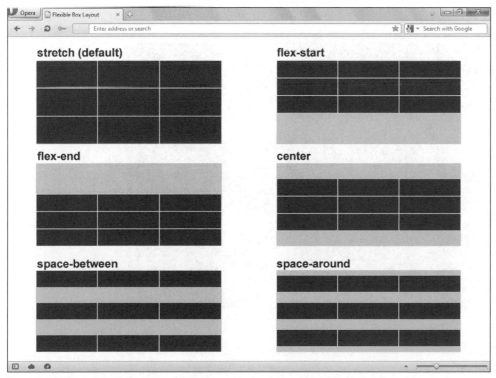

Figure 10-12 How each align-content value affects a Flexbox layout with multiple rows

To demonstrate a practical usage of this tool, you could use it together with the `justify-content` property to create a basic, evenly spaced grid of boxes (assuming a flex container with a specified width and height):

```
.container {
    width: 960px;
    height: 600px;
    display: flex;
    flex-wrap: wrap;
    justify-content: space-around;
    align-content: space-around;
}

.container .item {
    width: 240px;
    height: 120px;
}
```

With this minimal amount of code, you can create a result that looks like Figure 10-13. The `space-around` values of `justify-content` and `align-content` ensure that the leftover space is distributed evenly around each element, both horizontally and vertically.

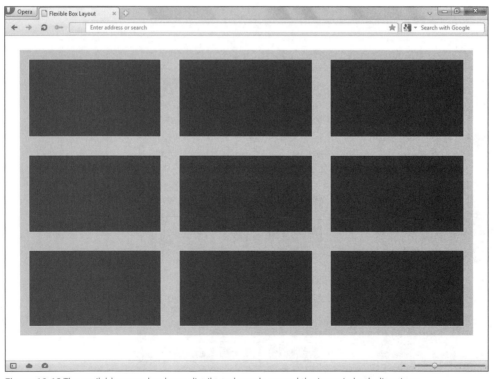

Figure 10-13 The available space has been distributed evenly around the items in both directions.

Defining Flex Factors

As I mentioned near the start of this chapter, the fundamental functionality of the Flexbox layout mode is a flex item's capability to "flex" its width or height based on the available space. Well, you'll be pleased to know that, true to form, the Flexbox module offers a great level of control over how your items should flex their sizes.

I'm hoping you've been pleasantly surprised as to how simple the various Flexbox properties and their respective functionalities have been so far, but at this point things start to get a little more complex.

The first issue to come to terms with is that when an item flexes its width or height, it does so based on the available space in the flex container. And how this available space is distributed between each item is determined by three factors: the *initial base width*, the *grow factor*, and the *shrink factor*. Each of these factors has a dedicated property:

- The `flex-basis` property takes a width value and sets the initial size of the flex item before free space is distributed based on the grow and/or shrink factors.

- The `flex-grow` property accepts a positive integer value, which controls what proportion of the available space is given to the targeted flex item, therefore determining how much this item will grow relative to the other items in the flex container.

- The `flex-shrink` property also takes a positive integer value, which determines how much a flex item will *shrink* relative to the other items in the flex container when negative space is distributed.

To understand how the `flex-basis` value affects the grow and shrink factors, look at Figure 10-14 from the specification. When you are working with a `flex-basis` value of 0, all the space in the container is distributed proportionately among the flex items; whereas when you are working with a `flex-basis` value of `auto`, all the space in the container *minus* the space taken up by the content is distributed proportionately among the flex items.

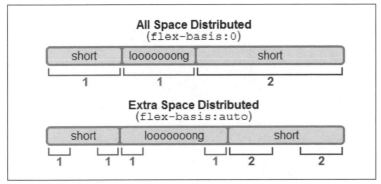

Image courtesy of the W3C.
Figure 10-14 In the top example, all the space in the container is distributed between the flex items based on their flex-grow factors of 1, 1, and 2, respectively. In the bottom example, only the leftover space is distributed between the flex items based on their flex-grow factors.

Although you can control each flexibility factor with the preceding properties, the specification suggests that you generally use the `flex` shorthand property instead, because when values are omitted from the shorthand, they are reset from their original initial values to accommodate the most common use cases. Table 10-1 describes these common use cases as outlined in the specification.

Table 10-1: Common Use Cases for the `flex` Property and How They Are Dealt With

Common Values	Longhand Equivalent `flex: <grow> <shrink> <basis>;`	Behavior
`flex: initial;`	`flex: 0 1 auto;`	Item is sized by `width`/`height` properties. It is not able to grow into available space, but it is allowed to shrink when there is insufficient space.
`flex: auto;`	`flex: 1 1 auto;`	Item is sized by `width`/`height` properties, but they are fully flexible and so can grow into available space or shrink when there is insufficient space.
`flex: none;`	`flex: 0 0 auto;`	Item is sized by `width`/`height` properties and is totally inflexible, meaning they cannot grow or shrink.
`flex: <pos-num>;`	`flex: <pos-num> 1 0px;`	The `flex-basis` is set to 0 so all available space can be proportionately distributed to items based on their specified grow values.

With this in mind, you can actually specify the `flex-grow` property using the `flex` shorthand property with a single positive integer value, which is likely to be the most common way in which you use the `flex` property. Consider the following code example:

```
.container {
    display: flex;
}

.container .item1
.container .item2 {
    flex: 1;
}

.container .item3 {
    flex: 3;
}

.container .item4 {
    flex: 2;
}

.container .item5 {
    flex: 3;
}
```

So what's going on here? First, the `flex` shorthand property uses a single integer value, which therefore resets the `flex-basis` value to `0`, meaning all the container's space is distributed between each of the five flex items based on their grow factors, which are 1, 3, 1, 2, and 3, respectively. To see the physical effects of these grow factors, look at Figure 10-15.

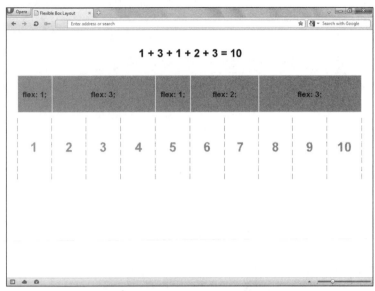

Figure 10-15 The container's space has been distributed among the flex items proportionately based on their grow factors.

As Figure 10-15 suggests, the best way to understand how the space is distributed is to divide the container's space into sections based on their flex grow factors. For example, the grow factors in this case are 1, 3, 1, 2, and 3, which add up to a nice, round total of 10. The following list details how the space is divided from here:

- The `flex` values add up to 10, so the available space is divided into 10 sections.

- Items with a `flex` value of 1 get one-tenth of the available space (equivalent to 10 percent in this instance).

- Items with a `flex` value of 2 get two-tenths of the available space (equivalent to 20 percent in this instance).

- Items with a `flex` value of 3 get three-tenths of the available space (equivalent to 30 percent in this instance).

So, specifying flexible and proportional widths (which is likely to be the most frequent way you use the `flex` property) is a basic task when broken down. It's only when you tap into the additional functionalities of the `flex` property in terms of the flex basis and shrink factor that your efforts could require a little more thought.

Creating a Flexible Box Layout

It's all well and good learning about Flexbox on a property-by-property basis, but a module this new and substantial is unlikely to stick in the memory if you don't apply what you've learned and see how these rules could function in a real-life project. Well, you're in luck, because that's exactly what I'm going to tackle next!

I hope that by the end of this section you will be able to recognize just how useful Flexbox can be, as well as how pleasantly easy it is to apply to your layout.

To begin, look at Figure 10-16, which shows the basic layout for the example in the next few pages. You can find the working demo (`1001-flexible-box-layout.html`) on the companion website at `www.wiley.com/go/ptl/css3`. Be aware that you must view it in Firefox 22+ because that is currently the only browser to offer complete, unprefixed support for the entire module.

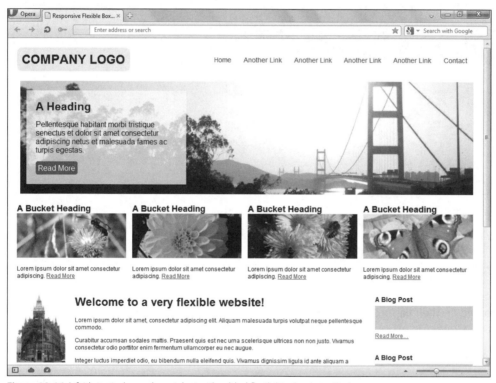

Figure 10-16 A fairly typical page layout, but with added flexibility thanks to Flexbox

Let's start with the markup, which I heavily edited down for simplicity:

```
<div class="container">
    <header>
        <nav>
            <ul><!-- Links --></ul>
        </nav>
    </header>

    <section class="runner">
    </section>
```

```
<section class="buckets">
    <!-- Buckets -->
</section>

<section class="main">
    <article class="content">
        <!-- Main body content -->
    </article>

    <aside class="sidebar-left">
    </aside>

    <aside class="sidebar-right">
    </aside>
</section>

<footer>
</footer>
</div>
```

A fairly familiar structure there, so let's get styling. The first step is to establish a flex formatting context and define the directional flow of the document:

```
.container {
    width: 960px;
    margin: 0 auto;
    display: flex;
    flex-direction: column;
}
```

The new `display` value of `flex` ensures that all the container's direct children will now play by Flexbox rules! Additionally, the `flex-direction` property states that the flex items will be stacked vertically in a column.

Now, because all the container's direct children are content containers in their own right, I simply went ahead and applied the `display: flex;` rule to all these direct children, ensuring that *their* contents then become flex items as well:

```
.container > * {
    display: flex;
}
```

You may find this difficult to believe, but that's *most* of the structuring work done—just like that! No floating or specifying widths for each element; the initial values of the various flex properties take care of that. Figure 10-17 shows how the layout looks currently, with barely a style applied! Bear in mind that I added some `height` values and a `background-color` to the `header`, `.runner`, and `footer` elements, simply to make them visible.

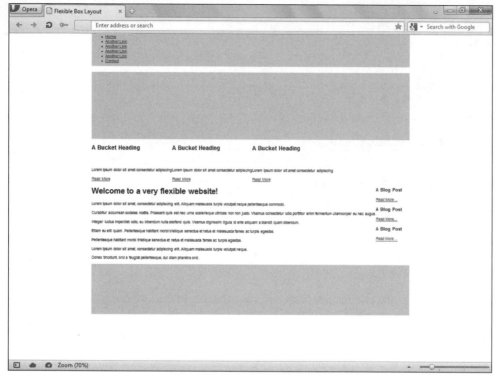

Figure 10-17 The layout after only a few lines of CSS

Moving on, the navigation links could obviously use some attention. The first step is to establish a flex formatting context for the navigation list items by applying the `display: flex;` rule to their parent `ul` container. Again, this does most of the work for you, but after applying some padding to the `li` elements, some of the links are forced onto two lines, presenting the age-old issue of vertical alignment on single- and multiple-line navigation items. As demonstrated by the following code and Figure 10-18, this is an absolute cinch to fix when working with Flexbox!

```
nav ul {
    display: flex;
    align-items: center;
}
```

Next up, the buckets just need a little tweak because they're currently all bunched to the left of their container, leaving excess space at the end of the row. The fix couldn't be simpler because you can simply use the `justify-content` property to distribute this excess space evenly between the three buckets:

```
.buckets {
    justify-content: space-between;
}
```

Finally, the main content block is obviously a bit of a mess at the moment, but again, not much is required to fix things up!

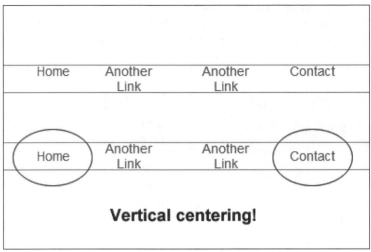

Figure 10-18 The vertical alignment issue (top) is easily amended using the align-items property (bottom).

It's usually desirable for the actual main content of the page to come first within the content container, which is why the markup is structured in this format, with the two sidebars following. Previously, you might have used some absolute positioning to hack the columns into the correct order, but as I described earlier, you now have a legitimate tool for amending the visual order of your content. It's wonderfully easy to apply in this case, too.

```
.sidebar-left {
    order: -1;
}
```

You may have been expecting to specify an `order` value of 1, 2, and 3, respectively, on each of the columns, but remember; negative integers are valid too! This places the left sidebar at –1 on a linear ordering scale, with the other two columns both at a position of 0 in this scale, causing them to rely on the source order.

The last issue to address is the width of these main content columns, which aren't ideal currently. To ensure these widths are suitable, you can use the `flex` property, which distributes the total space in the main content container to each column proportionately, based on the `flex` value that you specify for each:

```
.sidebar-left {
    order: -1;
    flex: 1;
}

.content {
    flex: 6;
}

.sidebar-right {
    flex: 2;
}
```

All the `flex` values add up to nine, so to understand how the width of each column is calculated, simply split the container's width into nine sections. The `.sidebar-left` element gets one of these nine sections, the `.content` element gets six of these sections, and the `.sidebar-right` element gets two of these sections. You can see the result of these amendments in Figure 10-19.

Figure 10-19 The main content columns have been assigned varying portions of the container's available space.

And that's it! How unbelievably easy was that? I hope you share my excitement about the Flexible Box Layout module now that you've seen the ease in which it tackles some of the oldest and most famous CSS layout pitfalls.

Examining Browser Support for Flexbox

The Flexbox spec has already undergone a couple of major overhauls in terms of property names, syntax, and even some functionality, which has caused wariness toward the module from both front-end developers and browser vendors. However, developers still appear eager to experiment with it, and the browsers are beginning to seem equally eager to provide support for it, with a couple even opting to remove their vendor prefixes!

Most browsers picked up support for Flexbox back when it used an older syntax, so they're still very much in a period of transition in terms of offering support for the updated module.

At the time of writing, Firefox is the only browser to provide complete unprefixed support for the entirety of the updated Flexbox module, although Opera also offered this level of support before its switch to WebKit. Chrome and Opera 15 currently support the new syntax but with the `-webkit-` prefix, while IE10 and Safari unfortunately still use the old syntax (both with prefixes). Table 10-2 shows the full picture.

Table 10-2: CSS Flexible Box Layout Browser Compatibility

Browser	Old Syntax	New Syntax
Chrome	4+ (prefixed)	21+ (prefixed)
Firefox	2+ (prefixed)	22+
Opera	No Support	15+ (`-webkit-` prefix)
Safari	3.1+ (prefixed)	No Support
IE	10 (prefixed)	No Support

Summary

Flexbox is new, it's exciting, and it's innovative, but more than anything else, it's just what CSS needs right now to tackle the responsive movement head on and to finally qualify as a comprehensive tool for laying out web pages.

As I touched on in the preceding section, Flexbox started to gain support from browsers and also hit the blog and tutorial circuit while it was still using the old syntax, so when it was subject to such a major overhaul, a lot of front-end developers dismissed it as unstable until further notice. That thinking is understandable, but the situation is a lot more stable now, as emphasized by a couple of the browser vendors opting to remove their prefixes for these properties, a move that I hope will give you the confidence to go ahead and start experimenting with Flexbox.

The web is obviously a long way away from making Flexbox the de facto tool for layout, but I for one hope that after the other browsers start to offer support and drop their prefixes, the industry gets past the initial fear and wariness of this module and pushes it straight into the mainstream. It will take a bit of getting used to for sure, but after a few projects, the ease and speed at which you throw your layouts together will make floats and clearfixes a distant memory!

Further Reading

CSS Flexible Box Layout Specification
`http://www.w3.org/TR/css3-flexbox/`

Old Flexbox and New Flexbox: How to Tell
`http://css-tricks.com/old-flexbox-and-new-flexbox`

Using CSS Flexible Boxes
`https://developer.mozilla.org/en-US/docs/CSS/Tutorials/Using_CSS_flexible_boxes`

Chapter 11

Grid Layout, Regions, and Exclusions

The layout modules discussed in the two preceding chapters, Multi-column Layout and Flexbox, are both reasonably well-rounded and are right on the edge of breaking into the mainstream. In contrast, the remaining CSS3 layout modules to be addressed are much newer and more cutting edge, with significant changes to their respective specifications a very strong possibility before they get anywhere near mainstream usage—if they make it that far, of course.

Some flaws and issues need to be worked out (particularly in the case of Regions and Exclusions) before many developers will accept them as legitimate layout mechanisms, but the tools they propose and the results that can be achieved with them are nothing short of mind-blowing when you consider that issues such as vertical alignment have only recently been addressed!

This chapter tackles the concepts behind three very exciting layout modules and touches on the technical side of each in terms of the tools on offer and their respective syntaxes; however, I avoid deep analysis of each and every property because they are likely to be subject to subtle or even major changes before these modules become usable, so the focus in this chapter remains conceptual.

CSS Grid Layout allows you to define rows and columns directly in your stylesheet to form a grid within which you can arbitrarily place your content, regardless of its position in the source. CSS Regions propose a solution for laying out your content in whatever way you wish, allowing you to specify several elements (or regions) within your page for your content to flow between. The last of these modules, CSS Exclusions and Shapes, provides you with full control over how your content wraps and the shape it should mold to, allowing the creation of visually rich, magazine-like layouts.

The first of these modules to be discussed is the CSS Grid Layout module.

Introducing CSS Grid Layout

While Regions and Exclusions are likely to generate the most excitement and anticipation, the Grid Layout module certainly qualifies as an unsung hero, offering a powerful yet extremely flexible and accommodating solution for laying out adaptable web pages.

Grids were actually a mainstay of web page layout many years ago, but those grids were rigid, uncompromising, and aggravatingly inflexible. Worst of all, they had to be defined in the markup, and I'm sure you've been well versed in the evils of presentational markup. The old school among you have probably divined that I'm talking about HTML tables! That's right; tables were effectively used as grids within which you would place the various elements of your design, which is precisely the concept of CSS Grid Layout.

Evidently, the two methods are a product of the same school of thought, but this is where the similarities end, because CSS Grid Layout brings with it an overwhelming amount of additional (and necessary) functionality.

What Is Grid Layout?

CSS Grid Layout enables you to define a grid using rows and columns, within which you can position the elements of your layout, all completely independent of the content!

> Before I continue, I need to clarify the browser support situation early on. This module was proposed by Microsoft, and it is Microsoft's Internet Explorer 10 browser that currently offers the only sliver of support. However, IE10's implementation is now slightly outdated because the specification has since been updated, although the changes are mostly property name tweaks and other such subtleties. As a result, the current version of the spec doesn't have any major browser support at the time of writing, so I put the emphasis on images rather than live demonstrations in this section to avoid confusion.
>
> It's also important to note that this module is very much in development as I write this and further changes are likely, so you should take the syntax with a sizable pinch of salt and focus more on the concept.

To create a CSS grid layout, you must first create a *grid element*, the contents of which then become *grid items*. This is similar to the Flexbox model, but instead of a flex container and a flex item, you have a grid element and a grid item.

You can then arbitrarily place these grid items into any slot on your grid, regardless of the element's position in the source, which opens the door to a functionality that has long been outside the scope of CSS—complete freedom over the visual order of elements, entirely independent of the source order. Sure, Flexbox touched on this capability with the `order` property, but that is limited to ordering the elements within the various flex containers in your layout. The placement of elements into a grid, however, allows you to position an element that is first to appear in your markup into a grid slot that sits at the bottom right of your page, for example. Ideal for layouts that need to adapt!

Creating a Grid Element

Creating a grid element couldn't be more straightforward because this process simply makes use of yet another new value of the `display` property. This value of `grid` is applied to an element and transforms it into a block-level grid element. You can also use a value of `inline-grid` to create an inline-level grid element:

```
/* Block level grid element */
.container {
    display: grid;
}

/* Inline level grid element */
.container {
    display: inline-grid;
}
```

Defining the Grid

Now that you have a functional grid element, you are free to start defining the columns and rows that you want to make up your grid. For this, you can use the `grid-definition-columns` and the `grid-definition-rows` properties.

> In the previous version of the spec (and therefore in IE10's implementation), these properties were called `grid-columns` and `grid-rows`.

In their simplest form, these properties can take a series of space-separated length values, determining the width of each column (or height of each row), as demonstrated in the following code snippet:

```
.container {
    display: grid;
    grid-definition-columns: 20px 600px 20px 300px 20px;
    grid-definition-rows: 100px 1fr;
}
```

This example outputs the grid that you see in Figure 11-1, which shows five columns and two rows.

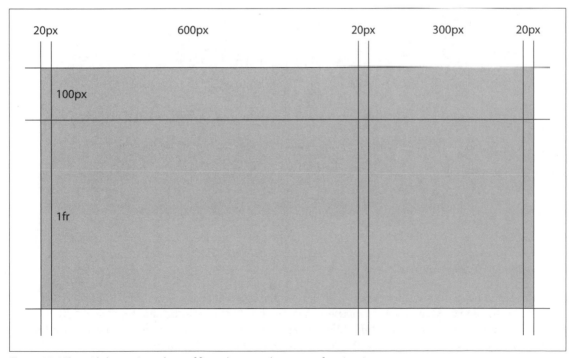

Figure 11-1 The grid element is made up of five columns and two rows of varying sizes.

The grid has two main columns: a 600px-wide main content area and a 300px-wide sidebar, surrounded by 20px gutters. In terms of rows, the first is exactly 100px tall, and you're probably wondering what the second row parameter, 1fr, is all about. It means 1 *fraction unit*, which ensures that this row occupies the remainder of the free space.

To really understand the fr unit, think of the flex property and how it was used in the preceding chapter to proportionately distribute available space. For example, if you were to add a third row to the equation, with a value of 2fr, this third row would get two-thirds of the remaining space, while the original second row would get only one-third of the available space. Figure 11-2 clarifies this arrangement visually.

```
.container {
    display: grid;
    grid-definition-columns: 20px 600px 20px 300px 20px;
    grid-definition-rows: 100px 1fr 2fr;
}
```

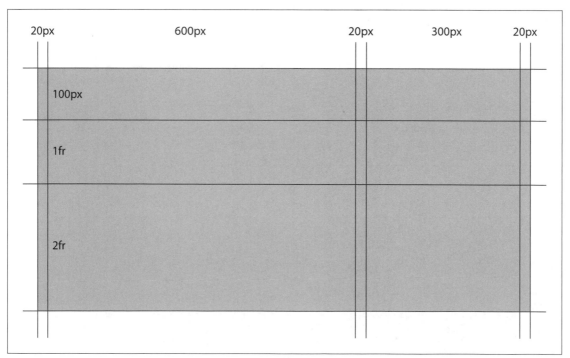

Figure 11-2 The additional third row takes up twice as much of the available space as the second row.

Another healthy modification that can be made involves the first row, which is currently 100px tall. It's very rarely a good idea to have fixed height elements because they should generally be allowed to adjust their height according to the amount of content they contain. You can easily remedy this situation by replacing the 100px value with auto, which ensures that the first row takes the height of its content:

```
.container {
    display: grid;
    grid-definition-columns: 20px 600px 20px 300px 20px;
```

```
    grid-definition-rows: auto 1fr 2fr;
}
```

Positioning Elements into the Grid

Next, you need to position your content into the grid areas formed by the columns and rows. Again, this is simply done thanks to the `grid-column` and `grid-row` properties. Consider the following example:

```
header {
    grid-column: 1;
    grid-row: 1;
}
```

The preceding code would place your header element in the first column and the first row; however, you need to understand that the numbers actually refer to *grid lines* rather than the actual column or row area. For example, a `grid-column: 2/5;` rule would position an item between grid lines 2 and 5, which means the item would span across three columns. Figure 11-3 illustrates further.

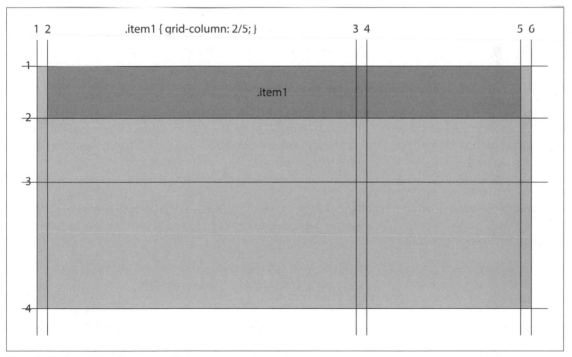

Figure 11-3 The grid item is positioned between grid line 2 and grid line 5

If you want to be more explicit you can use a longhand method. The `grid-row` and `grid-column` properties are actually shorthand solutions for specifying the `grid-row-start` and `grid-row-end` values and the `grid-column-start` and `grid-column-end` values. The following example explains this further.

```
.content {
    grid-column: 2/5;
```

```
    grid-row: 1/auto;
}

/* Longhand method... */

.content {
    grid-column-start: 2;
    grid-column-end: 5;
    grid-row-start: 1;
    grid-row-end: auto;
}
```

> Bear in mind that I have only included the `auto` value for clarity and it can be omitted as it is the initial value. It simply ensures that the element doesn't span across more than a single cell.

So far, so simple. The syntax for the grid definition properties can get a lot more complex, though, with the introduction of named grid lines, size ranges, and repeating column systems. As I said earlier, I don't want to get too deep into the syntax, but I feel it's important to have a basic understanding of these aspects at this point to ensure you're being as efficient as possible in your experimentations and getting the most out of this module's functionality. In that spirit, the following section introduces you to those concepts.

Making Your Grid Flexible and Adaptable

Defining your grid using fixed-length values is nice and easy to understand, but it doesn't allow for much flexibility or make adaptive behavior much easier, which defies the purpose of this module. Fortunately, the grid definition properties accept a range of possible value types that ensure your grid is highly flexible and optimized for adaptive behavior when it comes to displaying on small or wide-screen devices.

One of these additional functionalities is the capability to assign names to your grid lines that you can then use to position grid items instead of using integer values. These names are specified in between your column width values, as logic would suggest. Take a look at the following code and Figure 11-4 to see exactly how these names are applied to each grid line:

```
.container {
    grid-definition-columns: "sidebar" 150px "main" 450px "last"
}
```

You can then refer to these grid names when positioning your grid items, as shown in the following snippet:

```
.sidebar {
    grid-column: "sidebar";
}
```

Note that you should always specify the grid line names in quotation marks. The naming of your lines makes the grid easier to manage and will prove invaluable when you make the layout adaptable, because your `.sidebar` element will always want to be associated with the grid line titled `"sidebar"`, whereas you would have to change a simple number value each time the layout is shuffled.

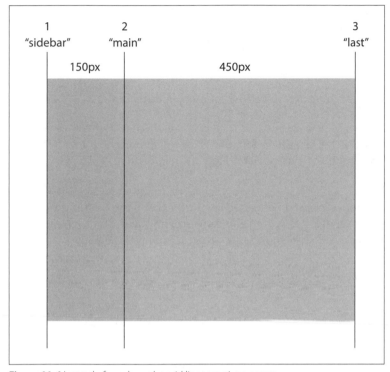

Figure 11-4 Instead of numbers, the grid lines are given names.

I already touched on the flexible nature of the `fr` unit and the `auto` keyword, but two additional keywords provide yet more options for controlling your column widths and row heights. The `min-content` keyword ensures your column shrinks as far as it can while respecting the *min-content* widths of the grid items that it contains. For example, if the greatest min-content width of all the grid items in a column is `100px`, the column shrinks to this width.

> The *min-content* width of a grid item refers to the longest word or fixed-width element that it contains.

The other keyword I alluded to is the `max-content` value. As you would imagine, this keyword ensures that your column expands to the widest *max-content* width of the grid items that it contains.

> The *max-content* width of a grid item refers to the greatest possible width that an element is allowed to expand to. This maximum width is achieved when inline content is allowed to wrap only when forced; that is, no soft wrap opportunities are taken.

Another value type accepted by the grid definition properties is the `minmax()` function, which allows you to specify a size *range* rather than an explicit value. For example, you may want to allow a column to fill the remainder of the available space, but not to ensure its min-content width is respected. Thanks to the `minmax()` function, doing so is trivial, as the following code demonstrates:

```
/* Syntax - minmax(min-value, max-value) */

.container {
    grid-definition-columns: auto 20px minmax(min-content, 1fr);
}
```

This code outputs a grid with three columns. The first takes the width of its content, the second is exactly 20px wide, and the third should take up the remaining space while ensuring that the min-content widths of its grids items are respected.

The final functionality of the grid definition properties to be addressed involves repeating column/row systems. The `repeat()` notation does the job here and enables you to avoid the unnecessary bytes that a repetitive column or row system would otherwise require. The following code shows how to apply this function:

```
.container {
    grid-definition-columns: 1fr repeat(3, 150px 10px);
}

/* This is the same as... */

.container {
    grid-definition-columns: 1fr 150px 10px 150px 10px 150px 10px;
}
```

As should be apparent from the preceding code, this `repeat()` function takes a basic column system of 150px 10px and repeats it three times.

So, all these value types allow for an abundance of fluidity and flexibility throughout your grid, which is exactly what was necessary for this module to work on a platform that is constantly having to reform and adapt.

Before signing off on CSS Grid Layout, I want to briefly touch on the `grid-area` shorthand property that provides a very useful method of compacting all your positioning values to sit within a single rule.

The `grid-area` property is a shorthand method of specifying both the column and row positions of a grid item. It accepts four parameters, which represent the `grid-row-start`, `grid-column-start`, `grid-row-end` and `grid-column-end` properties respectively. The following example should help to clarify this.

```
.content {
    grid-area: 1/1/3/3;
}

/* Equivalent to... */
```

```
.content {
    grid-row-start: 1;
    grid-column-start: 1;
    grid-row-end: 3;
    grid-column-end: 3;
}
```

This code places the grid item in the first column and the first row and ensures it spans across two columns and two rows.

To conclude on grid layout, I've barely touched the surface in terms of what this module is capable of, but I hope this description has given you an idea of the immense potential that it is waiting to fulfill. It's an extremely powerful mechanism and possesses the tools that appear to provide the perfect solution for the most complex of layouts—not to mention its immense flexibility, enabling layouts to adapt as they should do, completely independent of source order.

Now to get even more cutting edge as the discussion moves on to CSS Regions!

Introducing CSS Regions

Initially developed by Adobe, the CSS Regions module is highly ambitious, proposing solutions for extremely demanding and impressive layouts that are reminiscent of design-focused and aesthetically rich magazine spreads where text has the freedom to flow and roam as it wishes.

To reiterate my earlier caution, this module is still very much in the early stages of development and has several issues that need to be addressed, so in terms of technical functionalities, I provide only a basic outline and not an in-depth examination of the various syntaxes in this chapter.

What Are CSS Regions?

I've given you several teasers relating to this module so far, but now it's time to explain in depth the real concept and purpose of the CSS Regions module.

Regions allow you to control the flow of your content like never before, enabling it to travel seamlessly between several elements (or regions) anywhere on your page. The concept simply involves the formation of a *region chain*, through which your content will flow from the first to the last, or until the content has reached an end. For example, your content would begin by filling the first specified region until it's full, before moving on to fill the second region and then the third and so on, all regardless of where these regions appear on your page. Figure 11-5 illustrates this concept.

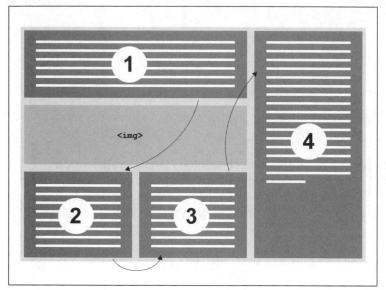

Figure 11-5 The content flows through the region chain in the order specified, starting with region one and finishing in region four.

Pretty cool, eh? This module is also designed to work in conjunction with any of the other layout mechanisms such as Flexbox or Grid Layout because it does not define a new layout mode in itself.

How Do Regions Work?

First, you need some content; an `article` element filled with paragraphs, images, and other content should suffice. This is the content that you want to flow between the various regions around your layout.

You need to specify in your stylesheet that this content is to flow through your region chain (that will be created soon after). The following code introduces the `flow-into` property, which requires you to name this content flow:

```
/* flow-into: your_flow_name; */

article {
    flow-into: my-first-flow;
}
```

With that, the `article` element is placed into what is referred to as a *named flow*. You can use your specified name to add other elements to your named flow. For example, if you have another `article` element that you also want to be part of the same group of content that flows through the same region chain, you can simply repeat the rule in the preceding snippet for this additional element (ensuring the same name is used):

```
article.one, article.two {
    flow-into: my-first-flow;
}
```

These two `article` elements are now part of the same named flow and will flow through the region chain that they are associated with. The next stage is to create the actual regions and make this association with the named flow.

Unfortunately, this creation process isn't as elegant as you may have envisioned because it simply involves revisiting the markup and adding empty `div` elements to act as the regions. I say "unfortunately" because it is rarely justifiable to add empty elements to your markup, especially when their sole purpose is to assist the visual appearance of the content.

In their defense, these `div` elements certainly serve a legitimate purpose and are vital to the layout functioning, rather than simply serving as targets for decorative styling. However, I'd still like to see whether a CSS-only alternative is feasible because the current method is likely to sit uncomfortably with many developers.

Anyway, for now you're stuck with empty `div` elements, so let's get them into the markup:

```
<div class="region1 region"></div>
<div class="region2 region"></div>
<div class="region3 region"></div>
<div class="region4 region"></div>
```

> Any block-level element can become a region, but a `div` is as good as any.

You can style these `div` elements as normal to prepare them for the content that will inhabit them. So, the next logical step is to transform them into a region chain, which is done by simply associating them with a named flow. This sees the introduction of the `flow-from` property, which must match your previously specified `flow-into` value to link the named flow with the regions:

```
.region {
    flow-from: my-first-flow;
}
```

This code snippet ensures that the named flow will now populate the region chain one by one, in the order that they were specified in the source.

And there you have it! It's a fairly basic process, but the additional functionality that it offers in terms of content layout is highly impressive, exciting, and somewhat inspiring.

The ease and simplicity of using regions comes with an obvious compromise in the form of empty HTML elements that are required to act as the region blocks. As I said previously, this module is still finding its feet and is likely to undergo significant changes before it becomes a usable technique.

You can experiment with regions now using WebKit Nightly and the `-webkit-` prefix for the `flow-into` and `flow-from` properties. I certainly advise you to play around to whet your appetite, which I hope encourages you to keep an eye on how the spec progresses and whether the major browsers start to pick up support.

Introducing CSS Exclusions

The final new layout module to be discussed, also proposed by Adobe, is the Exclusions module, which is the most ambitious, the most innovative, and definitely the "cool kid" among the CSS3 layout gang!

What Are CSS Exclusions?

The Exclusions module used to be called *Positioned Floats*, which gives you some idea as to the type of functionality it allows. The core concept involves creating *exclusion areas*, around which your text/inline content can flow, much the same as a floated image. However, an exclusion box is not limited to being floated left or right for its surrounding text to flow around it; it can be positioned anywhere within the container and still enable the surrounding text to wrap around its shape. Figure 11-6 should clarify this theory.

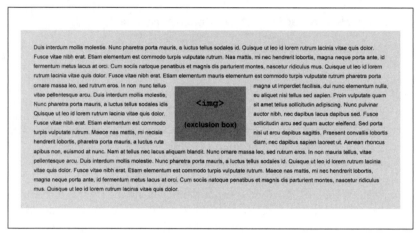

Figure 11-6 The text wraps around the exclusion box, which has been arbitrarily positioned in the middle of the content.

This relatively basic concept feels long overdue; however, the wow factor is introduced when the module's full title is revealed, which is CSS Exclusions and *Shapes*. The shapes aspect of this module allows you to specify shapes and custom polygons for the exclusion boxes, providing you with an immense amount of control over how your content should flow. More on this later.

How Do Exclusions Work?

First, you need some content and an exclusion box, which both require some markup:

```
<div class="container">

    <article>
        <p>Lorem ipsum dolor sit amet...</p>
        <p>Consectetur adipiscing elit...</p>
        <!-- etc. -->
    </article>

    <blockquote class="exclusion">
        "Whoa, I'm surrounded by inline content!"
    </blockquote>

</div>
```

As implied by the associated `class` attribute, the `blockquote` element is to be used as the exclusion area in this example. As with regions, an exclusion has to be a block-level element.

Also as with regions, exclusions do not define a new layout mode, so you can use them in conjunction with other layout modes and integrate them into these modes. In the following example, you use CSS Grid Layout to create the basic structure and to position the exclusion box, because it should be fresh in your memory from earlier in the chapter.

You could simply position the `blockquote` in the middle of the article by using good old absolute positioning, but that's obviously a very explicit method and there are now much more flexible means of positioning elements, so why not take advantage?!

First, you need to define the grid and position the grid items:

```
.container {
    display: grid;
    grid-definition-columns: repeat(3, minmax(min-content, 1fr));
    grid-definition-rows: repeat(3, minmax(min-content, 1fr));
}

article {
    grid-area: 1/1/4/4;
}

.exclusion {
    grid-area: 2/2;
}
```

Unless you have a memory like a sponge, the values of the `grid-area` **shorthand property in the preceding code block are probably proving to be a bit of a head scratcher. Here's how they translate when written in full:**

```
grid-area: 1/1/4/4;
/* Equivalent to... */
grid-row-start: 1;
grid-column-start: 1;
grid-row-end: 4;
grid-column-end: 4;


grid-area: 2/2;
/* Equivalent to... */
grid-row-start: 2;
grid-column-start: 2;
grid-row-end: auto;
grid-column-end: auto;
```

As you can see, it's well worth learning the shorthand `grid-area` **property because it can save several lines of unnecessary code.**

So, now you have a grid with three columns and three rows, with the actual article content taking up all the available space and the `blockquote` exclusion area positioned to sit in the second column and second row. Figure 11-7 illustrates the current layout situation.

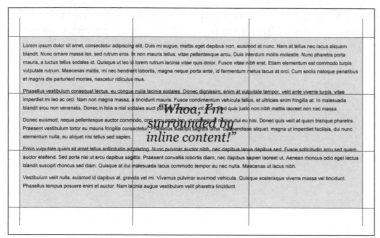

Figure 11-7 The content spans across all three columns and all three rows, and the blockquote element is currently dumped on top.

As you can see from Figure 11-7, the `blockquote` element is simply placed on top of the text and has no effect on its surroundings whatsoever. Obviously, the surrounding text should wrap around the `blockquote` element, so you need to transform it into an exclusion box, which sees the introduction of the `wrap-flow` property:

```
.exclusion {
    /* Other styles */
    wrap-flow: both;
}
```

The `wrap-flow` property causes the element to become an exclusion box, and a value of `both` ensures that the text wraps around all sides of this exclusion area, as Figure 11-8 demonstrates.

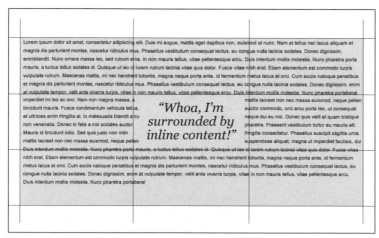

Figure 11-8 The wrap-flow: both; rule transforms the blockquote into an exclusion box and forces the text to wrap around it.

The other values of the `wrap-flow` property and their effects are detailed in the following list, with the explanations assuming a left-to-right writing mode. Figure 11-9 shows the effect of each value.

- `auto` is the initial value and applies no change to the exclusion box, ensuring the surrounding content flows as normal.

- `both` ensures that content wraps around all sides of the exclusion box.

- `start` wraps content around the left side of the element but leaves the area to the right empty.

- `end` wraps content around the right side of the element but leaves the area to the left empty.

- `maximum` ensures that content wraps around the element at the side with the largest available space, leaving the area on the other side empty.

- `clear` ensures that both the areas to the left and right of the element are empty.

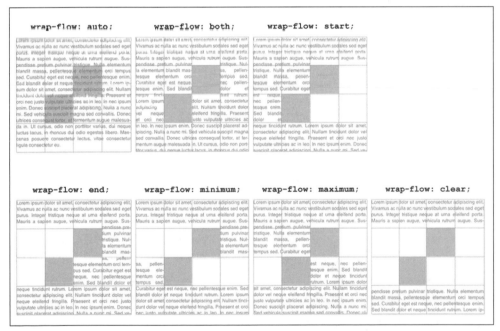

Sample images courtesy of the W3C.
Figure 11-9 The effects of each wrap-flow value on the way the content wraps around the exclusion box

Playing with Shapes

Excitingly, this module also sees the introduction of shapes to CSS. With the new properties proposed, you will be able to specify custom shapes not only for exclusion areas, but also for any block-level containers. This means you can shape your content areas in any way you want!

The shaping of exclusion boxes and floated elements is handled differently from other standard block-level elements. For example, exclusion boxes and floats make use of the `shape-outside` property, whereas other block-level elements are shaped using the `shape-inside` property.

> Bear in mind that because experimenting with shapes in CSS is virtually impossible at this time, some of the code examples and images used in this section are courtesy of an excellent article written by **Arno Gourdol** (`http://www.adobe.com/devnet/html5/articles/css3-regions.html`). This article, along with the specification, should be the first resources you visit after finishing this chapter.

Look at how the following code forms the results shown in Figure 11-10:

```
Shaping Exclusions and Floats
.exclusion-circle {
    wrap-flow: both;
    shape-outside: circle(50%, 50%, 50%);
}

.exclusion-heart {
    wrap-flow: both;
    shape-outside: polygon(150px, 32px, /* ...more points */);
}

Shaping Other Block-Level Elements
.content-circle {
    shape-inside: circle(50%, 50%, 50%);
}

.content-heart {
    shape-inside: polygon(150px, 32px, /* ...more points */);
}
```

How cool is that? I don't want to go too far into the shape functions because their syntaxes are likely to be changed before you're able to experiment with them, but I want to touch on the ones used in the preceding code.

The `circle()` function takes three parameters: x and y coordinates to determine the center of the circle and another to specify the radius length. The `polygon()` function simply accepts a series of points that are linked to form a custom shape.

Furthermore, two other basic shapes are available in the form of the `rectangle()` and `ellipse()` functions, and finally, the `url()` notation enables an element to take the shape of an image through use of its alpha channel.

The potential that these shape properties possess is somewhat overwhelming because the possibilities are seemingly endless, but with the freedom that these functionalities allow for, designers need to be careful that these new toys aren't misused.

Figure 11-10 The two exclusion boxes have been shaped into a circle and a heart, with the content flowing around them (top). The two content boxes have also taken these shapes (bottom).

A Caveat on Exclusions and Shapes

I use this phrase a lot throughout this book, but the Exclusions and Shapes module really does provide extremely powerful new tools that open up many new possibilities. However, as the saying goes, with great power comes great responsibility, and developers need to be careful that this module doesn't hinder the flexible and adaptable direction that the web is moving in.

Along with Regions, these tools seem to aspire to the rich quality of pixel-perfect magazine layouts, an approach that appears to contradict the idea of embracing a medium as flexible as the web. If or when these specs get picked up by the major browsers, their adoption should be accompanied by a clear message that reinforces the need for these features to be adaptable rather than fixed.

Summary

I know I sound like a broken record, but remember that the modules discussed in this chapter are in their infancy and the fundamentals of their functionalities are still being perfected. Feel free to experiment where possible, but don't be surprised if the modules have been only partially implemented by the browsers that claim to have support for them. Also, expect to encounter bugs and unexpected behavior.

Although that advice may sound a little offputting, experimentation (where possible) at this stage is extremely important, because it's your feedback that will influence the spec editors into making the appropriate amendments. Just be sure to keep these tools away from production sites, unless you can absolutely guarantee graceful degradation.

Further Reading

CSS Grid Layout Specification
http://www.w3.org/TR/css3-grid-layout/

Giving Content Priority with CSS3 Grid Layout
http://24ways.org/2012/css3-grid-layout/

CSS Regions Specification
http://dev.w3.org/csswg/css3-regions/

Rich Page Layout with HTML and CSS3
http://www.adobe.com/devnet/html5/articles/css3-regions.html

Adobe Homepage for CSS Regions
http://html.adobe.com/webstandards/cssregions/

CSS Exclusions and Shapes Specification
http://dev.w3.org/csswg/css3-exclusions/

CSS Exclusions Overview by Adobe
http://adobe.github.com/web-platform/samples/css-exclusions/

Bruce Lawson on Regions and Exclusions
http://www.brucelawson.co.uk/2011/css-regions-css-exclusions/

Chapter 12

Going Responsive with CSS3 Media Queries

The last decade has seen an astonishing advancement in the area of handheld devices, both in terms of technology and popularity. Ten years ago, the only thing I used my mobile phone for was to make the odd call and to try and beat my top score on Snake. Now I have what is effectively a minicomputer in my pocket, complete with camera, countless apps, and most importantly, easy access to the Internet.

The rapid nature of this progression left developers and their tools a few steps behind, because suddenly everyone owned a smartphone and was using it to browse the web. This was not supposed to happen; everything on the web was designed to be viewed on a large, desktop monitor or perhaps a laptop, but certainly not something that can fit in the palm of your hand! Subsequently, billions of smartphone users were trying to navigate websites that had been optimized for desktops on a tiny device, forcing them to zoom, pan, and swipe their way around these fixed-width designs, resulting in an exhausting and unbearably frustrating user experience.

As a result, designers needed a solution for optimizing their websites for smaller screens. When the concept of *responsive web design (RWD)* was introduced, it seemed to tick all the boxes. New features in CSS3, such as the additional range of media queries, play a fundamental role in the RWD process. Looking further ahead, the new layout mechanisms proposed in CSS3 are geared toward this responsive movement, aiming to embrace the fluidity and the freedom that a platform like the web offers. I use this chapter to explore how these new mechanisms can aid your website's ability to adapt and the ease with which they do so. To achieve this, I take the multicolumn layout from Chapter 9 and the flexbox layout created in Chapter 10, and make the necessary adjustments to improve the experience on smaller screens, demonstrating just how much easier these layout mechanisms make the responsive process. Before I get to those examples, I analyze exactly what RWD is and, I hope, eradicate any misplaced fear or intimidation you may feel toward it. I also discuss CSS3 media queries in depth to explain what they do, how they work, and how they should be used.

What Is Responsive Web Design?

RWD is not some scary algorithm or technology that magically enables your website to adapt to various different screen sizes; it's simply a *concept* that defines a *collection* of techniques and ideas that allow your website to respond sensibly to whatever situation it finds itself in.

The term itself was pioneered by Ethan Marcotte with his groundbreaking book, *Responsive Web Design*, within which he identified three core aspects that contribute to making a responsive website:

- A *fluid layout* does most of the work for you, ensuring your layout can grow or shrink to a certain extent when required. A fluid layout involves percentage-based values rather than fixed pixel widths, enabling the elements to adjust their widths according to the space available.

■ A fluid layout can only shrink or grow so far before it starts to break. These issues can be fixed with the help of *media queries* (covered in the next section), which can apply separate CSS rules to different screen widths.

■ Finally, you need *flexible images*; your 600-pixel-wide image isn't going to look too good on a 300-pixel-wide screen, so it needs to be able to shrink itself down to fit the width of the screen. You achieve flexible images simply by placing `max-width: 100%;` on all images; this setting then ensures that images will never be wider than their containers and will never extend beyond their true dimensions.

Before moving on, I want to drive home the point that the purpose of making a website responsive is so that it is able to adapt to *any* screen size. Not just your iPhone, your iPad, and your laptop, but for everything in between, too. This is why a fluid layout is essential; it allows your website to respond to *any* screen size, rather than a predefined list of currently popular devices.

If it doesn't have a fluid layout, it's not responsive.

When you have a fluid layout, you can test it by simply dragging your browser window to the point where something starts to break or where the fluid layout alone is no longer sufficient. Each time you drag your browser window and something breaks, you simply fix it with help from a media query.

Using Media Queries to Design for Device Differences

As I alluded to already, a *media query* can test for various conditions and deliver a different set of CSS styles based on whether those conditions are true (or false). For example, you could say, "if the browser width is currently between 300px and 600px wide, apply these styles." I get to *how* you can say that very soon.

Even if you're new to RWD, it's likely that you've come across media queries in some form already because they've actually been around for a long time; CSS3 just added a whole lot more features to play around with. Have you ever used a separate stylesheet for specifying styles for print? If you have, you used a media query to do so.

You can use media queries in the HTML when linking to a stylesheet with the `media` attribute, or you can use the `@media` rule directly in your CSS stylesheet. The following example demonstrates the most basic of media queries—the first using the `media` attribute and the second using the `@media` rule:

HTML `media` **Attribute**
```
<link rel="stylesheet" media="print" href="print.css">

/* Or... */
```

CSS `@media` **Rule**
```
@media print {
    div {
        property: value;
    }
}
```

The first method is appropriate when you want to link to a separate stylesheet just for print, whereas the second method can simply be added at the bottom of your main stylesheet so that it can override the preceding styles for the specified condition (`print`).

Most of the time, it's best to keep everything in a single CSS file so you don't have to manage multiple stylesheets and force your website to call several files. Moreover, in the case of responsive web design, you may have a few breakpoints that require only tiny fixes, and you don't want separate CSS files that contain only four or five lines of code!

Okay, take a look at something a little more advanced (and useful):

```
@media screen and (min-width: 500px) and (max-width: 700px)
```

I replaced `print` with `screen` and added a couple more conditions to be tested for, which are all linked by the `and` operator. This statement basically translates to "if the medium is a screen and the browser width is currently somewhere between 500px and 700px, apply the following styles."

Understanding Media Types and Media Features

In the preceding examples, `print` and `screen` are examples of media *types*, whereas the width and height conditions are media *features*.

The complete list of acceptable media types is `screen, print, aural, braille, handheld, projection, tty, tv, embossed,` and `speech,` in addition to the `all` keyword. The `not` media type is stated explicitly; the `all` keyword is applied to the query by default.

The complete list of acceptable media features is `width, height, device-width, device-height, orientation, aspect-ratio, device-aspect-ratio, color, color-index, monochrome, resolution, scan,` and `grid`.

Furthermore, as previously stated, you can use the `and` operator to test for multiple conditions, and you can use commas as an *or* operator if, for example, you want to apply the same styles to two different size ranges. Finally, you can use the `not` keyword at the beginning of a query to test whether the specified conditions are false as opposed to true. Take a look at the following code example:

```
@media screen and (min-width: 350px) and (orientation: portrait), print
```

This media query basically translates to "apply these styles if the medium is using a screen to view the website, the current viewport width is at least 350px, and the orientation of the device is in portrait mode." The use of the comma then ensures that these styles are used for print as well, but this is not required for the initial part of the query to be true.

Now you know how to create a media query and how they work. The next step is to get a grip on the theory of *mobile first*.

Applying the Mobile-First Approach

When RWD first started to take off, designers were creating desktop-optimized designs as normal and then stripping them down and shoe-horning them into the restricted dimensions of handheld devices. I'm not saying that this approach is categorically wrong, but I think that it makes the whole process more wearing, more tedious, and more *forced*. Furthermore, if you're taking things away from the design and deeming them unimportant for the mobile site, you need to question why they need to be on the desktop site in the first place. Instead, I generally favor the *mobile-first* approach.

If you start with your most restricted dimensions and work out, you are forced to really think about the importance of your content and what really needs to be present and focused on. This way, the mobile site has everything it needs, and the desktop site is rid of the unnecessary stuff that it *doesn't* need—that is, the clutter and the distractions.

Just remember that less space does *not* mean less content. Nothing is more frustrating, from my experience, than when you're looking for something on a mobile site and find that barely any information is available and you need to access the desktop version to get anything of any value. The mobile-first approach ensures that everything you need (and only what you need) is on every form of the website.

The concept was spearheaded by Luke Wroblewski and backed up by an astounding amount of research and statistical information, as the following list suggests:

- Home usage of PCs decreased by 20 percent between 2008 and 2010 due to mobile usage.

- There was a 600 percent growth in traffic to mobile websites in 2010.

- The average smartphone user visits up to 24 websites a day.

- Google mobile searches grew by 130 percent in the third quarter of 2010.

- Pandora's mobile traffic accounted for 70 percent of its overall traffic in March 2012, compared to 52 percent in October 2011 and 40 percent in June 2011.

All this information is in addition to the fact that mobile devices are now selling in much bigger numbers than PCs and are fast becoming the primary method of browsing the web; so it makes sense to optimize for them, doesn't it?

> **All the statistics are courtesy of Luke Wroblewski and his fantastic book, which I thoroughly recommend:** *Mobile First*, **A Book Apart, 2011** (`http://abookapart.com/products/mobile-first`). **I also recommend his regularly updated website at** `http://lukew.com/ff`.

Of course, if your website's traffic bucks the trend and is still heavily desktop, mobile first probably isn't the best methodology to go with. Start with some research, analyze the statistics, and use them to help establish your direction.

So how would you use media queries to apply this mobile-first methodology? First, apply your styles as normal and ensure the design renders appropriately at the smallest width you want it to. Then simply grab the edge of your browser window and drag it out to the point at which you think the design needs to be tweaked—say this occurs when the viewport is 500px wide. This is your first breakpoint and can be specified as shown in the following snippet:

```
@media screen and (min-width: 500px) {
    /* Styles for viewports that are 500px wide or more */
}
```

Then simply drag the browser window out again until you reach a point where you feel the design needs fixing up again and add another breakpoint, as follows:

```
@media screen and (min-width: 735px) {
    /* Styles for viewports that are 735px wide or more */
}
```

Can you guess what to do next? That's right—simply drag the browser window out until the design breaks again and add another breakpoint. And repeat.

Also, don't be afraid to use a media query for tiny fixes. If one element needs tweaking, tweak it; media queries aren't just for major layout alterations.

By applying these methods, you satisfy my golden rule when it comes to responsive design: **don't** base your breakpoints on currently popular devices. Remember, the whole point of RWD is to deliver a design that adapts appropriately to *any* screen size. If you focus your breakpoints around device widths, you are ignoring the in-between sizes, and in a world with countless handheld devices of all shapes and sizes, that is not a wise thing to do. Instead, ignore popular devices and create your breakpoints based on where the design needs them.

To give you an idea of what to look for when determining your breakpoints, look at Figure 12-1. The fluid layout shrinks the elements down to fit into the smaller viewport, but this is no longer suitable as the images are now too small and everything is in need of some breathing space.

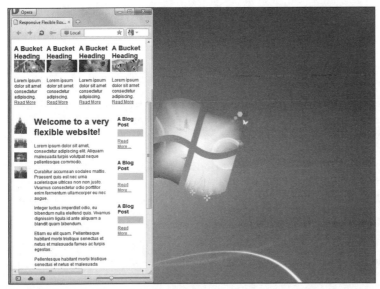

Figure 12-1 This fluid layout is no longer doing the job. It needs a media query to help adjust the layout.

Using the Viewport Meta Tag

One more tiny ingredient is essential for your responsive design to work correctly. In fact, without it, your media queries won't work at all on most mobile devices because the default behavior for most mobiles is to zoom out of websites so the sites are displayed in full. If the devices didn't do that, you would see only the top left section of a desktop-optimized website.

To counter this behavior, you need to add a viewport `meta` tag, which prevents the mobile device from zooming out:

```
<meta name="viewport" content="width=device-width">
```

This tag basically tells the browser that the width of your design is appropriate for the width of the device, so it doesn't need to zoom out. This tag usually suffices, but some browsers may forget what you told them earlier and apply a zoom when the orientation of the device is changed between portrait and landscape. Fortunately, you can easily remedy this situation by using the `initial-scale` parameter, which allows you to set an initial zoom value for the page, where a value of 1 prevents any default zooming behavior:

```
<meta name="viewport" content="width=device-width, initial-scale=1">
```

If you add the preceding line of code into the `<head>` of your responsive site, you are all set.

Before moving on, I want to briefly touch on the `maximum-scale` parameter, which allows you to set the extent to which the user can zoom in to your website. In some websites you see that this parameter is set to a value of 1, which basically disables the ability to zoom in to your website. This is very bad practice. No matter how optimized your website is, there are always those who need to zoom in that little bit more to be able to read your text comfortably. Don't forget about them!

Making a Multicolumn Layout Responsive

In Chapter 9, you learned about using the Multi-column Layout module to divide your text into columns that flow into each other without any modification of the markup. In this chapter, you look at the module from a different angle and discover its benefits when used in a responsive context.

As I mentioned earlier, the new layout models are geared toward the responsive movement, and that is certainly accurate in the case of Multi-column Layout. Remember, the fundamental ingredient that lays the foundations for any responsive website is a fluid structure, and the beauty of the Multi-column Layout is that it's wonderfully fluid by default.

You may recall the reason for this fluidity is that when you specify the widths for the columns, whether by using an explicit width or by declaring the number of columns, the specified value is only an *optimal* width, leaving the browser to decide the computed width, which is only *based* on your value.

Let's revisit the example from the end of Chapter 9 and turn it into a responsive design that should look presentable on any sized device. Because my example is already optimized for desktop screens, I have to contradict my advice from the previous section and reverse-engineer the design to suit smaller devices.

If you're bracing yourself for a lengthy tutorial, you can stop bracing. Seriously, you'll be amazed by how easy it is to make this layout adapt to its surroundings so effortlessly. To begin, check out Figure 12-2, which reminds you what I'm working with here, and you can take a look at the live demo `1201-responsive-multi-column.html` on the companion site at `www.wiley.com/go/ptl/css3`.

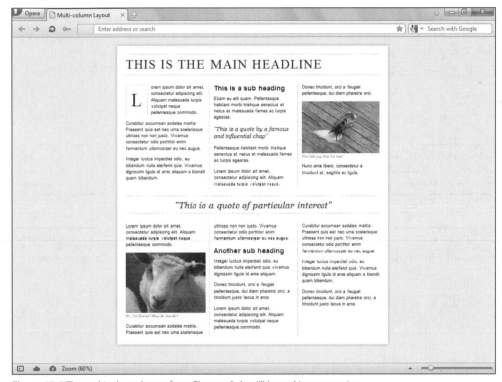

Figure 12-2 The multicolumn layout from Chapter 9 that I'll be making responsive

And this is how I left it in terms of the code:

```
.container {
    width: 920px;
    padding: 20px;
    columns: 3; /* Shorthand of column-count: 3; */
    column-gap: 1.8em;
    column-rule: 2px dotted #ccc;
}
```

The first modification that needs to be made should be obvious because it involves a pixel-based fixed width, which must be replaced when working responsively. You simply need to replace the `920px` fixed width by a percentage value to ensure a fluid container. However, if you want to restrict your layout so that it adapts to smaller screens but doesn't go any wider than what you originally intended, you can always re-introduce your `920px` value, but using the `max-width` property instead. But remember, responsive design isn't just for smaller screens; when done properly, it's supposed to optimize your design for wider screens, too.

While I'm on the subject of fixed widths, I need to deal with another one lurking in the preceding code example. You also should convert the `padding` value of `20px` to a percentage to adjust according to the current browser width. However, this value, which totals 40 pixels when you take into account the padding on both sides, currently adds to the container width of 920 pixels to make an overall width of 960 pixels; this behavior is far from ideal when working with percentage values that need to be adjusted for smaller screens.

This issue can be addressed by the `box-sizing` property, which is an absolute luxury when you're working in a responsive environment because it actually alters the traditional box model and allows you to specify `padding` and `border` values that don't add to the specified width of the container. For example, if your `width` is `960px`, your `padding` is `10px`, and your `border` is `5px`, the container's total width is still only 960 pixels:

```
.container {
    width: 100%;
    padding: 2.5%;
    box-sizing: border-box;
    columns: 3; /* Shorthand of column-count: 3; */
    column-gap: 1.8em;
    column-rule: 2px dotted #ccc;
}
```

A `box-sizing` value of `border-box` ensures that the total width of the container (inclusive of padding) is 100 percent, not 105 percent. Figure 12-3 demonstrates the behavior of the fluid, percentage-based layout.

Figure 12-3 The layout now expands to fit the size of the screen on which it is being viewed.

This width works fine at this size, but if you start to reduce (or increase) the screen size, the three-column layout fast becomes unsuitable, as Figure 12-4 illustrates.

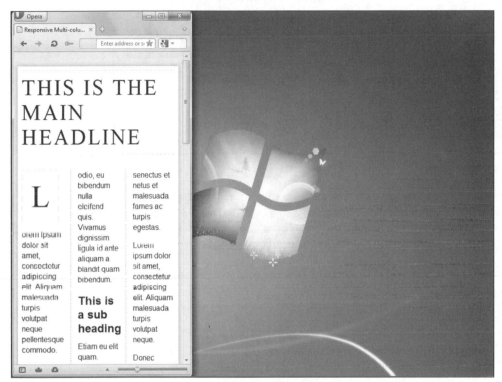

Figure 12-4 The three-column layout just doesn't work with smaller viewports.

Fortunately, the fix is easy. All you need to do here is specify an optimal `column-width` value rather than a `column-count` value. A column with an explicit width value always expands to fill the available space if there is any, so the adaptive behavior that you usually have to work so hard to achieve is already built in to the default functionality! Figure 12-5 shows how this affects the column-based layout.

```
.container {
    width: 100%;
    padding: 2.5%;
    box-sizing: border-box;
    columns: 250px; /* Shorthand of column-width: 250px; */
    column-gap: 1.8em;
    column-rule: 2px dotted #ccc;
}
```

Now you have a suitably responsive design, which you achieved using a fluid layout alone and without even a single media query in sight! However, while you don't have any major layout changes to make, little tweaks are always required at smaller widths, and this example is no different.

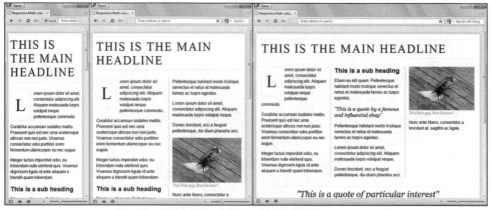

Figure 12-5 The columns now automatically adapt to the space available at all widths.

As the viewport shrinks to a certain width, a few elements of the design (notably the main headline and the main quote) look slightly big and overpowering for such a small viewing area. A couple of simple media queries will soon sort these minor issues; all you need to do is shrink the viewport until you feel changes are needed and then apply these changes to this width and below using a media query:

```
@media screen and (max-width: 805px) {

    h1 {
        font-size: 2.4em;
        margin-bottom: .5em;
    }

}

@media screen and (max-width: 600px) {

    h1 {
        font-size: 2em;
        margin-bottom: .4em;
    }

    blockquote.important {
        margin: 0 0 .5em;
        font-size: 1.8em;
    }

}
```

The first media query comes into action whenever the viewport is 805 pixels wide or less and performs a simple aesthetic fix on the main headline, decreasing the size slightly as well as its bottom margin. The second media query applies when the viewport is 600 pixels wide or less and makes the main headline slightly smaller again. This second set of styles also corrects the margins and decreases the font size on the important `blockquote` element when the layout adjusts to a single column. Figure 12-6 shows the final result.

Figure 12-6 The final result of the responsive restructuring, complete with media query–based tweaks.

Making a Flexbox Layout Responsive

Again, the Flexible Box Layout module is set to make your life an easier one when it comes to coding maintainable, responsive websites. The whole premise of RWD is fluidity and flexibility, so I suppose it would be a disappointing surprise if a module called Flexible Box Layout was to let you down here!

The capability of proportional widths and elements to "flex" their sizes makes Flexbox fluid by default. Add to this the dream-like alignment and ordering functionalities and you have at your disposal a tool that is ready-made for adaptable layouts, giving it a considerable head start over alternative options.

For this section, I refer you back to Chapter 10 where I created a basic Flexbox layout (see Figure 12-7 for a reminder). Once again, I'm going to demonstrate the ease with which this can be transformed into a responsive layout, before correcting the various imperfections at smaller screen widths using media queries. Again, you can find the working demo (`1202-responsive-flexbox.html`) on the companion website.

The first step is reminiscent of the previous section because the fixed-width, pixel-based values need to be replaced with fluid percentage values. Fortunately, because Flexbox handles widths using its own initiative, they are few and far between in this layout. The following snippet shows the current state of the code:

```
.container {
    width: 960px;
    padding: 0 10px;
    box-sizing: border-box;
    margin: 0 auto;
    display: flex;
    flex-direction: column;
}
```

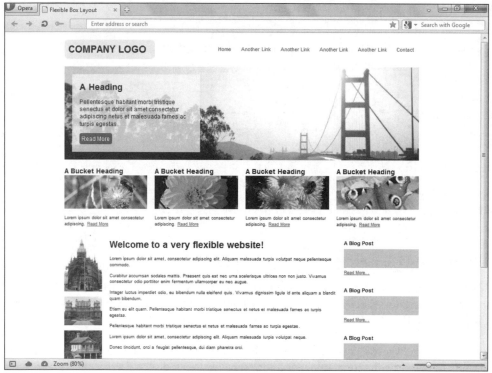

Figure 12-7 The Flexbox layout that I am going to transform into a responsive design (shot at 80% zoom to show more of the lower layout section)

Just a couple of amendments to make here; of course, the `width` value must be changed to `100%`, but I'm going to add a `max-width` value as well to prevent the layout from stretching beyond a comfortable width. Finally, the `padding` value should also be converted to a percentage value to ensure that it's proportional to the width of the viewport. Remember, due to the magic of the `box-sizing` property, you are free to add whatever `padding` value you like without having to amend the specified width.

```
.container {
    width: 100%;
    max-width: 1280px;
    padding: 0 2%;
    box-sizing: border-box;
    margin: 0 auto;
    display: flex;
    flex-direction: column;
}
```

With this tiny amendment, the fantastically fluid nature of Flexbox is illustrated perfectly, because a simple percentage-based width on the main container allows the entire layout to shrink with the viewport by a considerable distance before any significant changes are required. Figure 12-8 shows that the fluid layout can adapt right down to almost 700px, thanks to one simple change!

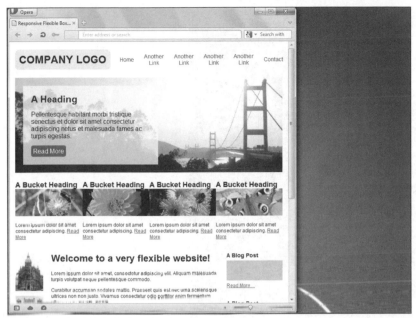

Figure 12-8 The default fluidity of Flexbox allows the layout to adapt extremely well without any major modification to the code.

Moving on, the only other fixed width that needs attention is the one applied to the buckets. Despite having a pixel-based width, these elements actually shrink in conjunction with the viewport due to the default behavior of flex items, which is to flex their sizes according to the available space. However, this shrinking process causes the buckets to eat up the entirety of the available space, meaning no space is left to sit between these elements (see Figure 12-8). You could specify explicit margins between the buckets, but doing so leaves you with the age-old problem of an additional, unwanted margin on the first or last element.

A more sensible method is to convert the pixel width to a percentage value that leaves enough space to act as margins between the buckets. For example, there are four buckets, so I chose a width of 24%, which obviously totals only 96 percent; this leaves 4 percent of the available space to be distributed *between* each of the buckets (thanks to the `justify-content: space-between;` rule on the bucket's container element). Figure 12-9 illustrates the result of this amendment.

```
.buckets {
    justify-content: space-between;
}

.buckets div {
    width: 220px;
    width: 24%;
}
```

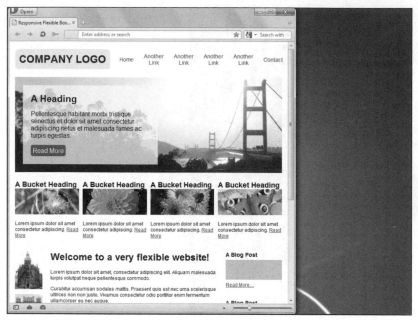

Figure 12-9 The buckets now shrink (and grow) proportionately while maintaining the spacing in between them.

Another slight tweak involves the `.runner` element. Way back in Chapter 3, I discussed the `background-size` property and, more specifically, its `cover` value. When utilized here, it applies a degree of responsiveness to the runner's background image, allowing it to shrink with its container while ensuring it always covers the element's parameters entirely. Furthermore, positioning it to the right edge of the element ensures that the focal point of this background image (the bridge) remains visible when the element's width is reduced:

```
.runner {
    background: url(images/runner.jpg) right no-repeat;
    background-size: cover;
}
```

After those initial few tweaks, the layout has effortlessly transformed into a fluid and adaptable design, ready to be perfected with some media queries!

The first major issue to address is the navigation because this soon forces a horizontal scroll bar as the viewport's width is reduced. In this case, I feel the nav will sit quite comfortably if it drops down a level and sits between the logo and the runner. By adjusting the width of the browser window, you can determine where this change needs to take place and add in the first media query, which will apply its styles when the viewport is under the specified `max-width`:

```
@media screen and (max-width: 720px) {

    header {
        flex-wrap: wrap;
    }

}
```

As you can see, the media query applies its styles when the device viewing the site has a screen and when the viewport is 720 pixels wide or less. This example also serves to remind you that it's okay to use a media query for minor issues that just need a line or two to correct (although I recommend revisiting the default styles in these instances to see whether the issue can be addressed initially).

To continue, because the navigation menu needs to drop onto a new row, you must overrule the default wrapping behavior of a flex container to allow its flex items to wrap onto new lines. In this case, the `header` element is the flex container, and the `wrap` value of `flex-wrap` must be specified to enable the flex items it contains (the nav) to drop onto a new row when space becomes insufficient. Figure 12-10 shows the result of this amendment.

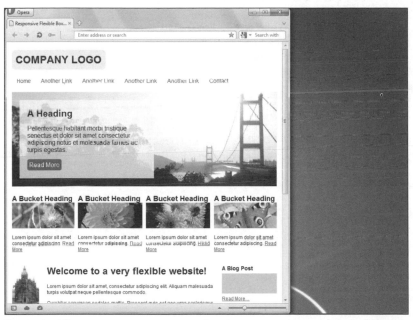

Figure 12-10 The nav wraps onto a new row when the viewport width is reduced to 720 pixels or less.

This technique provides a nice little interim solution to the depleting space, but it only delays the issue because the available space will once again become insufficient to accommodate the nav, despite enjoying a whole row to itself now!

The eventual solution to your navigation woes requires a bit more thought and effort, but with Flexbox's handling of everything so far, it's about time you were made to work for something! I'm going to use a tactic that is growing ever popular in responsive designs, which is to hide the actual navigation links and replace them with a button that allows users to toggle the nav in and out of view. Figure 12-11 demonstrates the desired effect.

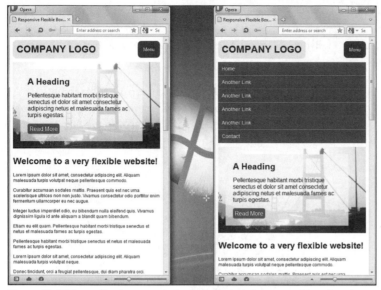

Figure 12-11 The nav has been restyled to fit the reduced screen width and can be toggled in and out of view.

After the button is added into the markup, it must be hidden by default before becoming visible at the appropriate width—the same width at which the navigation will be hidden:

```
@media screen and (max-width: 463px) {

    /* Display the Menu button */
    .nav-btn {
        display: block;
    }

    /* Hide the navigation links */
    nav {
        display: none;
    }

}
```

I used a bit of basic jQuery to achieve the show/hide functionality when the menu button is clicked:

```
jQuery(document).ready(function(){
    $(".nav-btn").click(function() {
        $("nav").toggleClass('vert-nav');
    });
});
```

This code ensures that when the `.nav-btn` element is clicked, the class `.vert-nav` is applied to the nav element. Then you can use this new class to show the navigation and style it more appropriately for the vastly reduced width:

```css
@media screen and (max-width: 463px) {

    .nav-btn {
        display: block;
    }

    nav {
        display: none;
    }

    .vert-nav {
        display: block; /* Display nav when menu button is clicked */
        width: 100%;
    }

    nav ul {
        flex-direction: column;
        align-items: stretch;
    }

    /* ...irrelevant nav link styles */

}
```

The next major issue to address is the main content area because the current three-column layout will soon be too much to accommodate as the viewport's width is reduced. Again, thanks to the way Flexbox works, this issue is wonderfully easy to fix. The first fundamental change that is required is to change the directional flow of the main content area from the default row value to a column display. This change then renders the three elements on top of each other in a column, rather than side by side in a row.

Additionally, the original order of these three elements was amended so that the left-hand sidebar could sit on the left of the content area, despite appearing after it in the source. For the column display, this order simply needs to be returned to normal, to ensure the content is set on top:

```css
@media screen and (max-width: 622px) {

    .main {
        flex-direction: column;
    }

    .sidebar-left {
        order: 0;
        /* This is returned to the initial value, ensuring it will now
            render in source order */
    }

}
```

Finally, I felt that as the viewport width got smaller and smaller, it became increasingly important to push the actual content of the page as close to the top as possible to avoid the need for excessive scrolling to even find the content. I therefore made use of the tremendously useful order property once again and moved the buckets to sit below the main content area, while also amending their widths and allowing them to wrap onto a second row to make them more legible.

Fortunately, these changes fit within an existing `@media` rule set quite nicely:

```
@media screen and (max-width: 463px) {

    /* ...existing vertical nav styles... */

    .buckets {
        flex-wrap: wrap;
        order: 1;
    }

    .buckets div {
        width: 48%;
    }

    footer {
        order: 2;
    }

}
```

To summarize, a fully fluid layout was achieved with the amendment of a single value, only three media queries were required, and the necessary amendments were made effortlessly thanks to the functionality that Flexbox offers. Figure 12-12 provides an overview of the finished and fully responsive product.

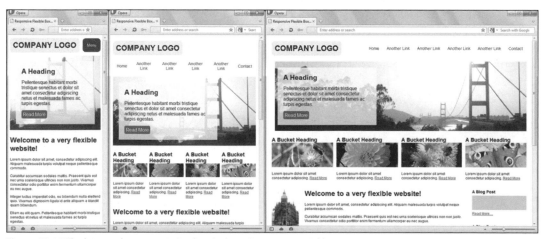

Figure 12-12 The layout adapts appropriately, whatever the viewport width.

A Word on CSS Grid Layout

In addition to the Multicolumn and Flexbox Layout modules, the CSS Grid Layout is also set to ease the responsive process, offering effortless reshuffling and reordering of content without any modifications to the source. Browser support for the most recent incarnation of this module is currently nonexistent, with IE10 the only browser to offer any level of compatibility at present, albeit with an older syntax. However, support is reportedly imminent in the WebKit browsers as well Firefox, so keep a close eye on the situation (as well as changes to the spec) and start playing around with it as soon as possible to get a feel for its functionalities in a responsive context.

The Here and Now of RWD

The options discussed in this chapter are obviously the stars of the future, but for now you have to make do with floats and positioned layouts, which are much less flexible when it comes to scaling down and rearranging content. In contrast to my examples, which had to be reverse-engineered for smaller screens, a mobile-first approach will help with these issues, forcing you to focus on the importance and hierarchy of your content right from the start, making the reordering of elements less of an obstacle when the content has to adapt for wider screens.

The ongoing RWD explosion is so robust that an endless list of responsive resources is available to assist with the limited layout mechanisms currently on offer, from grids and frameworks to scripts and plugins.

Frameworks such as Bootstrap and Skeleton are proving increasingly popular because they offer fast-tracks and shortcuts that speed up the responsive process. Bootstrap, in particular, is a great piece of kit and contains everything you need, but remember, you don't always need everything! I advise against using comprehensive frameworks such as these *blindly*, without knowing what everything does and whether it's all essential for your site. Experienced web developer Rachel Andrews wrote an article that hit the nail on the head regarding this issue, pleading with the industry to "[s]top solving problems you don't yet have." (You can find a link to the article in the "Further Reading" section of this chapter.)

These tools can be extremely useful and can often be exactly what you need, but just as often they can add a lot of unnecessary bloat to your website. You need to explore and understand the frameworks to ensure that they are implemented appropriately and can showcase their considerable power and capabilities effectively.

Summary

Although there is a certain degree of dissent from some corners, it's generally agreed that RWD—and its "one web" philosophy—is the most appropriate way for the web to progress and address the ever-growing issue of varying screen widths.

At the core of a responsive design is a fluid layout, which has been made increasingly painless to achieve thanks to grid systems, frameworks, and, of course, the new CSS3 layout modules. The other key ingredients are flexible images and media queries, the latter of which allows you to make alterations (both minor and major) to address imperfections as the fluid layout alone becomes insufficient below (and above) certain screen widths.

The final, essential element for a functional responsive design is the viewport `meta` tag, which ensures that the media queries are obeyed by mobile devices.

Further Reading

Ethan Marcotte's Responsive Web Design Article
`http://alistapart.com/article/responsive-web-design`

Luke Wroblewski's Mobile First Presentation (PDF)
`http://static.lukew.com/MobileFirst_LukeW.pdf`

Ethan Marcotte's Responsive Web Design Book
`http://www.abookapart.com/products/responsive-web-design`

Luke Wroblewski's Mobile First Book
`http://www.abookapart.com/products/mobile-first`

Seven Deadly Mobile Myths (PDF)
`http://globalmoxie.com/jhc/prez/mobile-myths.pdf`

CSS Media Queries Specification
`http://www.w3.org/TR/css3-mediaqueries/`

Deciding What Responsive Breakpoints to Use
`http://www.tangledindesign.com/blog/deciding-what-responsive-breakpoints-to-use/`

Rachel Andrews' "Stop solving problems you don't yet have"
`http://www.rachelandrew.co.uk/archives/2012/03/21/stop-solving-problems-you-dont-yet-have/`

Brad Frost's extensive collection of responsive resources
`http://bradfrost.github.com/this-is-responsive/resources.html`

Part IV

Pushing the Limits

Chapter 13

Getting Creative with Pseudo-elements

If you can remember all the way back to Chapter 1, you will recall the in-depth discussion of advanced CSS selectors. Well, it's 12 chapters on, and you finally get to enjoy the sequel! Pseudo-elements belong in the same bracket as selectors because they target aspects of the markup you use to style; however, despite their fundamental similarities, pseudo-elements hold much greater potential and open a new realm of possibilities for creative web designers to jump right into.

Pseudo-elements in their earliest form were actually first seen in the first CSS specification, with a couple more added in CSS 2.1. Their syntax was modified slightly in CSS3 to accentuate their difference from pseudo-classes (although this move hasn't gone as well as planned).

So what are pseudo-elements doing in a book on CSS3? Well, they may have been around for a long time, but finding a legitimate use for them has always been somewhat difficult. When CSS3 came along with all its new bells and whistles, though, it effectively injected a whopping shot of potential into pseudo-elements, suddenly making them an exciting prospect, full of possibilities.

With the help of these other CSS3 functionalities, I demonstrate how you can use pseudo-elements to really push the limits of what CSS is capable of doing. This chapter begins by establishing the difference between pseudo-elements and pseudo-classes before demonstrating how you can use the former to enhance your typography, generate content, and perform other neat tricks that do not compromise the semantic value of your markup!

Distinguishing Pseudo-elements and Pseudo-classes

You may remember reading about the many pseudo-classes in Chapter 1, and are wondering how they differ from pseudo-elements enough to warrant positions at opposite ends of this book. There is a significant difference, and one that is important to understand, as shown by the specification's attempt to emphasize that difference. More on the latter point soon, but first, let's nail down the two terms and their respective definitions.

What Is a Pseudo-class?

A *pseudo-class* is a method of targeting specific elements (or states of an element) without having to use a class in HTML. As described in Chapter 1, you can use them, for example, to select the fourth list item, every odd list item, empty div elements, or hover states. The following code demonstrates what each of these particular examples would look like in your CSS:

```
/* Select the fourth list item */
ul li:nth-child(4)
```

```
/* Select all odd list items */
ul li:nth-child(2n+1) /* or... */ ul li:nth-child(odd)

/* Select empty div elements */
div:empty

/* Select an element's hover state */
a:hover
```

What Is a Pseudo-element?

A *pseudo-element* targets areas of an element and treats them as elements in their own right, as if they actually exist as separate entities in the HTML. For example, you can use pseudo-elements to select the first line or letter of a paragraph, or the areas before or after an element. The following code shows how these examples should appear in your code:

```
/* Target the first line of a paragraph */
p:first-line

/* Target the first letter of a paragraph */
P:first-letter

/* Target the areas before or after an element */
div:before
div:after
```

After you consider these examples, you can see that pseudo-*classes* simply provide more control in terms of targeting elements, whereas pseudo-*elements* allow for the targeting and styling of nonexistent, "ghost" elements, which is a totally different ballgame.

Syntactical Differences

I hope the preceding explanations have cleared things up somewhat, but you can easily see why some developers muddle the two and often use the terms interchangeably. The spec editors foresaw this situation and attempted to emphasize the difference to quash any confusion, opting to describe slightly different syntaxes for the two selector types, suggesting a single colon for pseudo-classes and a double colon for pseudo-elements. The following code shows this ideal solution in action:

```
/* The spec's syntax for a pseudo-class */
p:first-child

/* The spec's syntax for a pseudo-element */
div::after
```

As I said, this seems like the ideal solution to prevent confusion and assist developers in understanding the difference between the two, but we don't live in an ideal world!

Both the single colon syntax and the correct double colon syntax are supported across the board in the current versions of the major browsers, but IE7 and 8 support pseudo-elements with only a *single* colon.

Logic then dictates that authors need to include only the single colon method to ensure that the pseudo-elements work in all the browsers that support them. Adding the double colon syntax would have the sole purpose of satisfying the spec, while taking up unnecessary bytes in the process.

Although the official line is still to use the double colon method for pseudo-elements, the universal support and the vast usage of the old single colon syntax suggests that the issue is too far gone for any retreat. Almost everything I've read on the subject uses the latter option, and for these reasons, I also use the single colon syntax throughout this chapter.

Exploring the Current Range of Pseudo-elements

You now know what pseudo-elements are in comparison to pseudo-classes, but what makes up the pseudo-element arsenal? The following list describes the modest collection at your disposal:

- `:first-line` targets the first line of text in an element (introduced in CSS 1).
- `:first-letter` targets the first letter in an element (introduced in CSS 1).
- `:before` allows you to target the area before an element and insert generated content (introduced in CSS 2.1).
- `:after` allows you to target the area *after* an element and insert generated content (introduced in CSS 2.1).

> Initially, CSS3 introduced the `selection` pseudo-element, which targets and styles the background and text color of selected areas. Because this was new in CSS3, it required the double colon syntax to work in the browsers that support it; however, despite maintaining a decent level of browser support, this new pseudo-element has since been dropped and is no longer a part of the new Selectors specification.

Enhancing Your Typography with Pseudo-elements

The two initial pseudo-elements that have been lurking in the background, unsuccessfully threatening to break into the mainstream since the inception of CSS, are `:first-line` and `:first-letter`, which are obviously typography-based.

> Unfortunately, no pseudo-element targets the first *word* of a block of text, despite appearing just as useful as the existing type-based pseudo-elements if its use in print is anything to go by.

In this section, I show you how to enhance your body copy with these pseudo-elements, before demonstrating how you can get a bit more creative with them to create bold and beautiful typography.

Drawing Users into Your Copy

An extremely common strategy in print works such as newspapers and magazines is to apply strikingly different styles to the first paragraph, first line, or first letter of large bodies of text to make them stand out. The purpose of this design is to grab the readers' attention at a glance and draw them into bodies of copy that can otherwise appear intimidating and uninviting.

These initial styling techniques that draw readers into copy are applied tastefully and effectively in newspapers, with magazines employing more extravagance and flair in their use of these techniques.

Using a basic example, I want to demonstrate how these techniques that are commonly used in print can make the transition to use on the web. Figure 13-1 shows the basic layout and styling that I explain how to achieve using the `:first-line` and `:first-letter` pseudo-elements, with a bit of help from a pseudo-class, too. You can also find a corresponding demo file, `1301-body-copy.html`, on the companion website at `www.wiley.com/go/ptl/css3`.

Figure 13-1 The first paragraph is a different color, the first line is bigger and bolder, and the first letter is decoratively styled, all to grab the readers' attention and draw them into the copy.

After you form your basic layout and implement your design, you're ready to apply the finishing touches that aim to enhance the readability of your content:

```
HTML
<article class="container">
    <h1>This is the main headline</h1>
    <p>...</p>
    <p>...</p>
    <p>...</p>
</article>
```

CSS
```css
.container {
    background: #333;
    font-family: Arial, Helvetica, sans-serif;
    color: #feffb2;
    text-align: justify;
    columns: 2;
}
```

The first stage is to change the color of the first paragraph, with the goal of easing the readers into the content. This change requires a simple pseudo-*class* that targets the first p element in the article for styling:

```css
.container p:first-of-type {
    color: #fff;
}
```

The pseudo-class used here must be :first-of-type to target the first paragraph; the :first-child selector wouldn't work because the h1 is actually the first child of the container, not the first paragraph.

Now it's time to move on to the pseudo-elements. Next, you need to target the first line of the copy to make it subtly larger and bolder; however, a simple selector of p:first-line would not suffice in this situation because it would target the first line of every paragraph in the article!

Instead, you must combine the pseudo-element with the previous pseudo-class to target only the first line of the first paragraph. The following snippet shows how this is done:

```css
.container p:first-of-type:first-line {
    font-weight: bold;
    font-size: 1.3em;
}
```

Finally, you need to use the same technique to target and style the first *letter* of the article's body copy, as demonstrated in the following code:

```css
.container p:first-of-type:first-letter {
    float: left;
    padding: .2em;
    margin-right: .1em;
    border: 2px dotted #ccc;
    border-radius: 10px;
    font-size: 3em;
}
```

Fairly simple stuff, and best of all, these two type-based pseudo-elements are supported across the board, including IE7 and up! Despite this impressive browser support and the fact that they have existed since CSS 1, these tools are criminally underused, and their potential has gone largely untapped. However, I plan to use the next example to illustrate how you can push these pseudo-elements to their limits and create outcomes that are much more creative and striking than simple body copy introduction.

Getting Creative with Type-based Pseudo-elements

The preceding example demonstrates some pretty standard usage of the `:first-line` and `:first-letter` pseudo-elements, but if you let your imagination roam, you can get much more creative with these tools and create really striking and customized typography that your instincts will tell you can't possibly be real text.

The following example shows you how to create an arresting `blockquote` design using only CSS and *semantic* HTML. To see the final goal, peek ahead at Figure 13-6.

The first step is to mark up the text as you might normally find it, independent of the fact that it will be presented so mindfully in the final rendering:

```
<article class="container">
    <blockquote>
        <strong>Imagination</strong> is <em>more important</em> than
        <strong>knowledge</strong>
    </blockquote>

    <b>Einstein, A.</b>
</article>
```

If you have only a passing familiarity with the HTML5 specification, it's likely that you are wincing at the way in which the quotation's credit has been marked up in the preceding code block. I share your anguish, but the seemingly ideal `<cite>` element has been slightly redefined in HTML5, with the spec stating that it is only for referencing bodies of work (books/papers/television shows) and not people. What's worse is that the current recommendation for referencing a person is to use the also-redefined `<b>` element or the semantically meaningless `<span>` element. In my humble opinion, this is a frankly ludicrous solution, but this is currently the official line, so I'm going with it for now. I suggest that you read this article by Jeremy Keith and make your own decisions: `http://24ways.org/2009/incite-a-riot/` (the piece is admittedly old but still as relevant as the day it was written).

Right—back to CSS! Figure 13-2 shows where things stand after some basic styling to the `blockquote` container.

This result is nice, but it's also very safe and not very adventurous; the use of pseudo-elements can push this piece of text much further. The first stage is to target the first line and adjust its font and size as per the final design shown in Figure 13-6.

```
blockquote:first-line {
    font: 1.85em "Sketch Block";
    color: #fff79e; /* A pale yellow */
}
```

With just a few lines of code, things are already looking noticeably more impressive, as shown in Figure 13-3.

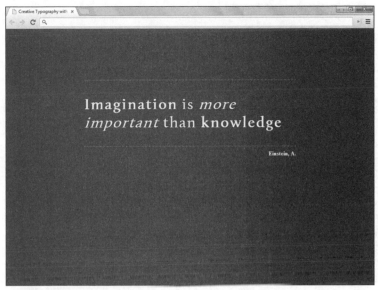

Figure 13-2 The blockquote after some basic styling

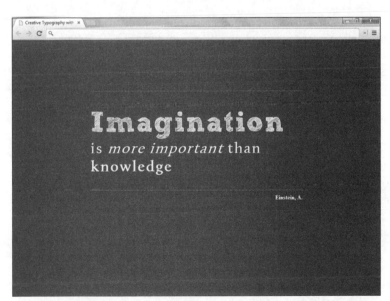

Figure 13-3 The first line has been styled to take on a different font and size from the rest of the text.

As the final design suggests, the next step is to attack the first letter of the quotation, which acts as the focal point from a design perspective. First, I simply increase the font size and convert it to lowercase, as shown in Figure 13-4:

```
blockquote:first-letter {
    font-size: 2.9em;
    text-transform: lowercase;
}
```

Figure 13-4 The first letter now stands out as it should, but the current state is still a way off from the final design.

As you can see, this first letter requires further attention to ensure it matches the desired outcome. To reach this outcome, you need to use some special positioning rules to hack it into place:

```
blockquote:first-letter {
    font-size: 2.9em;
    text-transform: lowercase;
    float: left;
    line-height: .52em;
    margin-right: -18px;
}
```

The first letter is now floated to the left so that the rest of the text can flow around it. I also applied a `line-height` value to correctly position the letter vertically and a negative `margin-right` value to ensure that it covers up the *i* from the word *is* (Figure 13-5 illustrates further). Note that this use is obviously only appropriate in tailored situations, not when styling general `blockquote` elements!

> Unfortunately, the `line-height` **property has no effect on the floated letter in Firefox, so it requires a negative** `margin-top` **value to do the job instead.**

The last major part of the puzzle is the word *knowledge*, which is targetable through its inline `<strong>` container and a pseudo-*class*. You simply need to adjust it to the appropriate size and font before converting it to uppercase:

```
blockquote strong:last-child {
    font: 2em "Museo 700";
    text-transform: uppercase;
}
```

Figure 13-5 The first letter has been maneuvered into place and now covers up the *i* from the word *is* so it can act as its replacement.

For the final touches, I applied a subtle underline to the emphasized text, used a 2D transform to slightly rotate the whole `blockquote`, and added some styling to the credit (including an additional `:first-letter` pseudo-element for good measure). The following code shows how these finalities are implemented, and Figure 13-6 demonstrates the final result:

```
blockquote {
    /* Other styles */
    transform: rotate(-3deg);
}

blockquote em {
    border-bottom: 2px dotted #858585;
}

blockquote + b {
    float: right;
    margin-top: 10px;
    font: 1.6em CallunaRegular;
}

blockquote + b:first-letter {
    color: #fff79e;
    font-size: 1.3em;
    font-style: italic;
}
```

To see the color version (albeit minimal) and the full code, look at the live demo (`1302-creative-typography.html`).

Figure 13-6 The final implementation of the customized blockquote design

When you use custom fonts on the web, bear in mind that different browsers and different operating systems can vary in the way they render these fonts—sometimes quite significantly. The main font I've used in this example appears to fall into this offending category, so for the best result when viewing the demo file, open it in Chrome on a Windows machine if possible. In a real-life scenario you cannot afford to be so lax; if the rendering of a font in a particular browser has a serious impact on usability, you must find a fix or use a different font.

I hope this section has emphasized just how useful these type-based pseudo-elements can be (particularly in terms of maintaining semantic values), whether you're looking to subtly enhance the opening to your body text or implementing customized and abstract typographic designs.

Using Pseudo-elements to Generate Content

The real attention grabbers in this chapter are the `:before` and `:after` pseudo-elements that were introduced in CSS 2.1. They allow you to create actual ghost elements, complete with basic content, that do not make up part of the source.

In their most basic form, they can be used to append text before or after an element. This is achieved through use of the `content` property, which is required for these faux elements to render on your page.

You can use these tools for something as simple as navigation link dividers that have no place in the actual source content. The following code shows how this might be done, with Figure 13-7 demonstrating the result. The corresponding demo is on the companion website (`1303-nav-separators.html`).

HTML

```
<nav>
    <ul>
        <li><a href="#">Home</a></li>
        <li><a href="#">Link</a></li>
        <!-- More links -->
        <li><a href="#">Contact</a></li>
    </ul>
</nav>
```

CSS

```
nav a {
    font: 1.2em Arial;
    padding: 20px;
}

nav a:after {
    content: "/"
    padding-left: 40px;
    color: #ccc;
}
```

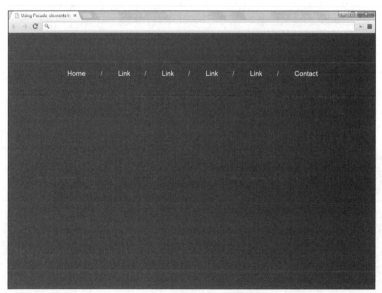

Figure 13-7 The nav links are now separated by slashes without the actual content being compromised.

This technique allows you to reuse this same markup in other areas of your site, such as the footer, for example, where you are free to display the links in a completely different format, such as columnar, without having to mess about with hiding aspects of the code!

To further demonstrate how content can be generated using pseudo-elements, I want to revisit the previous typography example and add in some quotation marks to surround the text because they're not present in the markup. The following code shows how the :before and :after pseudo-elements help to achieve this effect, and Figure 13-8 illustrates the results (check out the demo file, `1304-before-after-quotes.html`).

```
.container:before {
    content: """;
    font-size: 13em;
    position: absolute;
    left: -100px;
    color: #666;
}

.container:after {
    content: """;
    font-size: 13em;
    position: absolute;
    right: -100px;
    top: 150px;
    color: #666;
}
```

The `:before` and `:after` **pseudo-elements are appended onto the quote's** `.container` **element, because otherwise the first quotation mark would be considered the first letter of the** `blockquote` **rather than the letter *i* as intended.**

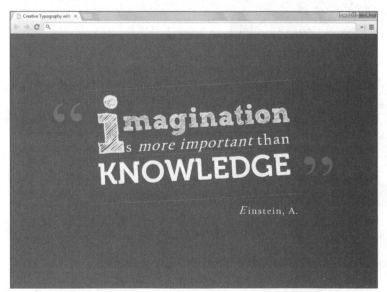

Figure 13-8 The quotation marks are added before and after the blockquote using the appropriate pseudo-elements.

Here's another method of generating content through pseudo-elements that could prove particularly useful in certain situations. Rather than specifying an explicit string as the value for the `content` property, you can use the `attr()` function, which allows you to specify an attribute of the element whose value should be outputted in the pseudo-element.

For example, in a print stylesheet, you may want to output the value of the `href` attribute after all `a` elements so that the links are still evident when the page is printed. The following code shows the `attr()` function in action:

```
@media print {
    a:after {
        content: attr(href);
    }
}
```

Additionally, for a friendlier format, you can combine this function with string values as shown here, with Figure 13-9 demonstrating how this would render in a print stylesheet:

```
@media print {
    a:after {
        content: " ("attr(href)")";
    }
}
```

This is a paragraph containing a link.

This is a paragraph containing a link (page.html).

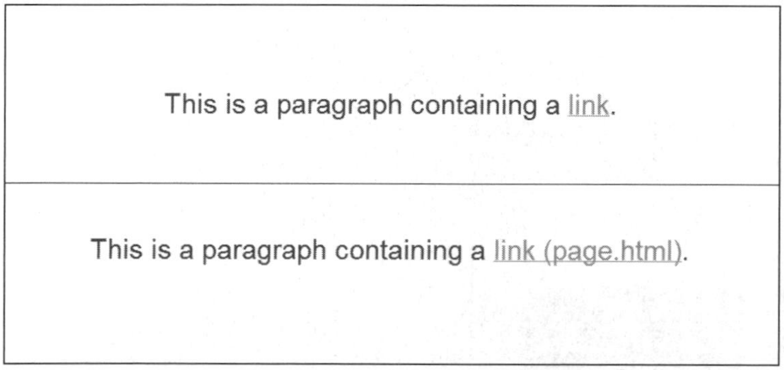

Figure 13-9 The links appear as normal on screen (top), but in print the href value is generated after the a elements (bottom).

Pushing Pseudo-elements to the Limit

Although the `content` property is required for the `:before` and `:after` pseudo-elements to render, it doesn't have to contain a value. Instead, you can simply specify the property with empty quotation marks and style this ghost element as if it were an empty element, but without the drawbacks of having an actual empty element in your markup.

To understand, take a look at the following code and the output in Figure 13-10, which goes some way to outlining the kinds of possibilities these tools create:

HTML
```
<div></div>
```

CSS
```css
div {
    width: 200px;
    height: 200px;
    background: blue;
    position: relative;
    margin: 0 auto;
}

div:before {
    content: "";
    width: 300px;
    height: 300px;
    background: red;
    position: absolute;
    left: -350px;
}

div:after {
    content: "";
    width: 300px;
    height: 300px;
    background: green;
    position: absolute;
    left: 250px;
}
```

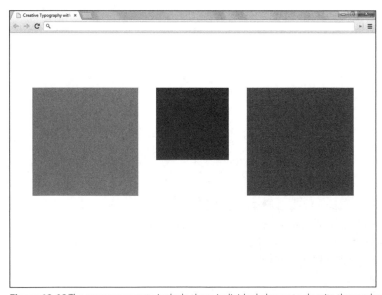

Figure 13-10 The page appears to include three individual elements, despite the markup containing only a solitary div.

As you can see, the markup contains just a single div element; however, the :before and :after pseudo-elements effectively transform this solitary div into three separate elements that can each be styled independently. This capability opens the door to much more complex creativity with CSS without having to add additional presentational markup.

A Contemporary Clearfix

One of the most loathed and frequent occurrences of additional markup to satisfy presentational needs is the infamous *clearfix*, which usually consists of an empty `div` with a class for styling, as shown in the following snippet:

HTML
```html
<div class="clearfix"></div>
```

CSS
```css
.clearfix {
    clear: both;
}
```

This method of clearing floats breaks the core principle of separating content and style as soon as it leaves the stylesheet and enters the markup. Fortunately, the `:after` pseudo element provides the perfect solution for your clearfix woes because it simply generates a faux element after the element that needs clearing, instead of resorting to adding an actual physical element. The following code explains more, with the result clarified in Figure 13-11:

HTML
```html
<div class="container clearfix">
    <div>A floated element</div>
</div>
```

CSS
```css
.container div {
    float: left;
}

.clearfix:after {
    content: "";
    display: block;
    clear: both;
}
```

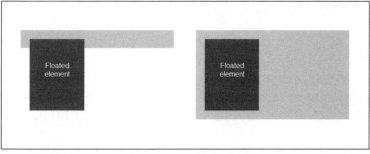

Figure 13-11 The container collapses (left) before the float is cleared using the :after pseudo-element (right).

Creating Scalable Icons and Shapes

Another innovative use of the `:before` and `:after` pseudo-elements is the creation of complex shapes without any additional, nonsemantic markup. Figure 13-12 demonstrates a small collection of the possible shapes and icons that you can create using just a single HTML element.

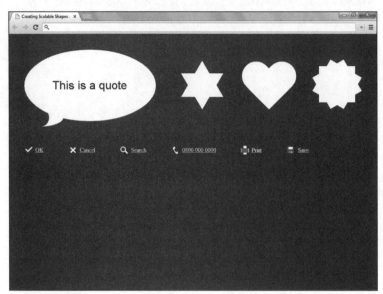

Figure 13-12 A selection of shapes and icons, with each one created using a single HTML element and CSS pseudo-elements

In this section I show you how to create the `blockquote` speech bubble, the OK icon, the print icon, and the save icon; you can find the code for all the others in the demo on the companion website (`1305-scalable-icons.html`).

Creating a Speech Bubble

The first step is to form the main ellipsis shape, which is a nice place to start because it simply uses the `border-radius` property:

HTML
```
<blockquote class="speech-bubble">This is a quote</blockquote>
```

CSS
```
.speech-bubble {
    background: #fff;
    padding: 80px;
    border-radius: 50%;
    display: inline-block;
    position: relative;
}
```

Now comes the challenging part because you need to create the bubble's "tail" and position it appropriately. Of course, this step involves zero modification to the markup, requiring only the introduction of a pseudo-element:

```
.speech-bubble:before {
    content: "";
    width: 50px;
    height: 50px;
    position: absolute;
    bottom: -15px;
    left: -20px;
    border-radius: 50%;
    border-left: 40px solid transparent;
    border-right: 40px solid #fff;
}
```

To understand what's going on in the preceding block of code, look at Figure 13-13, which shows how this pseudo-element would render if the `border-left` and `border-right` colors were both gray (as opposed to the colors specified in the previous code).

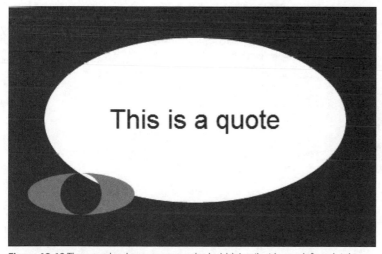

Figure 13-13 The pseudo-element creates the bubble's tail with gray left and right borders to illustrate how it works.

This example should make the way the tail is formed much more apparent. From Figure 13-13, the left border and background colors are changed to transparent, while the right border color (which forms the visible tail) is specified as white to match the main bubble's color.

When this tail is absolutely positioned into place, the job is done!

Creating an OK Icon

Beneath the surface, the OK icon is actually ridiculously simple and easy to implement. To begin, look at the following code, which demonstrates how a single pseudo-element is sufficient to create the check mark shape:

HTML
```
<a class="ok">OK</a>
```

```
CSS
.ok {
    padding-left: 30px;
    position: relative;
    color: #fff;
}

.ok:before {
    content: "";
    position: absolute;
    left: 3px;
    width: 15px;
    height: 7px;
    border-left: 4px solid #fff;
    border-bottom: 4px solid #fff;
    transform: rotate(-45deg);
}
```

As this code suggests, the pseudo-element is simply a transparent, 15×7 pixel rectangle with white borders to the left and bottom. This shape is then rotated 45 degrees counterclockwise, creating the appearance of a check mark. Figure 13-14 illustrates further.

Figure 13-14 A transparent rectangle with white borders (left), which is then rotated (middle) before the top and right borders are removed (right)

Creating a Print Icon

Again, the print icon is deceptively simple, although this icon does require both the :before and :after pseudo-elements to create the aspects of this shape:

```
HTML
<a class="print">Print</a>

CSS
.print {
    padding-left: 30px;
    position: relative;
}

.print:before {
    content: "";
    position: absolute;
    left: 7px;
    top: -2px;
    width: 9px;
    height: 24px;
```

```
        background: #fff;
    }

    .print:after {
        content: "";
        position: absolute;
        left: 0;
        top: 5px;
        width: 19px;
        height: 12px;
        border-left: 2px solid #ddd;
        border-right: 2px solid #ddd;
        background: #777;
    }
```

The first aspect of this icon, formed by the :before pseudo-element, is simply a narrow white column, whereas the second aspect, created by the :after pseudo-element, is simply a gray, horizontal rectangle with slightly lighter-colored left and right borders. Figure 13-15 breaks this down and shows how the icon comes together.

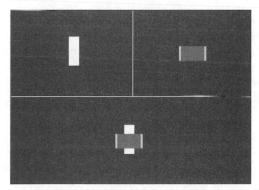

Figure 13-15 First, a white vertical rectangle is created (left), before a gray horizontal rectangle (right) is placed over the middle to create a basic printer shape (bottom).

Creating a Save Icon

Finally, I walk you through the creation of the save icon, which arguably *looks* the most complex of this collection. Again, let's start with the code before breaking it down to see how the icon comes together:

HTML
```
<a class="save">Save</a>
```

CSS
```
.save {
    padding-left: 30px;
    position: relative;
}

.save:before {
    content: "";
```

```
        position: absolute;
        left: 0;
        width: 12px;
        height: 7px;
        background: #fff;
        border-bottom-left-radius: 4px;
        border: 4px solid #125ea5; /* Blue */
        border-top: 1px solid #125ea5; /* Blue */
        border-bottom: 11px solid #125ea5; /* Blue */
    }

    .save:after {
        content: "";
        position: absolute;
        left: 5px;
        bottom: 2px;
        width: 3px;
        height: 4px;
        border-left: 2px solid #ccc;
        border-top: 1px solid #ccc;
        border-right: 5px solid #ccc;
    }
```

As with many of the other examples, this icon showcases a creative use of borders, which allow the shape to give the initial impression that it is made up of more than simply two pseudo-elements. The `:before` pseudo-element creates the small white rectangle and applies blue borders to form the main part of the floppy-disk icon; the `:after` pseudo-element then creates a small transparent rectangle, which uses gray borders and sits at the bottom of the icon. Figure 13-16 illustrates this effect visually.

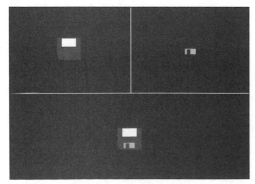

Figure 13-16 The first pseudo-element is a white rectangle with blue borders (left), and the second pseudo-element is a transparent rectangle with gray borders (right).

These shapes and icons use various CSS3 techniques to push pseudo-elements to their current limits, and it's a wonderfully creative and innovative use of these tools. However, this use is currently highly experimental and relies on support for various CSS3 functionalities such as the `transform` property, so they are not to be thrown straight into production sites. Furthermore, don't move heaven and earth simply to avoid using an image; if it's the easiest option and is the only way to guarantee complete browser support, go ahead and use an image.

Pushing the Limits Even Further and Knowing When to Stop

You can push and expand even further on the techniques described here to create truly mind-blowing outputs. Figure 13-17 showcases famous logos that have also been created using CSS3 and pseudo-elements, although they cannot claim to utilize only semantic markup. You can analyze and dissect these examples at the following link: `http://www.tangledindesign.com/blog/tag/famous-logos-in-css3/`.

Figure 13-17 Famous logos re-created using CSS3 and pseudo-elements

I certainly encourage you to conduct similar experimentations and exercises with the capabilities of CSS3, as I learned a huge amount from my own practice, but make sure you use them only as a learning tool and aren't tempted to throw them into "real-world" situations. Although these examples clearly showcase the power that CSS is now able to yield, you need to ensure that your creative talents do not run out in front of your rational thinking.

A logo is an image, and it should always be an image. I think it's inarguably awesome that CSS is now capable of replicating It, but CSS is not the appropriate tool for rendering a logo.

Summary

Although pseudo-elements aren't new to CSS3, their uses are completely dependent on the capabilities of CSS as a whole. As CSS has advanced by staggering amounts, pseudo-elements have thus become much more powerful than they were when first introduced.

The `:first-line` and `:first-letter` pseudo-elements can be used to subtly enhance blocks of text, allowing you to ease readers into your copy through attractive and inviting styling. These elements can also be used much more creatively to assist with implementing heavily designed typography without having to resort to images or nonsemantic markup.

The `:before` and `:after` pseudo-elements allow for much more complex styling without the drawback of presentational markup. For example, with a bit of imagination, you can create any number of shapes and icons using only a single, semantic element, potentially making developers less dependent on images in the not-too-distant future.

However, you must always remember that just because you *can* create almost any shape that comes to mind with the help of pseudo-elements, this doesn't mean you *should*. If it's easier and more sensible to use an image, then use an image!

Further Reading

Pseudo-elements in the CSS Level 3 Selectors Specification
`http://www.w3.org/TR/css3-selectors/#pseudo-elements`

An introduction to CSS pseudo-element hacks
`http://nicolasgallagher.com/an-introduction-to-css-pseudo-element-hacks/`

Chapter 14

Using Preprocessors to Push CSS3 to the Limit

CSS is renown for its simplicity and low entry barrier, offering a relatively gentle learning curve as far as the basics are concerned. However, this level of simplicity is a result of trade-offs in terms of scope and functionality, the frustrations from which are all too familiar to experienced web designers. A common example of a feature from the wish lists of front-end developers is the capability to specify variables, the benefits of which are evident if you're familiar with programming languages such as PHP; if you're not, sit tight because I discuss their uses further into the chapter.

Variables are actually being introduced to native CSS and are currently at the working draft stage of development (you can read more details on CSS variables in Chapter 16), but in the meantime, you can tackle the need to specify variables with the help of *CSS preprocessors*.

As well as variables, CSS preprocessors address a whole host of other limitations and restrictions imposed by standard CSS, and provide a method of writing stylesheets with all the flexibility and functionality you've ever dreamed of (and a whole lot more)! And they do all this before processing the code into a standard CSS stylesheet that browsers can recognize and deal with as normal.

This chapter addresses what exactly preprocessors are and why they exist before exploring some of the more popular preprocessors around in terms of what they're capable of and their syntaxes. I then demonstrate how you can use them to push CSS3 to the limits and simply make your life easier.

From making effortless wholesale changes with variables to reusing entire chunks of code with mixins, CSS preprocessors come packed full of features that are of great use to front-end developers.

What Is a CSS Preprocessor?

A CSS preprocessor is an alternative method of writing a stylesheet and uses its own associated coding syntax, rather than CSS, to afford significant amounts of additional functionality, before processing this code into a standard `.css` file that browsers can work with.

The obvious benefit is that these preprocessed languages can ultimately offer whatever syntax and functionality they like, as long as they can be processed into a standard `.css` stylesheet afterward; this, therefore, allows them to offer functionality that would otherwise be inaccessible using standard CSS.

What Can CSS Preprocessors Do for You?

A minority of developers still question the need for preprocessors, but the fact that they exist at all and have such a large user base suggests that they certainly have a place in CSS development today. Some of the defiant few are undoubtedly struck with fear and intimidation at the word *preprocessor,* but others raise legitimate concerns, such as blogger Miller Medeiros, who eloquently discusses the potential pitfalls on his website (`http://blog.millermedeiros.com/the-problem-with-css-pre-processors/`).

However, an overwhelming amount of support exists for CSS preprocessors, which speaks volumes about their usefulness in a world that is so wary of change, particularly when it involves something as fundamental as writing CSS.

So *why* are preprocessors needed? The last few years have seen a growing emphasis applied to modular, scalable, and DRY (for *don't repeat yourself*) CSS concepts, encouraging the abstraction of reusable styles into chunks that can be called on where required. With variables and, more notably, *mixins*, CSS preprocessors tie in with this ideology perfectly and ensure that modular CSS development is an absolute breeze.

Another way in which the web has experienced a slight transition is the shift toward proportional layouts that rely on base values to calculate widths, font sizes, and line heights that are all relative to each other. Again, preprocessors make this proportional process far simpler than it could ever be with standard CSS. For example, you could quite feasibly set up your stylesheet to calculate all sorts of values automatically based on one specified base value.

So you know what preprocessors aim to achieve and you know why they're here. Next, what preprocessing options do you have to choose from?

Choosing the Right Preprocessor for You

A number of CSS preprocessing options are available, but the two main players are LESS and Sass, with Stylus following in a distant but outright third place (see Figure 14-1). I discuss LESS and Sass in this section before continuing with the latter throughout the rest of the chapter.

The two leaders are not very different in terms of functionality or syntax, which has, in turn, made the choice of which to use ever more challenging. Subsequently, usage stats are also evenly matched, with support coming from all angles for both LESS and Sass. A very general opinion that I have garnered from a bird's-eye view on the subject is that LESS is perhaps more inviting for first-timers with a slightly lower entry barrier, whereas Sass may hold slightly more power overall. Ultimately, however, the choice simply comes down to personal preference. Study the differences and make your own informed decision.

One of the main reasons why LESS is sometimes perceived as the easier option is that it uses the exact same syntax as standard CSS; it is simply an extension of the basic language, adding many more functionalities and possibilities.

Sass, on the other hand, began life a little differently, offering a leaner syntax without the extraneous features of standard CSS such as brackets and semicolons; this is called the *indented syntax* and uses the `.sass` file type. This more concise method totally makes sense to me and is hardly a drastic difference from CSS syntax, but the perceived gap between this method and standard CSS was enough to make people favor LESS. As a result, Sass released a new, additional syntax that reintroduced the brackets and semicolons to more closely resemble standard CSS and bring the entry barrier that bit lower. This newer syntax uses the `.scss` file type, which stands for *Sassy CSS,* and has grown to be the more popular of the two Sass syntaxes by a considerable amount (see Figure 14-2).

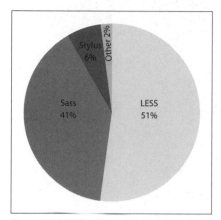

Figure 14-1 LESS and Sass lead the way with Stylus topping the list of less popular alternatives (statistics from css-tricks.com)

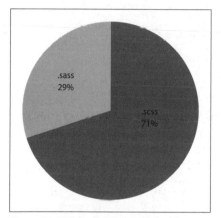

Figure 14-2 Of the two Sass syntaxes, the .scss syntax is considerably more popular than the .sass syntax (statistics via css-tricks.com).

To help you really understand the various syntaxes, the following sections go through the basic functionalities of preprocessors and show you how each syntax handles them.

Declaring Variables

One of the most basic and sought-after functionalities boasted by preprocessors is the capability to declare variables. Variables are a pivotal part of scripting languages such as PHP and JavaScript and have long been billed as a highly appropriate addition to CSS. They are indeed on their way to native CSS (see Chapter 16 for more details), but for now, they remain as one of the biggest draws for preprocessors.

Variables are extremely simple to implement, as shown by the following code, which demonstrates how each of the previously discussed preprocessor syntaxes handle them, and how this code is compiled into real CSS.

LESS
```
@baseColor: #0367a0;

header {
    background: @baseColor;
}
```

Sass (.sass and .scss)
```
/* .sass */
$baseColor: #0367a0;

header
    background: $baseColor


/* .scss */
$baseColor: #0367a0;

header {
    background: $baseColor;
}
```

CSS Output
```
header {
    background: #0367a0;
}
```

As you can see, the LESS syntax uses the @ sign to specify variables, whereas Sass uses the dollar sign ($), which should feel very natural if you've ever worked with variables in PHP. To offer my personal viewpoint on these differences, I much prefer Sass's dollar sign syntax because it has no predefined meaning in CSS, whereas LESS's @ sign is a potential cause for confusion because this symbol is also used in CSS to define keyframe rule-sets and media queries.

Doing Functions and Simple Math

Preprocessors allow you to do a lot more with variables than simply make global changes with ease. Using an extensive list of functions and basic math operations, you can calculate values throughout your stylesheet that are relative to your base values. Look at the following example to understand how these operations are handled by LESS and Sass.

> For simplicity, rather than describing both Sass syntaxes for each example, I continue with just the younger and more widely used .scss syntax.

LESS
```
@baseColor: #0367a0;
@padding: 20px;

.main-content {
    background: lighten(@baseColor, 50%);
```

```
        padding-right: (@padding / 2);
}
```

Sass
```
$baseColor: #0367a0;
$padding: 20px;

.main-content {
    background: lighten($baseColor, 50%);
    padding-right: $padding / 2;
}
```

CSS Output
```
.main-content {
    background: #a5ddfd;
    padding-right: 10px;
}
```

The preceding code illustrates the ease with which you are able to develop complex and varied color palettes based on a single main color. In this particular example, the `lighten()` function takes the `$baseColor` variable and makes it lighter by a strength of 50%. A vast range of additional color functions such as `darken()`, `saturate()`, and `hue()` allows you to develop your color palette much further. In terms of the two syntaxes, they both handle functions in the same way, although they each have their own list of functions that they support.

The math operation that takes place in the preceding example uses the initial `$padding` variable and divides it by two in order to get the appropriate result. This is a basic example, but you get the idea; you can also use the +, -, and * operators, too, which enables you to add, subtract, and multiply, respectively.

In terms of the syntax for math operations and functions, the only difference between the two is that LESS encloses math operations in parentheses.

Using Mixins

One of the most powerful features of CSS preprocessors—and one of their biggest draws—is *mixins*. This feature is like an advanced variable in that it allows you to set aside entire rule-sets that you can reuse again and again wherever appropriate, simply by referencing the mixin's name. These mixins can also take *arguments* that allow you to manipulate the values within the mixin from their defaults whenever this mixin is called on. LESS and Sass handle this feature rather differently, as the following code suggests:

LESS
```
.block-item(@bg: #fff) {
    width: 100%;
    float: left;
    background: @bg;
}

.main-content {
    .block-item(#eee);
}
```

Sass

```
@mixin block-item($bg: #fff) {
    width: 100%;
    float: left;
    background: $bg;
}

.main-content {
    @include block-item(#eee);
}
```

CSS Output

```
.main-content {
    width: 100%;
    float: left;
    background: #eeeeee;
}
```

You can see that these reusable styles are abstracted into a mixin that can be referenced whenever these styles are required. Also included is an optional argument that, in this example, allows you to set a variable for the default `background` value, which can then be adjusted when the mixin is called to another particular rule-set. In this example, the default `background` value is set to `#fff`, which is changed to `#eeeeee` when the mixin is called within the `.main-content` rule-set.

Using LESS, you define a mixin simply by using a class selector within which you can add your styles, just as if you were writing standard CSS. This class selector is then included within other rule-sets as if it were a property, to include all the rules it contains.

Sass does things a little differently, because it uses the `@mixin` rule to explicitly define the rule-set as a mixin before assigning a name and specifying optional arguments. This chunk of code is then called on within other rule-sets using the `@include` rule and by referencing the specific name of the mixin.

Sass's `@mixin` rule is a little more capable than LESS's simple class selector method because just as with other @ rules in CSS, you can add multiple selectors and rule-sets within it, not just one set of properties and values.

The purpose of this basic example is to help you grasp the concept of what mixins are and what they can do. I show more of what they're capable of later in the chapter.

Selector Inheritance

The selector inheritance feature is unique to Sass, but the way it is implemented is similar to the way in which LESS's mixins work. What this particular feature does is allow you to reuse existing rule-sets within other rule-sets; however, rather than simply duplicating the styles, Sass actually rewrites your selectors when it compiles to standard CSS to avoid unnecessary repetition of CSS and inevitable bloat. The following code illustrates further:

Sass

```
.quote {
    font: italic 1.3em Georgia;
    color: fff;
    background: #333;
}
```

```
.quote-important {
    @extend .quote;
    border-top: 1px dotted #ccc;
    border-bottom: 1px dotted #ccc;
}
```

CSS Output
```
.quote, .quote-important {
    font: italic 1.3em Georgia;
    color: #fff;
    background: #333;
}

.quote-important {
    border-top: 1px dotted #ccc;
    border-bottom: 1px dotted #ccc;
}
```

As is apparent, styles from the .quote rule-set are included in the .quote-important rule-set using the @ extend keyword; however, rather than simply duplicating these styles, the selectors are grouped together so you specify the styles only once. The process is effortless, yet the output is wonderfully efficient!

Nested Selectors

Quite often in stylesheets, you see repetitive selectors as you target elements deeper into your source. The following code shows a standard and common example of this:

```
nav { /* styles */ }
nav ul { /* styles */ }
nav ul li { /* styles */ }
nav ul li a { /* styles */ }
nav ul li a:hover { /* styles */ }
```

This code has a lot of repetition, with the nav, for example, targeted in each of the four selectors. CSS preprocessors eliminate this inefficient requirement of standard CSS because they allow *nested* selectors, as shown by the following code. Both LESS and Sass handle nested selectors in the same way.

```
nav {
    /* styles */
    ul {
        /* styles */
        li {
            /* styles */
            a {
                /* styles */
                &:hover {
                    /* styles */
                }
            }
        }
    }
}
```

This example provides a more logical and less repetitive way of writing your CSS selectors, while ensuring that the outputted CSS is still as it should be. Notice also the & symbol, which, when used in a selector, targets its parent; this use is ideal for using pseudo-classes within nested rule-sets. In this particular example, the immediate parent is the a selector, so a :hover pseudo-class is applied to this selector.

Here, the previously discussed .sass syntax has a big advantage over the .scss version (and LESS), because although the brackets help to maintain a clear structure, keeping track of them can become more and more difficult as you go deeper and deeper. The following code demonstrates how the .sass syntax would handle the previous example:

```
nav
    /* styles */
    ul
        /* styles */
        li
            /* styles */
            a
                /* styles */
                &:hover
                    /* styles */
```

You may have your own preference, but visually, I find this approach a lot simpler, a lot more readable, and much easier to maintain.

All the examples discussed so far aim to ease you into the world of preprocessing, but these functionalities have much greater and much more advanced uses, especially in terms of utilizing the new CSS3 features to their full potential. Stay tuned for more on this topic, but first, I want to address the elephant in the room, which is the dreaded installation process that you must endure to use CSS preprocessors.

As I mentioned previously, I continue the chapter using only Sass. There isn't much to choosing between the two main options, but my personal preference leans toward Sass due to minor differences such as more powerful mixins, the @extend feature, and the fact that variables are defined using the $ sign rather than the @ symbol, which already has meaning in standard CSS.

If you prefer the look of LESS, you can find everything you need to install and use it at http://lesscss.org/.

Getting to Grips with the Dark Side of Preprocessors

When a web designer finally bites the bullet and decides to get on the preprocessor hype, one of the biggest barriers that stands in the way is the installation process, which is completely alien and downright terrifying to the majority of web designers.

Sass is built in the Ruby programming language and can be run through the Command Prompt (CMD), or Terminal on a Mac.

You're probably frozen with fear at the mention of Ruby and CMD/Terminal, which are worlds away from the skill set of the average web designer! And now you're expected to use them to be able to write a simple CSS stylesheet? I must be joking, right?

I have to admit, when I first read up on preprocessors and realized what I had to go through to use one, I was intimidated, so I ignored them for a while in the hope that they'd soon fizzle out. They haven't—nor have they shown any signs of doing so.

I soon got over the scary words and decided it was time to get my hands dirty. Sure enough, I had to install Ruby and open the Command Prompt, through which I installed and ran Sass. I was pleasantly surprised at how easy this process was. As ever, when you take the time to understand it, there's really nothing to it.

In the following sections, I quickly run you through the setup process for both Windows and Mac machines.

Step 1: Installing Ruby

The first step is to install Ruby. Macs have this installed by default, so if you're in this camp, feel free to take a break and rejoin the action in a couple of paragraphs.

Windows users can simply go to the Ruby Installer website (`http://rubyinstaller.org/`), where you can download the latest version. Simply run through the installation process, click the Start menu button, and select Start Command Prompt with Ruby, as shown in Figure 14-3.

Now you should be looking at the dreaded Command Prompt window (CMD). Time for Mac users to start paying attention again, too; you need to open Terminal.

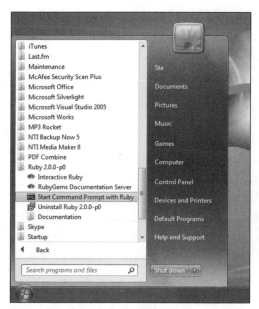

Figure 14-3 After Ruby is installed, click Start Command Prompt with Ruby.

Step 2: Installing Sass

The next stage is to install the Sass gem via CMD/Terminal. To do this, simply type the following line of code into your window and press Enter:

Windows (CMD)
```
gem install sass
```

Mac (Terminal)
```
sudo gem install sass
```

Allow 10 seconds or so for the command to be carried out, and then your successful installation of Sass is confirmed, as shown in Figure 14-4.

Step 3: Creating Your First Sass File

Now you need to create a Sass file. I used the `.scss` syntax, so my file is called `style.scss`. Remember, this file is processed into a standard `.css` stylesheet, so it is referenced in the `<head>` of the HTML as normal.

HTML
```
<link rel="stylesheet" type="text/css" href="style.css">
```

SCSS
```
$color: blue;
p {
    color: $color;
}
```

Figure 14-4 Sass has been successfully installed!

Save this file wherever you like, but you'll need to make sure you know exactly where it is to complete the next step.

Now that everything is set up, you need to tell the CMD/Terminal where your .scss file is and specify a standard .css file that will be automatically generated to contain the compiled CSS. You don't need to create the standard .css file yourself; this is automatically created for you in the next step.

Step 4: Compiling Your Sass Code

To make things easier, you can use the cd (change directory) command to locate the directory that contains your .scss file, as shown in Figure 14-5. To keep things simple, I saved my HTML file and .scss file to my desktop.

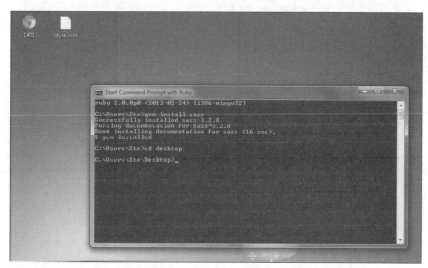

Figure 14-5 I am now operating within the desktop folder in the CMD, which is where my .scss file is located.

If you skip the optional cd command step, you will need to include the full file paths when referencing the .scss and .css files in the next part.

Now you need to tell Sass to *watch* the style.scss file so that as soon as any changes are made to this file, they are automatically compiled into a standard CSS file called style.css. The following code shows how this is done, with Figure 14-6 illustrating how this should look in CMD. Remember, I'm now working within the appropriate folder (my desktop in this case), so I don't need to worry about including the paths before the filenames in this command.

```
sass --watch style.scss:style.css
```

The CMD then reports that "Sass is watching for changes"—and that's it; you're all set to go! Whenever you make any more changes to the style.scss file, the code is automatically compiled into the standard style.css stylesheet.

I hope you agree that the Ruby/CMD approach is far less painful than it initially appears. If you don't, fear not, as there are several tools to help you out.

Figure 14-6 Tell Sass to watch the .scss file for any changes and then compile this code into a standard .css file (which has been automatically generated).

Helpful Tools

That's right—there are apps that do all this work for you, so in theory, you never need to go anywhere near CMD or Terminal. Despite this fact, I want to dispel the widespread misconception that the CMD installation process is dark, scary, and no place for your everyday web designer. In fact, you use just a couple of easy-to-understand commands, and you're away. For me, this is a simpler approach than using an app to do the job, but each to his own, so here's a list of tools that will help you out:

- **Scout** (`http://mhs.github.io/scout-app/`) is the best free option and is available for both Windows and Mac. It runs Sass in a self-contained Ruby environment, allowing you to avoid the Ruby and CMD setup process; instead, you can manage your Sass-based projects with just a few clicks!

- **CodeKit** (`http://incident57.com/codekit/`) is a reasonably priced option for Mac users and works with both Sass and LESS (as well as many other preprocessors). It combines a range of useful functionalities, such as image optimization and live browser reload, with a beautiful user interface to produce a real "wow" factor.

- **LiveReload** (`http://livereload.com/`) is a cheaper alternative that is available for both Mac *and* Windows, and again, it works with both LESS and Sass. As soon as you make changes to your Sass/LESS stylesheet, your code is compiled into a CSS file, and the browser automatically refreshes to display the changes!

- **Compass.app** (`http://compass.handlino.com/`) is another cheap option for both Windows and Mac users and serves the Sass preprocessor. It eliminates the need to install Ruby or open the CMD/Terminal, allowing effortless compiling of Sass into CSS.

This last tool is based on a Sass framework called Compass (`http://compass-style.org/`) that harnesses the power of Sass perfectly, offering a vast range of reusable code patterns and ready-made mixins that make implementation of certain CSS3 features a breeze. If you're serious about working with Sass, it's definitely worth a closer look. In the next section, I show how you can use these kinds of mixins to reduce the inevitable bloat when using experimental CSS3.

Making CSS3 More Efficient with Mixins

As you likely gathered from previous chapters, vendor prefixes are currently required to allow most of the experimental CSS3 features to work in all major browsers. This process can soon become tremendously tedious and ensures that your code is far more repetitive and swollen than it should be, which often leads you to question whether a CSS3 feature is really worth all the extra bytes.

Consider the following block of code, for instance, which includes each prefix required for a CSS transition to work in all major browsers (including older versions):

```
a {
    -webkit-transition: color 1s ease-in-out .5s;
    -moz-transition: color 1s ease-in-out .5s;
    -o-transition: color 1s ease-in-out .5s;
    transition: color 1s ease-in-out .5s;
}
```

> To remind you of the shorthand syntax for the `transition` property, the parameters in the preceding example stand for the `transition-property`, `transition-duration`, `transition-timing-function`, and `transition-delay` values (in that order).

The same line of code is repeated no less than four times, which makes cross-browser transitions an absolute nightmare to implement and maintain. Many CSS3 features would also require the `-ms-` prefix, so this scenario can be even worse.

Fortunately, CSS preprocessors eliminate this issue with the help of mixins because they allow you to specify all the prefixed transition properties only once and then enable you to simply `@include` them as required. Now look at the following code and revel in the ease of applying experimental CSS3 with Sass:

```
@mixin transition($property, $duration, $timing, $delay) {
    -webkit-transition: $property $duration $timing $delay;
    -moz-transition: $property $duration $timing $delay;
    -o-transition: $property $duration $timing $delay;
    transition: $property $duration $timing $delay;
}

a {
    @include transition(color, 1s, ease-in-out, .5s);
}
```

The prefixed transition properties are relocated to a mixin that has been aptly named `transition`, and their parameters are replaced by variables. The mixin also includes arguments that allow you to define the variable values when the mixin is later included. For example, the mixin is included in the `a` selector where the variable values can then be specified within parentheses, in the order they appear in the mixin.

This approach means that the bulk of the work is done in one fell swoop, and each time you want to add a transition to another element, you can simply `@include` the transition mixin rather than tediously add another prefix-ridden chunk of code!

This approach is already a much tidier and more effortless method of implementing a CSS3 feature that requires several vendor prefixes to work across all browsers, but you can push this method even further to really maximize the efficiency of your stylesheets.

For example, the flaw in this method as it stands currently is that you must declare values for each of the four variables whenever the mixin is included. You may remember that the only *required* transition parameter is the duration value, so on several occasions you may not need or want values for the other three parameters. With the mixin arguments written as they are in the preceding example, you must specify values for *all* the variables, which obviously isn't ideal.

To correct this situation, you can give the mixin arguments default values so that when the mixin is included, you need to specify variable values only when you want to change them from their default values. The following code should explain further.

Sass
```
@mixin transition($property: null, $duration: .4s, $timing: null,
                  $delay: null) {
    -webkit-transition: $property $duration $timing $delay;
    -moz-transition: $property $duration $timing $delay;
    -o-transition: $property $duration $timing $delay;
    transition: $property $duration $timing $delay;
}

a { @include transition; }

.cta { @include transition($duration: 2s, $timing: linear); }
```

CSS Output
```
.a {
    /* prefixed versions */
    transition: .4s;
}

.cta {
    /* prefixed versions */
    transition: 2s linear;
}
```

Now the mixin's arguments have default values, which are defined as `null` for the nonrequired parameters. Defining these default values ensures that these parameters default to their initial values unless otherwise specified when the mixin is later included. For example, in the `.cta` rule-set, the transition mixin is included, and the duration and timing-function variables are altered from their default values.

It's clearly evident how much easier and less painful this technique makes it to apply experimental CSS3 features that require several vendor prefixes.

Creating Proportional Layouts with Simple Math

You might recall that I discussed proportional and fluid layouts in depth throughout Part III of this book, but with preprocessors, these layouts can become wonderfully easy to maintain and amend, thanks to the dynamic nature of preprocessed code.

Next, I demonstrate how easy Sass can make it to control the width of your layout items when elements of the design are forced to change, as they so often do. The use of variables and basic math operations, two of the most basic preprocessor features, makes this process an absolute cinch.

Consider that you are coding a row of equal-width buckets that span the full width of your site. The following example shows you how the width of these buckets can be automatically calculated from a few base values:

Sass
```
$siteWidth: 100%;
$baseMargin: 2%;
$bucketItems: 4;

.buckets {
    width: $siteWidth;
}

.buckets div {
    width: $siteWidth / $bucketItems - $baseMargin;
    margin: 0 $baseMargin / 2;
    float: left;
}
```

CSS Output
```
.buckets {
    width: 100%;
}

.buckets div {
    width: 23%;
    margin: 0 1%;
    float: left;
}
```

So, all you need to set up this technique is a few variables that you can reuse throughout your stylesheet where needed. You work out the available space for each bucket item by dividing the overall site width by the number of buckets in the design. In this case, the available space would be 25 percent for each of the four buckets. Then you subtract the amount of room needed for the margins between the buckets using the base margin variable. This latter value is then, of course, applied as left and right margins for each bucket item.

As is apparent, this process is fairly simple, which means that whenever your layout is forced to change in terms of its overall width or if you need to add in extra buckets, everything is calculated automatically, meaning any future changes are as simple as altering one or two variable values.

Using Functions to Form a Dynamic Color Palette

The final example I want to walk you through involves variables and color functions. Again, the following example shows you how specifying a base value and working relatively from that value can make your life that bit easier.

A site design often has a leading color, from which the rest of the color palette is formed, whether they are different shades or hues, or are complementary. Preprocessors have a vast range of color functions that allow you to manipulate your leading color in whatever way you need to, without having to memorize a tireless list of hex codes. The following code block provides some inspiration as to how these color functions could be used:

Sass
```scss
$baseColor: #0367a0;

body {
    background: linear-gradient(lighten($baseColor, 60%), $baseColor);
}

nav {
    background: $baseColor;
    border: 5px solid complement($baseColor);
}

nav a { color: invert($baseColor); }

.bucket { background: desaturate($baseColor, 75%); }
.bucket:hover { background: $baseColor; }
```

CSS Output
```css
body {
    background: linear-gradient(#d7f0fe, #0367a0);
}

nav {
    background: #0367a0;
    border: 5px solid #a03c03;
}

nav a { color: #fc985f; }

.bucket { background: #405663; }
.bucket:hover { background: #0367a0; }
```

These are just a few examples to show how effortless it can be to create an entire color palette from just a single base color without having to memorize those forgettable hex codes. In theory, this technique also allows you to adjust the entire color scheme of a design by editing just a single variable value!

A Word of Caution on Preprocessors

The web industry has by no means accepted preprocessors unanimously, and many developers will no doubt remain defiant. I described some very useful functionalities and solutions that preprocessors provide you with, but despite this, they are unlikely to ever displace standard CSS entirely.

To ensure that preprocessors are used wisely, you need a deep understanding of CSS as a foundation; you must have a high level of skill and understanding of plain old CSS before you can use preprocessors properly. If you don't have this fundamental knowledge, preprocessors are easy to misuse, which could result in a sloppy final output that is far from what the code would have been if it were handcrafted.

Another issue commonly raised by those who are wary of preprocessors is the matter of working in teams. When multiple developers are working on one project with each adding bits and pieces to the CSS, everyone on the team needs to be on board with the same preprocessor and be able to use it effectively; otherwise, it would be more likely to harm the team's efficiency rather than assist it.

Summary

Preprocessors provide all the additional functionality you likely ever dreamed of, allowing you to write dynamic and efficient stylesheets that are easy to maintain and that make wholesale changes a breeze.

You have two main preprocessing options to choose from, LESS and Sass, with very little to separate the two, which has resulted in a very even market share. My opinion is that Sass's features are slightly more intuitive, although it really comes down to personal preference.

A vast range of new features is available to help you take CSS to the next level, from variables and functions to mixins and nested selectors. The initial stumbling block for most people is the installation process, which involves installing Ruby and using the Command Prompt/Terminal to run the preprocessor; however, I showed in this chapter that this process is not nearly as scary as it first comes across.

With all things considered, preprocessors can be extremely powerful and easily allow you to make the best of what CSS3 has to offer, but always be wary of who else will work on your project and whether those users will be able to work with preprocessed code as well.

Further Reading

Sass Documentation
`http://sass-lang.com/docs/yardoc/file.SASS_REFERENCE.html`

LESS Documentation
`http://lesscss.org/#docs`

Musings on CSS Preprocessing
`http://css-tricks.com/musings-on-preprocessing/`

Popularity of CSS Preprocessors
http://css-tricks.com/poll-results-popularity-of-css-preprocessors/

The Problem with CSS Preprocessors
http://blog.millermedeiros.com/the-problem-with-css-pre-processors/

Chapter 15

Creating Practical Solutions Using Only CSS3

Throughout this book I've introduced an extensive range of new CSS3 features—some right on the cutting edge and highly experimental, others more mature and already finding a place in the real world. I've explained what they do and how they work individually, but now it's time to bring them all together to showcase their immense power and capabilities and to really maximize their potential.

In this chapter, I show you how to create practical, aesthetically desirable, and *interactive* features that would usually be possible only through use of JavaScript (and plenty of it). Of course, these pure CSS examples show what can you achieve in an ideal world of complete browser support, but in the real world, it's just not yet feasible to implement such functionality with the need to maintain some kind of support for the older, noncompatible browsers. However, while the world waits for the bliss of browser support utopia, these experiments serve as examples that showcase just how far CSS has come and what the future holds for CSS development.

So, as I alluded to previously, you should now be well versed on the theory, but this chapter is all about the practical because it walks you through the creation of three common interactive elements that typically run on JavaScript, using only HTML and CSS3. The first of these examples is relatively simple as I describe how to create tabbed content. The second is more substantial as I walk you through the creation of a pure CSS *lightbox* feature. To finish, I crank up the "wow" factor as I explain the process of creating an animated, 3D image carousel!

> If you're unfamiliar with the term *lightbox,* it is simply a common way to refer to the technique of displaying particular content in a focused modal window, with everything "underneath" this window often blurred out to emphasize this focus on the modal content. In this case, lightbox refers to a gallery that allows you to cycle through full-size images without having to leave the current page.

Creating Tabbed Content Using Only CSS3

I start things off with a fairly basic example using a concept that I introduced in the first chapter and have revisited a couple of times since. This example involves triggering actions and style alterations on click, and is achieved through creative use of HTML radio buttons and the `:checked` pseudo-class. I show you how to use this technique to create tabbed content that would generally be achievable only through use of JavaScript. The general process is outlined in the following list, with the remainder of this section explaining each stage in detail. You can see the final result in Figure 15-1 and the working example (`1501-tabbed-content.html`) on the companion website at `www.wiley.com/go/ptl/css3`.

1. The first stage is to mark up the content using semantic HTML as well as the tab buttons.

2. The tabbed content panels are styled so that they sit on top of each other and are ready to be toggled in and out of view.

3. The radio buttons are styled to look like tabs rather than check boxes using a bit of creative CSS.

4. The next stage is where the magic happens, as the `:checked` pseudo-class is used to show the appropriate content when the corresponding tab has been clicked.

5. Finally, you can apply the final niceties through the use of other CSS3 features such as transitions and opacity.

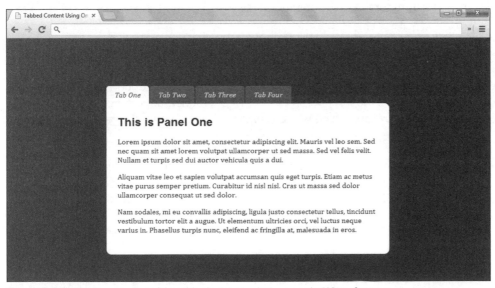

Figure 15-1 The final appearance of the tabbed content, which uses only CSS3 to function

The Markup

Unsurprisingly, you need to start with some content, which, of course, involves some HTML. The content is divided into four panels, which are marked up sensibly with semantics in mind, resulting in a relatively minimal amount of markup ready to be sparked into life by some creative CSS3. The following code block shows the markup you have to work with:

```
<article class="tabs">
    <div class="panels">

        <div class="panel">
            <h2>This is Panel One</h2>
```

```
            <p>...</p>
            <p>...</p>
        </div>

        <!-- .panel x4 -->

    </div>
</article>
```

> Don't be thrown by the use of the `article` element to contain this feature. The HTML5 specification allows you to use this element for *any* standalone content that still has meaning when abstracted from its surroundings, which is certainly the case here. The spec also explicitly states that the `article` element can be used for interactive widget features.

With the panels added, this feature is just lacking some tabs—a vital ingredient of creating tabbed content! At this point, of course, things get a little less semantic and a touch more creative, as the tabs are formed through the use of radio button `input` elements, which can either be checked or unchecked, opening many doors for the creative developer.

The catch is that `input` elements on their own do not suffice to make this technique visually satisfying because radio buttons are extremely rigid in terms of styling. Fortunately, HTML provides a convenient solution in the form of the `label` element. This element has total freedom in terms of styling, and most importantly, it can be coupled with an `input` element, allowing it to be clicked on behalf of the radio button. The following code should illustrate further:

```
<article class="tabs">
    <div class="panels">

        <input id="one" name="tabs" type="radio">
        <label for="one">Tab One</label>

        <input id="two" name="tabs" type="radio">
        <label for="two">Tab Two</label>

        <input id="three" name="tabs" type="radio">
        <label for="three">Tab Three</label>

        <input id="four" name="tabs" type="radio">
        <label for="four">Tab Four</label>

        <!-- .panel elements -->

    </div>
</article>
```

First, each `input` element is given a `type` value of `radio` and a matching `name` value of `tabs` to ensure that they are all part of the same group of radio buttons, meaning only one of these buttons can be "checked" at any one time.

Now you need to understand how the `input` and `label` pairs are coupled together. You can see that the `input id` value matches the `label` element's `for` value throughout, which ensures that these pairs are associated with each other, allowing the `label` element to be checked on behalf of its associative `input` element.

Your tabbed content is now ready for styling! Figure 15-2 shows how things stand currently with the markup stage completed; you evidently have a long way to go to mold this content into something that resembles interactive tabs!

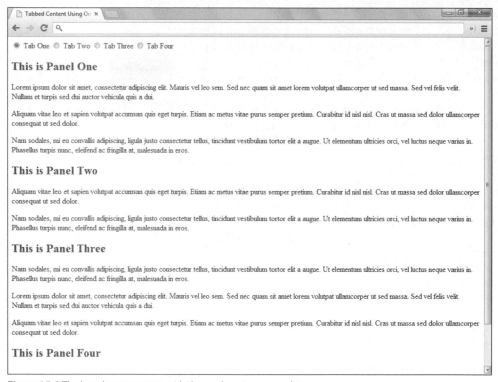

Figure 15-2 The bare-bones content with the markup stage complete

Applying Basic Styling to the Panels

With the panels and tab controls in place in the source, they need some sprucing up and some preparation to become functional.

The main issue to address is the positioning of the panels because they currently flow linearly, one after the other, which is obviously not appropriate for tabbed content. You need to position the panels so that they all lie on top of each other in a pile, which you can easily achieve through absolute positioning. With the addition of some basic, decorative styling, the panels begin to take some shape, as you can see in Figure 15-3, with the following code demonstrating how this effect is achieved:

```
.panel {
    width: 100%;
```

```
    position: absolute;
    background: #fff;
    border-radius: 0 10px 10px 10px;
    padding: 4%;
    box-sizing: border-box;
}
```

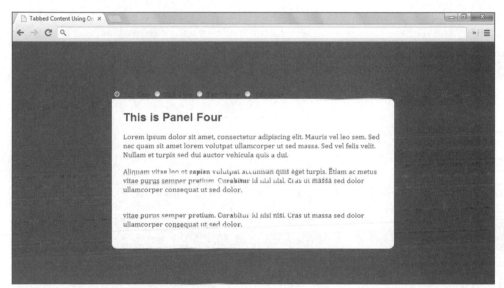

Figure 15-3 The panels now overlie each other and have been styled to resemble tabbed content.

There's nothing too out of the ordinary here. The panels have simply been positioned absolutely to ensure they overlie each other; bear in mind that the `top` and `left` properties do not need to be explicitly defined because they are set to 0 by default. One point to note is the use of the `box-sizing` property and its `border-box` value, which ensures that the `100%` width is inclusive of the `4%` padding, rather than in addition to it as with the normal box model laws. Finally, the `border-radius` of the panels is set to `10px` except for the top left corner, which allows it to line up with the leftmost tab after they have been styled.

Styling the Tabs

As I mentioned previously, to style the tabs, you must target the `label` elements rather than the actual radio `input` elements because the former element type has no restrictions in terms of styling and can also be clicked on behalf of the actual radio buttons.

Additionally, after styling the clickable labels, you still need to ensure that the radio buttons are not visible, which is surprisingly difficult to get right. There are obviously many methods of hiding elements, but they all have their flaws. The traditional `display: none;` method breaks the functionality in Mobile Safari, and the other popular method of positioning the elements offscreen by `-9999px` is rarely a good idea when you consider performance. Another alternative is the `opacity: 0;` method, which leaves the space taken up by the elements intact, but the actual elements themselves are invisible. In this particular instance, this latter method is the most appropriate because the space left by the invisible radio buttons has no visual impact on the design.

The following code shows how the tabs take shape, with Figure 15-4 illustrating the result:

```
input {
    opacity: 0;
}

label {
    cursor: pointer;
    background: linear-gradient(#666, #555);
    color: #eee;
    border-radius: 5px 5px 0 0;
    padding: 1.5% 3%;
    float: left;
    margin-right: 2px;
    font-style: italic;
}
```

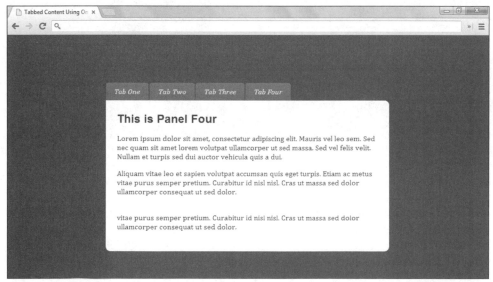

Figure 15-4 The tabs have now also been styled appropriately, nicely rounding off the aesthetic aspect of the tabbed content.

Now the tabbed content is really looking the part. All that's left is to make the tabs functional!

Making the Tabs Functional

To make the tabbed content work as it should, you need to display the appropriate panel based on which tab the user has clicked; for example, panel three needs to be displayed when Tab Three is clicked.

At this point, you can see the hotly anticipated return of Chapter 1 heroes: the general sibling combinator, the `nth-child()` selectors, and, of course, the `:checked` pseudo-class.

First, however, you need to hide the panels by default so that they can be brought into view only when their corresponding tab is clicked. You could use `display: none;` but this property cannot be transitioned as is desirable in this case, so instead you can hide the panels using the `opacity: 0;` method, which allows the panels to fade back into view using a transition.

```
.panel
    opacity: 0;
    /* Other styles */
}
```

With the panels hidden by default, you can then display them when they are triggered by the tabs. To achieve this effect, you need some pretty substantial selectors, as demonstrated by the following code:

```
.tabs input:nth-of-type(1):checked ~ .panels .panel:nth-child(1),
.tabs input:nth-of-type(2):checked ~ .panels .panel:nth-child(2),
.tabs input:nth-of-type(3):checked ~ .panels .panel:nth-child(3),
.tabs input:nth-of-type(4):checked ~ .panels .panel:nth-child(4) {
    opacity: 1;
}
```

These are some seriously long selectors, so let me break them down to really explain how they work. The first step is to select the `input` element when it is in a `:checked` state (after it has been clicked by the user):

```
.tabs input:nth-of-type(2):checked
```

So, this part of the selector targets the second `input` element within the `.tabs` container when it has been checked by the user. Now that you have selected the second `input` element in a `:checked` state, you need to make the corresponding second panel visible; this is possible thanks to the general sibling combinator, as shown in the following code:

```
.tabs input:nth-of-type(2):checked ~ .panels .panel:nth-child(2)
```

Remember, the general sibling combinator targets sibling elements that appear after the originally selected element (the checked radio input) in the source; in this case, you can target the `.panels div` because it is a sibling of the `input` elements and follows them in the source. Now that you've made it this far, you can easily select the appropriate panel and display it using the `:nth-child()` pseudo-class.

The full selector basically translates to "when the second radio input is checked, set the opacity of the second content panel to 1." Pretty simple!

The big issue now is that the panels are all hidden by default, resulting in just a row of tabs until one of them is clicked to display a content panel. Fortunately, this problem is extremely easy to correct because you can simply set one of the radio `input` elements to be checked by default so that one of the panels is displayed initially:

```
<input checked id="one" name="tabs" type="radio">
```

There it is—just the simple keyword `checked` within the `input` tag. Easy! Almost there now; all that's required to finish things off is a bit of TLC!

Applying the Finishing Touches

An integral part of creating tabbed content is applying active states to the tabs so the user knows which tab's content he is currently looking at, making this step essential for usability.

Remember, though, that the tabs are styled through the `label` elements rather than the actual `input` elements, so you can't simply target `input:checked` to apply the active state. Fortunately, CSS has another trick up its sleeve in the form of the adjacent sibling combinator, which targets the sibling that immediately follows an element. You may recall that the markup is structured in such a way that the `input` and `label` elements are coupled together in that order, so you can easily target the `label` element that immediately follows a checked `input` element. The following code explains further, with the result illustrated in Figure 15-5:

```
input:checked + label {
    background: #fff;
    color: #333;
}
```

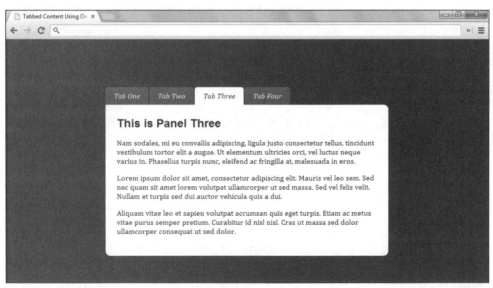

Figure 15-5 The tabs now have an active state to clearly indicate to the user which panel he's currently viewing.

In terms of appearance and functionality, this example doesn't really need to go any further, but I like to apply a bit of subtle enhancement to the interactive aspect of this feature, just to make it that little bit more satisfying to use. This comes in the form of a simple transition.

To avoid the text fading in and out (which doesn't look at all appropriate), you can apply the `transition` property in this instance to the `:checked` state rather than the `.panel` itself. This means the text fades in but not out, allowing a much smoother change between the content.

```
.tabs input:nth-of-type(1):checked ~ .panels .panel:nth-child(1),
.tabs input:nth-of-type(2):checked ~ .panels .panel:nth-child(2),
.tabs input:nth-of-type(3):checked ~ .panels .panel:nth-child(3),
```

```
.tabs input:nth-of-type(4):checked ~ .panels .panel:nth-child(4) {
    opacity: 1;
    transition: .3s;
}
```

And there you have it! Fully functional tabbed content with minimal HTML and just a few lines of extremely maintainable CSS. If you want to dig deeper into the code, don't forget to take a look at the live demo; you can refer back to Figure 15-1 for the final appearance of this feature.

This is a nice and simple way to start things off, showing how you can use a minimal amount of readable CSS3 to replace lines of JavaScript. The next tutorial, however, takes things to the next level.

Creating a Lightbox Feature Using Only CSS3

This example also uses CSS to trigger actions and style changes on click, but this time using a different method that was also first introduced in Chapter 1. This method uses the `:target` pseudo-class, which allows you to apply styles to an element if its `id` value sits at the end of the URL in your address bar. If you're struggling with the concept, don't worry because you'll soon understand as I take you through the tutorial.

The outcome is a fully functional lightbox gallery using, once again, nothing but HTML and CSS3. A rough outline of the process is described in the following list, with each stage discussed in depth throughout this section:

1. Naturally, the first stage involves laying the foundations for the thumbnail gallery markup, which is added further into the tutorial as you introduce some functionality.

2. Next, you play with CSS3's fun side to enhance the aesthetics and interactive satisfaction of the thumbnail gallery.

3. The markup is added for the actual lightbox gallery, which becomes active when the thumbnail images are clicked.

4. The next stage involves making this additional markup behave like a lightbox gallery using some creative CSS3, as well as adding essential navigation controls.

5. Finally, you add some finishing touches in terms of styling.

Figure 15-6 shows the final result in terms of the thumbnail gallery, and Figure 15-7 demonstrates the lightbox in action. Furthermore, as always, you can explore the code by accessing the live demo (`1502-lightbox.html`).

Figure 15-6 The final outcome of the thumbnail gallery—the thumbs have a sepia and grayscale effect applied by default; it is then removed when the images are hovered.

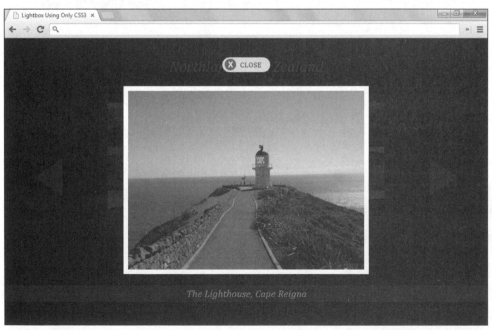

Figure 15-7 When a thumbnail image is clicked, the full-size image is shown in a lightbox window, complete with navigation controls.

Laying the Foundations for the Markup

When you have some images, the first job is to create the image thumbnail gallery, which you can simply mark up using an unordered list.

Usually, when creating a lightbox gallery, you would save thumbnail-sized images and the corresponding full-sized images; but in this instance, you don't really need to save two sets of differing sizes because you can just use some basic CSS to scale down the full-size images to be used as the thumbs. This approach will save you time, and providing your images aren't gargantuan, you may see performance benefits as the full-size images will have already loaded by the time you come to view them.

```
<ul class="gallery">

    <li>
        <a href=""><img src="images/1.jpg" alt="..."></a>
    </li>

    <li>
        <a href=""><img src="images/2.jpg" alt="..."></a>
    </li>

    <!-- etc. -->

</ul>
```

Nothing too drastic here; the images are simply marked up within an unordered list and are surrounded by a tags, which later allow them to link to their full-size counterparts. As you can see from Figure 15-8, the rendering of this code currently resembles nothing like a thumbnail gallery, so it is in desperate need of some CSS-based attention.

Figure 15-8 The "thumbnail" gallery is currently an unstructured list of full-size images.

Styling the Thumbnail Gallery

Now that the basic structure is in place, you can format the list of images to resemble an actual gallery of thumbnail-size images! After applying some basic styling to the page and the `ul` container, you use the `li` elements to form the gallery structure and contain the images to thumbnail proportions:

```css
.gallery {
    max-width: 600px;
    padding: 10px;
    margin: 0 auto;
    border: 1px dashed #ccc;
    background: #666;
    border-radius: 10px;
    box-shadow: 0 0 20px rgba(0, 0, 0, .5);
}

/* Clearfix for the ul container */
.gallery:after {
    content: "";
    display: block;
    clear: both;
}

.gallery li {
    float: left;
    width: 18%;
    margin: 1%;
}

.gallery li > a img {
    max-width: 100%;
}
```

As you can see, the `li` elements have been styled so that they take up 20 percent (including margins) of the container's total 620-pixel width (including padding), allowing for rows of five. The `img` elements within the `a` tags are then given a `max-width` value of `100%` to ensure that they are scaled down to fit into the available space—and just like that, you have a gallery of thumbnail images! Figure 15-9 shows how things currently stand.

You probably can't really tell in a colorless publication such as this, but the thumbnail gallery currently looks a bit bland and uninspiring, which is the perfect excuse to play with some CSS3!

Figure 15-9 The images are now appropriately sized and laid out in a gallery-like structure.

To spruce things up a little, you can apply some filters to the default state of the images and then remove these filters when the thumb is hovered to emphasize its focus. You can also apply a 2D transform to slightly increase the size of the thumbs on hover to provide an enhanced teaser before the user clicks an image to launch the full-size lightbox gallery. As you would expect, the additional inclusion of a transition ensures that these effects are nice and smooth. The following code demonstrates how these effects are achieved:

```
.gallery li > a {
    float: left;
    filter: grayscale(.5) sepia(.8);
    transition: .5s;
    position: relative;
}

.gallery li > a img {
    max-width: 100%;
    box-shadow: 0 0 5px rgba(0, 0, 0, .3);
    transition: .5s;
}

.gallery li > a:hover {
    filter: grayscale(0) sepia(0);
    z-index: 1;
}

.gallery li > a:hover img {
    transform: scale(1.4);
    box-shadow: 0 0 15px rgba(0, 0, 0, .8);
}
```

I should clarify why I instructed you to apply the effects to both the a and img elements rather than just the latter. The reasoning involves WebKit's handling of the filter functions because they do not seem to be compatible with 2D scaling. For example, if you place the grayscale and sepia filter effects directly onto the img element, the `scale()` transform that is performed on hover would cause the image to pixelate severely.

Fortunately, this method allows both the filter effects and the scaling to work correctly because they are applied to different elements. To further explain the result, when a thumbnail image is hovered, the grayscale and sepia effects are removed to reveal the thumb's full color, and it is also scaled up slightly to emphasize the focus and provide an enhanced teaser for the user. This presents the perfect middle ground between the default thumbnail image and the full-size lightbox view. Figure 15-10 provides some visual clarification.

Figure 15-10 The thumbs have partial grayscale and sepia effects by default, which are removed on hover in addition to a slight increase in size to enhance this initial experience.

> The `position: relative;` **rule on the** a **element and the** `z-index: 1;` **rule on its** `:hover` **state ensure that when the thumb is enlarged on hover, it appears on top of any other image that it overlaps.**

Adding the Lightbox Markup

Now that the thumbnail gallery is in place, you can add the lightbox structure to the HTML. To keep things organized, you group the full-size images with their thumbnail counterparts in the unordered list, as shown in the following code:

```
<ul class="gallery">

    <li>
```

```
        <a href="#img1"><img src="images/1.jpg" alt="..."></a>
        <article id="img1">
            <figure>
                <img src="images/1.jpg" alt="...">
                <figcaption>Matauri Bay</figcaption>
            </figure>
        </article>
    </li>

    <!-- etc. -->

</ul>
```

The full-size image and accompanying caption are naturally grouped within a `figure` element, which is then contained in an `article` element and placed below the thumbnail image in the markup. This containing `article` element effectively plays the part of the lightbox window.

The `article` element is obviously hidden by default and is brought into view only when the thumbnail image is clicked. Notice that the thumbnail image links to the `id` value of the `article` element, which is how the thumb triggers the display of the lightbox. To make this effect work, though, you need to introduce some more CSS, namely, the `:target` pseudo-class.

Making the Lightbox Functional

With the lightbox markup in place, the next step is to hide the `article` elements initially until they are triggered by a thumbnail image. Remember, a simple `display: none;` rule means that the element cannot be transitioned, so that method would be a bit restrictive. The `opacity: 0;` method of hiding elements, which you used a couple of times recently, would also not be suitable in this instance because the `article` element would still cover the thumbnail gallery beneath it, despite being invisible; this would obviously prevent the user from being able to click the thumbs.

Instead, you can apply a `width` and `height` of 0 to the `article` element as well as an `overflow` value of `hidden`, which effectively hides the entire element from view:

```
.gallery article {
    width: 0;
    height: 0;
    overflow: hidden;
    position: absolute;
    top: 0;
    left: 0;
}
```

Furthermore, because this element is actually inside a list item, you must explicitly position it in the top left of the page so that it doesn't sit in its default position at the top left of each individual list item, allowing it to eventually fill the entire viewport.

Now that the lightbox windows (the `article` elements) have been hidden, you can introduce some functionality to make the appropriate lightbox window visible when the corresponding thumbnail image is clicked.

To understand the process, consider that the first thumbnail image has been clicked. Remember that the `href` value for the thumb link is `#img1`, matching the `id` value of its associative `article` element. When this link is clicked, the `#img1` value is added to the end of the URL in the user's address bar and is referred to as a *fragment identifier*. When this fragment identifier is in place, the element with an `id` of `#img1` can be selected via the `:target` pseudo-class:

```css
.gallery article:target {
    width: 100%;
    height: 100%;
    text-align: center;
    background: rgba(0, 0, 0, .8);
    z-index: 1;
}
```

The selector in the preceding code example ensures that the styles are applied to any `article` element whose `id` value is currently the fragment identifier at the end of the URL. The following code should illustrate further:

```css
/* URL */
http://webaddress.com/gallery.html#img1

article:target {
    /* Styles are applied to the article element with an id of #img1 */
}
```

So, when an `article` element's `id` is the current fragment identifier in the URL, the element's `width` and `height` are set to `100%` to fill the entire page. The element is also given a slightly transparent black background to obscure the background and therefore emphasize the focus on the lightbox. Figure 15-11 shows the appearance of the first lightbox window as things stand.

Figure 15-11 The current appearance of the first lightbox window after the first thumbnail image is clicked

The fundamental lightbox functionality is now in place, but you have some way to go yet to make this feature usable. For example, after a thumb is clicked and the lightbox is activated, you are currently trapped with no way to exit the lightbox window! Evidently, it needs a few more controls in terms of navigation to satisfy the basic usability requirements. Time to add some more markup:

```
<ul class="gallery">

    <li>
        <a href="#img1"><img src="images/1.jpg" alt="..."></a>
        <article>
            <figure id="img1">
                <a href="#img2"><img src="images/1.jpg" alt="..."></a>
                <figcaption>Matauri Bay</figcaption>
            </figure>
            <nav>
                <a class="close" href="#close">Close</a>
                <a class="arrow prev" href="#img15">Previous</a>
                <a class="arrow next" href="#img2">Next</a>
            </nav>
        </article>
    </li>

    <!-- etc. -->

</ul>
```

To summarize what's new, in the preceding code you add a new `nav` element to the lightbox markup to contain navigation controls that allow you to close the lightbox window and cycle through the full-size images without exiting the lightbox.

The link that allows you to close the lightbox window has an `href` value of `#close`, although this value can theoretically be anything as long as it doesn't match any of the `article` element `id` values in the page. This value simply ensures that no `article` element is targeted via the fragment identifier in the URL and, therefore, the `article:target` styles are not applied.

The next and previous links simply link to the appropriate `article` elements to allow the user to navigate through the full-size images without having to exit the lightbox window. For example, the preceding code block demonstrates the markup for the *first* full-size image (#img1), so the Next link targets #img2 and the Previous link targets the *last* full-size image, which in this case is #img15.

This code also wraps the actual full-size image in a tags that link to the following full-size image to make navigation as seamless and effortless as possible. The result of these additions is illustrated in Figure 15-12, which also clearly highlights the desperate need for some more styling!

I know what you're thinking: manually adding and maintaining all those links for every image looks hideously tedious. And you're right. When you consider the bare-bones markup, writing this code from scratch doesn't make a lot of sense. However, the repetitive nature of this HTML enables this example to become considerably more dynamic using a programming language such as PHP, and therefore infinitely more maintainable, making it a feasible future solution for simple lightbox gallery requirements.

Figure 15-12 The navigation controls are currently basic text links with unintuitive positions and styling.

Applying the Polish to the Final Design

As Figure 15-12 highlights, the various elements within the lightbox window are in serious need of visual alteration, both in terms of enhancing the aesthetic value and improving the usability of the feature.

First, let's look at the actual full-size image, to which you can make a few subtle enhancements, as shown in the following code:

```
.gallery article img {
    max-height: 100%;
    max-width: 100%;
    box-sizing: border-box;
    border: 10px solid #fff;
    box-shadow: 0 0 20px rgba(0, 0, 0, .5);
    opacity: 0;
    transition: .7s;
}

.gallery article:target img {
    opacity: 1;
}
```

The first issue to address is the minor aesthetic enhancements such as the white border and the subtle shadow. Second, the addition of max-width and max-height values of 100% ensure that the full-size image is rescaled in proportion with the page if the viewport is too small to contain it at its full size. And finally, notice that the code sets the opacity of the image to zero and applies a transition to ensure any changes that occur are smooth and gradual. As you would expect, this change involves adjusting the image's opacity value to a maximum of 1, which occurs when its figure container element is targeted via the fragment identifier in the URL.

Figure 15-13 illustrates the updated appearance of the lightbox after some basic styling also has been applied to the `figcaption` element.

Figure 15-13 The full-size image and the caption have been subtly enhanced with some basic CSS.

The most obvious aspects of the design that are in great need of attention are the navigation controls. Let's start with the Close link:

```
article .close {
    position: absolute;
    top: 40px;
    left: 50%;
    margin-left: -50px;
    width: 100px;
    padding: 6px 6px 6px 25px;
    box-sizing: border-box;
    border-radius: 15px;
    transition: .5s;
    /* Other irrelevant/basic styles */
}

article .close:before {
    content: "X";
    position: absolute;
    top: 3px;
    left: 5px;
    padding-top: 3px;
    width: 24px;
    height: 21px;
```

```
    border-radius: 50%;
    /* Other irrelevant/basic styles */
}
```

This code uses an old-school method to center the `.close` link at the top of the page by applying an explicit width (`100px`), positioning it `50%` from the left, before applying a `margin-left` value of exactly half of the element's width (`50px`). Simple! From there, it adds some basic styling to create a prominent, off-white, rounded rectangle to contain the text.

However, Close buttons are almost always accompanied by assistive symbols, usually a cross. For this aspect of the design, you could resort to an extra element in the markup or perhaps a background image; instead, I suggest you opt to take advantage of what CSS offers and utilize the `:before` pseudo-element. This allows you to create a faux element containing an X character that is then styled appropriately to fit the look of a Close symbol. Figure 15-14 demonstrates the result.

Figure 15-14 The Close button is positioned in a prominent and accessible place on the screen and is completed by an assistive cross symbol for instant recognition.

Last but not least are the Next and Previous navigation controls. Again, they need to be fairly prominent and would benefit from a large target area for the user to click, so you can mold them into large arrows that clearly communicate their purpose in the lightbox context.

Because these two links share many of the same styles due to their visual similarities, they also share the class `.arrow` in addition to their individual `.prev` and `.next` classes:

```
article .arrow {
    position: absolute;
```

```
        top: 250px;
        width: 0;
        height: 0;
        border-top: 40px solid transparent;
        border-bottom: 40px solid transparent;
        text-indent: -9999px;
        transition: .4s;
    }

    article .prev {
        left: 50%;
        margin-left: -450px;
        border-right: 60px solid rgba(250, 250, 250, .1);
    }

    article .next {
        right: 50%;
        margin-right: -450px;
        border-left: 60px solid rgba(250, 250, 250, .1);
    }
```

Because the text within these Next and Previous links is no longer required, you can hide it using the `text-indent` method. In place of the text, large, light gray triangles are formed using a clever trick involving borders. With a `width` and `height` value of `0`, the borders of the element combine to create a triangular shape, which is illustrated further with the following code:

```
    /* Left-pointing triangle */
    border-top: 20px solid transparent;
    border-bottom: 20px solid transparent;
    border-right: 20px solid #fff;

    /* Upwards-pointing triangle */
    border-left: 20px solid transparent;
    border-right: 20px solid transparent;
    border-bottom: 20px solid #fff;

    /* etc. */
```

With these triangles positioned into place to play the part of navigation, you now have a fully functional and visually appealing lightbox feature, created from the bottom up using nothing but semantic HTML and CSS3. As usual, you can explore the full code in depth on the companion website, and if you need a reminder of the lightbox's final look, you can refer back to Figure 15-6 and Figure 15-7.

This example pushed the limits even further in terms of what you can achieve using nothing but CSS3 and a creative mindset, with a final product that is fully functional, easy to use, and built with highly readable code.

However, the final tutorial takes things even further because it adds an entirely new dimension along with delightfully satisfying touches of animation.

Creating a 3D Image Carousel Using Only CSS3

This last example packs a real punch and, for me, is by far the most visually impressive of the examples described in this chapter. To view it in its full glory and benefit from the animation aspect, you need to open the live demo (`1503-3d-carousel.html`), although Figure 15-15 demonstrates the final look and provides some idea as to how it functions.

Figure 15-15 The final result of the 3D image carousel

The following list outlines the general process of creating the 3D image carousel:

1. The first stage is to determine how many images your carousel will contain and to mark them up using sensible HTML.

2. Next, you use CSS3 to establish a 3D formatting context for your images to work in.

3. After forming the 3D environment, you can then rotate and position each image appropriately to form a 3D ring of images.

4. Next, add the navigation controls that allow the user to determine which image is currently at the forefront of the carousel.

5. To finish, apply the final niceties that will enhance the 3D illusion and emphasize the focus on the currently selected image.

Marking Up the Carousel

Nothing out of the ordinary is required when it comes to structuring the HTML for the carousel because it is simply a bunch of images organized into an unordered list, as the following code confirms:

```
<div class="container">
    <ul class="carousel">
```

```
        <li><img src="images/1.jpg" alt="Landscape 1"></li>
        <li><img src="images/2.jpg" alt="Landscape 2"></li>
        <li><img src="images/3.jpg" alt="Landscape 3"></li>
        <li><img src="images/4.jpg" alt="Landscape 4"></li>
        <li><img src="images/5.jpg" alt="Landscape 5"></li>
        <li><img src="images/6.jpg" alt="Landscape 6"></li>
        <li><img src="images/7.jpg" alt="Landscape 7"></li>
        <li><img src="images/8.jpg" alt="Landscape 8"></li>
    </ul>
</div>
```

The containing `div` is required to establish the 3D formatting context because 3D transformations are applied to the `.carousel ul` element as well as the `img` elements.

Establishing a 3D Formatting Context

If Chapter 7 is still fresh in your memory, you know exactly what to expect from this section; if not, you're about to be suitably refreshed!

The property that basically transforms an element into a 3D environment for its children to work within is the `perspective` property, which takes a pixel-based value. Remember, the `perspective` value sets the assumed viewing position in terms of distance from the screen, therefore determining the intensity of the 3D effect. For example, the lower the value, the closer the viewing position is to the screen and, therefore, the more intense the 3D illusion.

```
.container {
    perspective: 1000px;
}
```

With that, the `.container` element's children (namely the `.carousel` element) are now operating within a 3D environment; however, this doesn't extend any deeper to the `.carousel` element's children. To ensure that the images can also function within this same 3D environment, you need to preserve the 3D context at each new level, as follows:

```
.container {
    perspective: 1000px;
}

.container .carousel {
    transform-style: preserve-3d;
}
```

So, the original 3D environment is established with the `perspective` property on the `.container` element, and this is then preserved on the `.carousel` element so that *its* children can also function in the same 3D context.

Positioning the Images in a 3D Environment

With the 3D formatting context established, you can now rotate and translate the images in three dimensions, allowing you to position them into place to form a ring of images. First, though, they need to be positioned absolutely so that they all sit on top of each other in a pile, enabling them to be transformed from the same initial position:

```
.carousel img {
    position: absolute;
}
```

Now the images are ready for some 3D transformations! The number of images you work with is important here because it determines the angle at which each image needs to be rotated to result in a perfect circle of images.

As is evident from the markup, this carousel contains a total of eight images. There are obviously 360 degrees in a full circle, which means that to determine the angle at which each image should be rotated, you must divide 360 by 8 (the number of images). The result of this calculation is, of course, 45, which means that the carousel has eight sides and eight equal 45-degree angles.

```
.carousel li:nth-child(2) img { transform: rotateY(45deg); }
.carousel li:nth-child(3) img { transform: rotateY(90deg); }
.carousel li:nth-child(4) img { transform: rotateY(135deg); }
.carousel li:nth-child(5) img { transform: rotateY(180deg); }
/* etc. */
```

The first image needs to face the viewer, so it doesn't require a rotation value.

As you can see, the images are rotated in 45-degree increments, which eventually create a proportional circle of images. However, the images are currently rotated from the same initial, central position, resulting in the situation presented in Figure 15-16.

Figure 15-16 The images are currently rotated at different angles from a central point, forming a cluster of rotated images in the center of the page.

To resolve this situation, you need to move the images outward from this center position so that they form the circle of images, which is actually simple to achieve. Remember that when an element is rotated in a 3D environment, its entire coordinate system is rotated with it, including the z-axis, resulting in a collection of z-axes pointing in eight different directions. The images can then be moved along their respective z-axes until their edges meet, as per Figure 15-17.

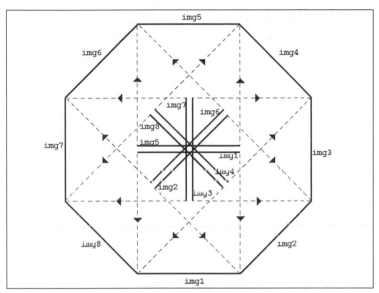

Figure 15-17 The images are moved along their respective z-axes until they form the eight-sided carousel shape.

To calculate the amount each image needs to be moved along its z-axis, you could use some trigonometry that I'm sure you practice every day for occasions such as these!

Don't worry—I'm not really going to make you do trigonometry. In truth, the easiest and most time-efficient method is that old standby, trial and error. In this particular example, the images are positioned so that a small amount of space appears between them, so calculating an exact value to ensure the image edges line up isn't necessary here.

After a couple of estimates, I found that the value that produces the most satisfying result is 680px. As a result, you can move each image 680px away from its currently central position using the translateZ() 3D transform like this:

```
.carousel li:nth-child(1) img {
    transform: translateZ(680px);
}

.carousel li:nth-child(2) img {
    transform: rotateY(45deg) translateZ(680px);
}

.carousel li:nth-child(3) img {
    transform: rotateY(90deg) translateZ(680px);
```

```
}

.carousel li:nth-child(4) img {
    transform: rotateY(135deg) translateZ(680px);
}

/* etc. */
```

After each image is translated by `680px` along its z-axis, the carousel begins to take shape. However, if you recall the cube tutorial from Chapter 7, you may remember that when an element is translated *toward* the user (as the first image is), it effectively makes the element larger and therefore pixelated. To counteract this effect, you need to push the entire carousel back by the same `680px` value to ensure that no images are scaled beyond their true size:

```
.container .carousel {
    transform-style: preserve-3d;
    transform: translateZ(-680px);
}
```

Figure 15-18 shows how the carousel stands currently with the preceding alterations in place.

Figure 15-18 Now that the images have been translated from their central position, the carousel shape resembles an actual 3D ring of images as was initially desired.

It's certainly getting there, but for me, it's still not instantly recognizable as a 3D carousel, and the initial wow factor is lacking. To remedy this and enhance the 3D illusion, you can apply a simple alteration. The `perspective-origin` property allows you to alter the vanishing point of the 3D context from its initial central value, so you can simply push it higher up, allowing the previously out-of-sight images to creep into view and reinforce the fact that you're looking at a 3D ring of images. The following code shows how to implement this amendment, while Figure 15-19 illustrates the visual result:

```
.container {
    perspective: 1000px;
```

```
        perspective-origin-y: -25%;
}
```

Figure 15-19 All the images are now partially visible, making the 3D carousel structure apparent and therefore enhancing the 3D illusion.

Making the Carousel Functional

To remain with the theme of using only CSS3 functionality, you can again opt to use the check box method of triggering actions and style alterations on click. I don't go into too much depth about the radio `input` elements because the section on tabbed content earlier in the chapter discussed them in great detail.

In short, you have eight radio buttons in total, one for each of the images in the carousel. When the fifth button is clicked, for example, the carousel rotates by the necessary amount to bring the fifth image to the forefront.

The important point to note here is that the images themselves are not affected when the buttons are clicked; it is the actual `.carousel` container that is rotated, allowing all its children to rotate with it. The following code shows how the radio `input` buttons trigger the necessary rotation of the `.carousel` container to bring each of the images to the front:

```
input[value="2"]:checked ~ .container .carousel {
    transform: translateZ(-680px) rotateY(-45deg);
}

input[value="3"]:checked ~ .container .carousel {
    transform: translateZ(-680px) rotateY(-90deg);
}

input[value="4"]:checked ~ .container .carousel {
    transform: translateZ(-680px) rotateY(-135deg);
}
```

Remember that the `.carousel` container was pushed backward along the z-axis by `680px` to ensure that none of the images pixelate; this rule still needs to apply here in addition to the rotation value. The rest is fairly simple: when the second button is clicked, the carousel is rotated by `-45deg`, which brings the second image (which is rotated by `45deg`) to the front of the carousel.

When this effect is in place, you want this carousel rotation to be animated rather than the changes snapping into place. Naturally, it is an elementary fix because a simple transition property does the job. Figure 15-20 shows the process of the animation when the fourth button is clicked.

```
.container .carousel {
    transform-style: preserve-3d;
    transform: translateZ(-680px);
    transition: 1s;
}
```

Figure 15-20 The animation obviously starts in the carousel's initial position, before rotating around until the fourth image is at the front.

Now that the carousel controls are in place and the animation is functional, the impact of this feature is substantial because the resulting visual effects are highly impressive and reminiscent of widgets that typically require Flash or JavaScript to work.

Before signing off on this tutorial, I have a couple more tricks up my sleeve to push this feature even further.

Applying the Finishing Touches

The carousel is looking good and is fully functional, but for me, it needs to do a better job of highlighting the image that is currently at the front of the carousel because this is the image the user should be focused on.

To achieve this result, you can scale down the images by default, as well as drop their opacity values, before bringing them to full size and opaqueness when the image is brought to the front of the carousel. When you also apply a transition effect to the `img` elements, the resulting animation is enormously satisfying.

The following code shows how the images are scaled down and made more transparent by default:

```css
.carousel img {
    position: absolute;
    border: 15px solid rgba(0, 0, 0, .8);
    opacity: .5;
    transition: 1s;
}

.carousel li:nth-child(1) img {
    transform: translateZ(540px) scale(.8);
}

.carousel li:nth-child(2) img {
    transform: rotateY(45deg) translateZ(540px) scale(.8);
}

/* etc. */
```

> Bear in mind that because the images are now smaller, the carousel as a whole is also smaller, meaning the images don't have to travel so far along their z-axes. As a result, the previous value of `680px` **has changed to** `540px` **throughout the code.**

Now that these changes are in place, the image at the front of the carousel needs to be at full size and opacity to emphasize its presence in comparison to the rest of the images in the carousel. The following code demonstrates how this effect is achieved:

```css
input[value="1"]:checked ~ .container .carousel li:nth-child(1) img {
    transform: translateZ(540px) scale(1);
    opacity: 1;
}

input[value="2"]:checked ~ .container .carousel li:nth-child(2) img {
    transform: rotateY(45deg) translateZ(540px) scale(1);
    opacity: 1;
}

/* etc. */
```

I appreciate that those selectors are outrageously long, but they're really not that complicated when broken down. The second one, for example, basically translates to "when the second radio button is clicked, select the image within the second list item and return it to its full size and opacity." You can see the result of these alterations in Figure 15-21.

Figure 15-21 The images have been scaled down by default and have had their opacity reduced, while the image at the front of the carousel is at full size and opacity to emphasize its focus.

Of course, you really need to view the live demo on the companion website to fully appreciate this feature, particularly in terms of the animation, but I hope the figures and accompanying descriptions have left you suitably impressed.

This example goes a long way to showcasing the immense power of CSS3 and what you can achieve with the new features it provides, without the need for any assistive JavaScript.

Summary

The tutorials described in this chapter demonstrate how the vast and diverse range of new CSS3 features can provide methods of producing not only stunning aesthetics, but also fully functional and interactive elements.

The tabbed content is an extremely simple concept and requires a minimal amount of HTML and CSS that reflect its elementary functionality. Your ability to produce a functional, interactive feature such as this with just a few lines of exceedingly readable CSS rather than lines of complex JavaScript could prove invaluable in years to come.

The lightbox example is considerably more substantial and, on the surface, appears very cumbersome and difficult to maintain, but with the help of PHP, it could easily become a dynamic script that takes seconds to amend. Despite these drawbacks, the CSS aspect of this example once again benefits from being readable, robust, and easy to maintain.

The final, 3D carousel tutorial is the ace in the pack because it combines a 3D environment with simple animations to produce a truly jaw-dropping result. This example really showcases the power of CSS3 and opens new doors for web designers that were previously locked tight if entering with CSS as the only key.

Despite these CSS3 heroics, I must once again finish with a stern word of caution. On several occasions throughout this chapter, I suggested that these examples could once be feasible in real-world scenarios in a future world of browser support utopia. But until then, they are simply experiments and should be treated as such.

Further Reading

More advanced CSS3 tutorials
```
http://dzineblog.com/2011/11/23-must-read-tutorials-for-advanced-
html5css3-coders.html
```

Chapter 16
The Future of CSS

I hope that this book has gone some way to showing you how much CSS is developing as a language to tackle age-old issues as well as to provide solutions for problems you didn't even know you had yet. On that point, though, it's important to note that the CSS Working Group is an extremely rational and sensible bunch and will develop only features that aim to solve *real-world problems*, not just features that look cool and exciting.

In terms of the future, CSS3 is actually the last numbered version of CSS, which could understandably lead you to think that the language's development is approaching a stage of actual completion. Of course, this couldn't be further from the truth because the development of CSS is as strong and vibrant as it's ever been. So what's the deal with CSS3 being the last version?

The truth is that the *way* in which CSS is being developed has altered to allow for a faster, more streamlined process, ensuring that new features are quicker to reach a stage that is considered stable enough for implementation by browsers.

There is no such thing as CSS4. That's right—despite what you may have seen around the web offering you a "sneak peak at CSS4."

CSS1 and 2.1 were large, collective specifications, but everything within has since been modularized, which you have probably noticed throughout this book as I referenced the individual modules. For example, CSS3 consists of a vast (and ever increasing) range of different modules (such as Backgrounds and Borders and Text Decoration) that level up independently. Most of these independent modules begin at Level 3 because they are simply developing their features from the earlier CSS versions; however, other modules, such as Flexbox and Grid Layout, are brand new and are therefore at Level 1.

Confusion has mounted as a result because some of these modules are starting to progress even further, with the Selectors module, for example, now at level 4, causing some to believe or assume that this means it is part of "CSS4." You now know that this is not the case; the new development format has simply allowed this module to progress slightly quicker than others, ensuring troublesome features have not held it back. Figure 16-1 illustrates this point.

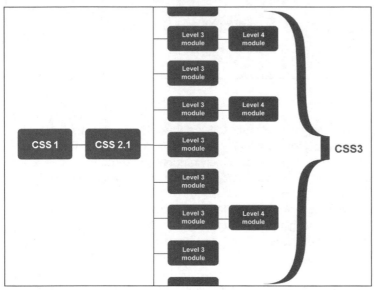

Figure 16-1 CSS was one big specification through versions 1 and 2.1, until it was modularized with CSS3.

So, with that myth expelled, what *is* the future of CSS? This chapter aims to give you an insight into that very question, offering snippets of extremely new modules, such as those that have already progressed to Level 4 (Selectors and Backgrounds and Borders, among others) as well as the lesser-developed Level 3 modules. With Regions and Exclusions, Grid Layout, Flexbox, and others, I already discussed cutting-edge modules that aim to form the future of CSS; but this chapter delves even further, reaching the furthest corners of CSS obscurity where possible future heroes lie in wait.

Just remember that this chapter aims to provide insight into the proposed functionalities of these features; the actual syntaxes of many of them are likely to be almost unrecognizable by the time they reach a usable stage. Some of them may not even make it that far.

CSS Variables

As you learned from Chapter 14, CSS preprocessors are full of useful functionalities, and stimulate good ideas that make the process of writing CSS a much easier one. The fact that developers feel the need to make use of these preprocessors suggests that CSS doesn't provide enough functionality in itself, so as a result, the CSS Working Group is beginning to consider aspects of preprocessors that would be particularly useful in native CSS.

The ability to define variables for use throughout stylesheets is certainly one of the functionalities that would be desirable in plain old CSS, without having to rely on a preprocessor. A brand new module aims to address this issue: the not-so-concisely named CSS Custom Properties for Cascading Variables module. The underlying functionality is naturally similar to the preprocessor version, but CSS's current implementation is rather different.

Variables are defined using *custom properties*, which you can then reference throughout your stylesheet as values. For example, consider a scenario in which the concept of variables would typically prove useful, such as a base color that is reused multiple times. The following code demonstrates how you might currently implement this functionality in your stylesheet:

```
header, footer {
    background: linear-gradient(#012274, #000);
}

h1 {
    color: #012274;
}

.sidebar div {
    border: 1px solid #012274;
}

/* etc. */
```

I'm sure you can see (and have no doubt experienced) how this repetition could soon become very tiresome and potentially very difficult to maintain. By declaring this color value using a custom property name, you can then refer to this custom property name throughout your stylesheet rather than a very forgettable hex code. The following code shows how CSS tackles the problem according to the *current* module draft. Remember, try not to focus too much on the syntax and concentrate instead on the concept and functionality that it presents.

```
:root {
    var-base-color: #012274;
}

header, footer {
    background: linear-gradient(var(base-color), #000);
}

h1 {
    color: var(base-color);
}

.sidebar div {
    border: 1px solid var(base-color);
}
```

The variables are declared on the `:root` pseudo-class using custom properties that are defined by the `var-` prefix. Your variable is now created and is ready to be referenced throughout the stylesheet. As is evident from the preceding block of code, the variable is referenced using the `var()` notation, with the custom property name stated within the parentheses.

Brand new modules are often intimidating and difficult to understand on the first read, but this one certainly bucks the trend in that regard. Variables are a familiar concept to most, thanks to Sass/LESS, JavaScript, PHP, and other programming languages, and this module simply extends this concept to CSS using a fairly friendly syntax. New, exciting, and cutting edge—but also extremely simple.

Someone who is at the forefront of the CSS Working Group and editor of many modules is Tab Atkins, Jr., who has suggested that other preprocessor functionalities could also prove to be useful additions to CSS. He outlined his plans for CSS in early 2013 in a blog post (http://www.xanthir.com/b4N80) within which he specifically mentions mixins and Sass's @extend feature. In addition to this, Tab recently led a discussion in the CSS mailing list in which the possibility of bringing color functions from Sass and LESS to native CSS was pondered very positively. These latter suggestions are obviously just pipe dreams at the moment, but keep your eyes open and you may find them drafted up in some form or another before too long.

Moving on, the variables module is clearly pretty bite-sized compared to most, so it's about time the discussion moved forward to tackle one of the bigger beasts: namely, Level 4 Selectors.

CSS Selectors: Level 4

I spent all of Chapter 1 discussing advanced Level 3 selectors, many of which are yet to hit the mainstream, but already you can find even more advanced selectors that are even more cutting edge, even if the majority of them are a world away from browser implementation.

The Selectors module is the most developed of those that have so far progressed to Level 4 and has by far the most coverage across the web as a result. A few of the features are even starting to gain some support in modern browsers already!

The module consists of an extensive list of new selectors, primarily made up of shiny new pseudo-classes with two or three new combinatory-based selectors, too. I show you the majority of what's in store through the following list, before expanding on a few of them with more specific examples:

- `:not(div, a)`—The eagle-eyed among you may notice that this negation pseudo-class was introduced in Chapter 1 with the Level 3 selectors; however, the Level 4 version allows for comma-separated selectors within the parentheses.

- `.main :matches(ul, ol) li`—This pseudo-class enables you to condense multiple rule-sets or long-winded selectors into something more compact and concise; this example is equivalent to a selector of `.main ul li, .main ol li {}`.

- `:any-link`—This hyperlink pseudo-class enables you to target every link in the document, including visited links and those that point to external addresses.

- `:local-link`—This pseudo-class selects all links to targets within the current document.

- `:valid-drop`—This drag-and-drop pseudo-class targets an element that is able to receive an item being dragged.

- `:invalid-drop`—Predictably, this pseudo-class enables you to target elements that *cannot* receive an item being dragged.

- `:placeholder-shown`—This pseudo-class enables you to style the placeholder text in form input fields.

- `:indeterminate`—Whereas the `:checked` pseudo-class enables you to target checked radio buttons and check boxes, this pseudo-class targets those that are neither checked nor unchecked.

- `:required`—This pseudo-class enables you to style UI elements that require input.

- `:optional`—And this pseudo-class enables you to target UI elements that do *not* require input.

- `:blank`—This pseudo-class targets elements that are empty, although unlike `:empty`, this pseudo-class includes those containing whitespace.

- :nth-column(n)—This pseudo-class enables you to select a particular column in a grid/column-based layout.

- :nth-last-column(n)—This pseudo-class does the same as the preceding rule but counting from the *last* column.

- a /attr/ b—The *reference combinator* is very cool, enabling you to select *element b* if its id value matches the specified attribute of *element a*.

- a! span—This selector actually targets all a elements that contain a span! Potentially very useful, although there is currently much doubt over where the exclamation mark should be placed in the selector.

This is a truly extensive list of brand new selectors, but believe it or not, it's not an exhaustive list. For the full rundown on Level 4 selectors, look at the current Editor's Draft (http://dev.w3.org/csswg/selectors4).

I want to expand on a few of the more interesting selectors from the preceding list that I feel would be of instant use if they were available today. The first of these is the :not() pseudo-class, which was originally unveiled in the Level 3 spec.

The Level 4 draft allows for a bit more flexibility with comma-separated values and chained selectors. Consider the following example:

```
ul li:nth-child(odd):not(li:nth-child(3n), li:first-child) {
    font-weight: bold;
}
```

The preceding selector would target all odd numbered list items in an unordered list, apart from the first item and those that are a multiple of 3. Figure 16-2 demonstrates this more clearly as it shows the resulting list.

Item1	Item16
item2	**item17**
item3	item18
item4	**item19**
item5	item20
item6	item21
item7	item22
item8	**item23**
item9	item24
item10	**item25**
item11	item26
item12	item27
item13	item28
item14	**item29**
item15	item30

Figure 16-2 Thanks to the negation pseudo-class, all odd list items are made bold except for the first item and those that are multiples of 3.

The `:matches()` pseudo-class is another instrument that seems as though it would be a natural addition to the CSS toolkit. The following snippet provides a simple example as to how it could make your life that little bit easier:

```
/* Current method */
ul li a:hover span,
ul li a:focus span,
ul li a:active span {
    background: #000;
}

/* Future method using :matches */
ul li a:matches(:hover, :focus, :active) span {
    background: #000;
}
```

And with one simple pseudo-class, you can condense three separate selectors into one, allowing for much more efficiency in your stylesheets. Figure 16-3 shows the result of the preceding example.

Figure 16-3 When the a elements are hovered, the background of the span element within them changes to black.

One of the most intriguing of the new selectors, in my opinion, is the reference combinator, which enables you to style an element based on an attribute value of *another* element. To understand this concept more clearly, consider the following snippet:

```
HTML
<label for="name">Name</label>
<input id="name" type="text">

CSS
label:hover /for/ input {
    border: 3px solid #000;
}
```

When a `label` element is hovered, this code adds a black border to the `input` element, but only if its `id` value matches the `label` element's `for` attribute value (you can see from the HTML that it does this because they are both set to `"name"`). Figure 16-4 illustrates the result of this example.

Finally, let's discuss the much-sought-after method of targeting a parent if it contains a particular element. This is not your average selector because it goes against the basic principle of a CSS selector, which is that the final part of the selector is the element that should be targeted. This particular functionality turns things on its head, as you can see from the following example:

```
figure! figcaption {
    border: 1px dashed #000;
    padding: 20px;
}
```

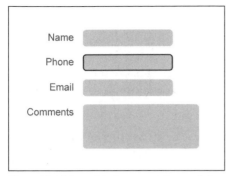

Figure 16-4 When a label element is hovered, the input element with an id value matching the label element's for value is given a black border.

The parent `figure` element is given a dashed border and some padding, but only when it contains a `figcaption` element. If a `figure` element lacks a `figcaption` child, it does not receive the additional styles, as demonstrated in Figure 16-5. And all this is courtesy of a solitary, additional exclamation mark!

> Bear in mind that as I mentioned previously, there is currently a note in the spec suggesting that the position of the exclamation mark within the selector is far from decided upon.

Figure 16-5 A figure element containing a figcaption is given a border (left), while those without are not (right).

I'd love to discuss many other selectors from the list, but any attempt to address the entire list in depth would be worthy of a book on its own. For more details, read the spec or simply head to Google because they're a hot topic as far as Level 4 CSS modules go!

The future isn't just about Level 4 and beyond, though; some Level 3 modules are just as distant from mainstream use. However, one of the L3 modules that is a little closer to browser implementation and that has slipped under the radar somewhat is the Conditional Rules module.

Browser Support Using CSS Conditional Rules

The issue of browser support occupies a front row seat in the mind of every web designer, with a constant stream of new and exciting features filtering their way into mainstream use, along with varying browser support. Traditionally, support for these features has been tested for using JavaScript-based solutions, before delivering alternative code based on the results of these tests. But finally, CSS has proposed a native solution to this age-old problem.

The syntax is relatively basic, as it introduces the `@supports` rule, within which you can specify rule-sets based on whether or not a feature is supported. The following code example illustrates further:

```
.modal {
    border: 1px solid #999;
}

@supports ( box-shadow: 0 0 10px rgba(0, 0, 0, .5) ) {

    .modal {
        box-shadow: 0 0 10px rgba(0, 0, 0, .5);
    }

}
```

As you can see, the CSS rule that the `@supports` rule must test for is specified in parentheses, and must consist of a property and value pair, rather than just a simple property type. The preceding example styles a modal box with a light gray border, unless the `box-shadow` property with an `rgba()`-based value is supported, in which case it applies a `box-shadow` instead of the border, as shown in Figure 16-6.

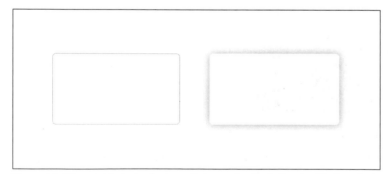

Figure 16-6 The modal window is given a light gray border (left), unless the box-shadow property/value pair is supported (right).

The functionality of this feature can be extended slightly thanks to some simple operators, as outlined in the following list:

- The `not` operator allows for negation, enabling you to apply styles when a property/value pair is *not* supported:

```
@supports not ( box-shadow: 0 0 10px rgba(0, 0, 0, .5) ) {

    .modal {
```

```
        border: 1px solid #999;
    }

}
```

■ The or operator allows you to apply styles when any of a range of property/value pairs are supported; it is ideal for multiple prefixed properties:

```
@supports ( -webkit-border-radius: 3px ) or
          ( -moz-border-radius: 3px ) or
          ( border-radius: 3px ) {

    .modal {
        -webkit-border-radius: 3px;
        -moz-border-radius: 3px;
        border-radius: 3px;
    }

}
```

■ Finally, the and operator enables you to apply styles when multiple property/value pairs must be supported:

```
@supports ( background: rgba(250, 250, 250, .7) ) and
          ( box-shadow: 0 0 10px rgba(0, 0, 0, .5) ) {

    .modal {
        background: rgba(250, 250, 250, .7);
        box-shadow: 0 0 10px rgba(0, 0, 0, .5);
    }

}
```

Obviously, to use the @supports rule to test for these conditions, you need this feature to be supported in the first place! However, the first signs of browser implementation are apparent because support in upcoming releases of Firefox and Chrome has been reported, so keep an eye out for this one.

Pseudo-elements: Level 4

The Level 4 Pseudo-elements module is an *unofficial draft*; that is, it has simply been drawn up by the guys at Adobe and presented to the CSS Working Group for discussion. Although this draft is effectively an outside suggestion up for review by the CSS WG, it proposes additional functionality for pseudo-elements that has already been widely suggested across the web.

The main feature of this module that could potentially prove very powerful is your ability to define multiple ::before and ::after pseudo-elements. The syntax proposed in this unofficial draft is extremely simple currently, but remember that this is likely to change over time.

You could use these multiple levels of faux elements to effectively create the illusion of any number of physical elements using only one *actual* element in the markup. The following code explains further, and Figure 16-7 shows the result:

HTML
```
<div>An Element</div>
```

CSS
```
div::before(3) { content:"1"; background: red; /* etc. */ }
div::before(2) { content:"2"; background: red; /* etc. */ }
div::before    { content:"3"; background: red; /* etc. */ }
div::after     { content:"4"; background: red; /* etc. */ }
div::after(2)  { content:"5"; background: red; /* etc. */ }
div::after(3)  { content:"6"; background: red; /* etc. */ }
```

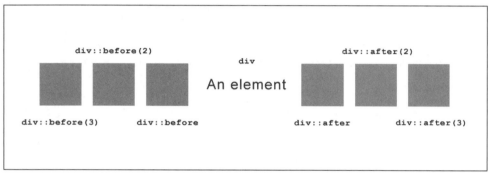

Figure 16-7 From just a single div element, the page features text surrounded by six other boxes.

Have Your Say

The best thing about the future of CSS is that *you* can help shape it if you're willing. The CSS mailing list (`http://lists.w3.org/Archives/Public/www-style/`) is an open forum for subscribers to discuss the development of CSS. You can comment on the existing drafts to express concern over possibly confusing aspects, or you can propose new ideas and discuss the ideas of others. Subscribing to the list is a great way to keep tabs on how the language is developing and get a first-hand view of discussions among the greatest CSS minds on the planet. However, the volume of mail you will receive from the list is extremely high, so you should take this factor into account before you make the decision to sign up.

Summary

Despite widespread belief to the contrary, the development of CSS is not working toward a mammoth release of one huge CSS4 specification. It has instead been modularized so that each set of related features can progress at its own pace, without the hindrance of waiting on more troublesome features to catch up.

Preprocessors have taken CSS development by storm, which has led to the possible addition of some preprocessing functionalities to native CSS. Variables are already well on their way, with more having been merely suggested in a positive light.

The Selectors module has advanced the furthest of all the new modules, with a Level 4 draft that is already in the early stages of being picked by browsers.

Other exciting features include the `@supports` rule and multiple-level pseudo-elements. There are, however, countless new features across a range of constantly updated modules, including those discussed earlier in this book, such as Filters, Flexbox, Regions, and more. The best way to keep track of everything regarding the development of CSS is to sign up for the CSS mailing list, but be warned that the volume of emails is substantial.

Unfortunately, this chapter has nowhere near enough scope to address everything in the pipeline for the future of CSS; as I mentioned previously, the stuff that is currently in development or simply yet to hit the mainstream would warrant a separate publication in itself! However, I hope that what I have included has given you enough of a taste to whet your appetite and get you excited for what looks like a very bright future for CSS.

Further Reading

CSS Custom Properties for Cascading Variables Module Level 1
`http://dev.w3.org/cocwg/css-variables/`

CSS Selectors Level 4
`http://dev.w3.org/csswg/selectors4/`

CSS Conditional Rules Module Level 3
`http://www.w3.org/TR/css3-conditional/`

CSS Pseudo-elements Module Level 4 (Unofficial Draft)
`http://dev.w3.org/csswg/css-pseudo/`

CSS Backgrounds and Borders Module Level 4
`http://dev.w3.org/csswg/css-backgrounds-4/`

Index